THE WORD UNHEARD

THE WORD UNHEARD

*Legacies of Anti-Semitism in
German Literature and Culture*

~

MARTHA B. HELFER

NORTHWESTERN UNIVERSITY PRESS
EVANSTON, ILLINOIS

Northwestern University Press
www.nupress.northwestern.edu

Printed in the United States of America

10 9 8 7 6 5 4 3 2 1

Library of Congress Cataloging-in-Publication Data

Helfer, Martha B., 1962–
    The word unheard : legacies of anti-Semitism in German literature and culture /
Martha B. Helfer.
      p. cm.
    Includes bibliographical references and index.
    ISBN 978-0-8101-2794-4 (cloth : alk. paper)
    1. German literature—18th century—History and criticism. 2. German
literature—19th century—History and criticism. 3. Antisemitism—Germany—
History—18th century. 4. Antisemitism—Germany—History—19th century.
5. Jews—Germany—Social conditions—18th century. 6. Jews—Germany—Social
conditions—19th century. 7. Antisemitism in literature. 8. Jews in literature.
I. Title.
PT149.J4H45 2011
830.93529924—dc23

                                    2011023274

For Steve

and

in memory of my mother

CONTENTS

ACKNOWLEDGMENTS

This project began many years ago, "vor grauen Jahren," to speak with Lessing's Nathan, and it began with Lessing's *Nathan,* with an unsettled feeling that I had as an undergraduate that I did not fully understand this text. At the time I ascribed this unsettled feeling to insufficient linguistic proficiency. But over the years I came to realize that the text *itself* was unsettling, that the text said something other than what I had been taught that it said. What was unsettling to me then remains unsettling to me today: but now I have a better understanding of why I felt so uneasy.

Many people provided help and support as I shaped this uneasy understanding into book form. I would like to thank the students at the University of Utah and Rutgers University who joined me in questioning literature. Much of the material in this book was presented in draft at conferences and lectures: I am grateful for audience feedback at meetings of the Modern Language Association, the German Studies Association, and the German Jewish Studies workshop at Duke University. Special thanks to Bill Donahue, Katja Garloff, Jonathan Hess, Dagmar Lorenz, Joe Metz, and David Wellbery, who read various chapters and helped sharpen my argument. Karin Schutjer and Eric Downing read the entire manuscript, and their astute comments have been tremendously helpful. Michael Levine has been a wonderful interlocutor who provided crucial input as the manuscript neared completion. Thanks, too, to my colleagues and friends in the Department of Germanic, Russian, and East European Languages and Literatures at Rutgers University for their support and for giving me a vibrant intellectual home. The University of Utah funded initial research for this project with Faculty Research and Career Development Grants. A sabbatical leave from Rutgers University enabled me to complete the manuscript, and I gratefully acknowledge this institutional support. Warmest thanks, too, to Sarah Goodman for her enthusiasm and understanding.

I am very thankful to Henry Carrigan Jr. for his strong editorial support of this project. I also would like to thank the superb staff at Northwestern University Press for their help in guiding the manuscript into print.

I am immensely grateful to my family for their love, encouragement, and good humor. Heartfelt thanks to Adam, Aisha, Rokaya, Riaz, Beth,

Bruce, Rebecca, Aaron, Tam, John, Ben, and Joe, for always being there for me. Warmest thanks to Jon Salmon for his support and good cheer. Loving thanks, too, to my in-laws, Joan Nowick and the late Arthur Nowick, for making me part of their family, and for being so interested in this project. My parents, Joanne and Larry Helfer, have been a huge source of comfort and support, and I am tremendously grateful for their love and care. My mother did not live to see this book in finished form, but her impact on my work has been profound. She taught me the power of language, and she taught me how to write.

Finally, my deepest thanks to my husband and soulmate, Steve Nowick, for his unwavering love, support, and encouragement, and for listening.

Some of the material in this book first appeared in essays published elsewhere, and I am grateful for the editors' and anonymous reviewers' comments that strengthened this work. Chapter 4 was published as "*Wer wagt es, eitlen Blutes Drang zu messen?*: Reading Blood in Annette von Droste-Hülshoff's *Die Judenbuche*" in *The German Quarterly* 71, no. 3 (1998): 228–53. Chapter 5 appeared as "Natural Anti-Semitism: Stifter's *Abdias*" in *Deutsche Vierteljahrsschrift für Literaturwissenschaft und Geistesgeschichte (DVjs)* 78, no. 2 (2004): 261–86. Chapter 6 was published as "Framing the Jew: Grillparzer's *Die Jüdin von Toledo*" in *The German Quarterly* 75, no. 2 (2002): 160–80. I thank the publishers for permission to use this material, which has been slightly revised for publication here.

INTRODUCTION: THE LANGUAGE
OF ANTI-SEMITISM

This is a book about language, about how to recognize and interpret the rhetoric of anti-Semitism in its literary articulations. It focuses on latent anti-Semitism in mainstream German and Austrian literature written during the early phases of the Jewish emancipation debate, the years 1749 to 1850. Most studies of pre-Holocaust literature analyze obvious, virulent expressions of anti-Semitism. I propose a more nuanced approach, and consider how subtle forms of literary anti-Semitism mirror, create, and subconsciously instill prejudice in an educated population. The following chapters present major new readings of seminal works by leading authors, including Gotthold Ephraim Lessing, Friedrich von Schiller, Achim von Arnim, Annette von Droste-Hülshoff, Adalbert Stifter, and Franz Grillparzer. Through careful textual analysis I reshape our understanding of this canonical literature, and demonstrate that disciplinary practices within the fields of *Germanistik* and German Studies have led to systematic blind spots in the scholarship on anti-Semitism to date. In unsettling this established reception history, *The Word Unheard* remaps the boundaries of German Jewish Studies and opens up new lines of interdisciplinary inquiry.

By concentrating on *latent* expressions of anti-Semitism in key canonical texts from the German literary tradition, *The Word Unheard* aims to reconceptualize our understanding of literary anti-Semitism in general. The close readings developed throughout this book comprise a methodology applicable across the humanities: its goals are to recognize expressions of anti-Semitism not readily apparent on a first reading, and to analyze how a text constructs the figure of the Jew discursively. (In referring to "the Jew" as a "discursive construct," I invoke the terminology of discourse analysis, which considers language as a social practice that inscribes ideologies and power structures.) In contrast to most other studies of Jews in German literature that are primarily sociohistorical or thematic in approach,[1] the main focus here is on rhetorical strategies, on the language of anti-Semitism. Drawing on Sander Gilman's foundational work; on recent studies of Jews, anti-Semitism, and anti-Semitic stereotypes in European literature; on discourse analysis; and on semiotic theory, I identify and interpret the discursive networks of anti-Semitism that inform the signifying systems of mainstream literary texts. For the most part, the anti-Semitic dimensions of these texts—canonical works of *Bildungskultur*—have not been recognized, much less analyzed, in the scholarship to date. Accordingly, two interrelated questions motivate the following readings: why have these anti-Semitic discourses escaped notice in German Studies as a discipline, and how do these hidden discourses of anti-Semitism construct meaning in literary texts?

In answer to the first question, I maintain that fundamental historical, epistemological, and disciplinary paradigm shifts have made these readings both possible and necessary. From historical and epistemological vantages, our post-Holocaust eyes cannot and do not read these texts as they were read in the eighteenth and nineteenth centuries. This is not to argue for a deterministic or teleological genealogy, but for a structural shift in cultural awareness. Something akin to a Marxian false consciousness rendered this latent anti-Semitism natural—hence only marginally perceptible—to a pre-Holocaust readership inured to anti-Jewish thought.

At the same time, disciplinary practices within the fields of *Germanistik* and German Studies have perpetuated this false consciousness, wittingly or unwittingly, up until the present. Historically, there has been a demonstrable resistance to reading the Jew in the German literary canon, and, oddly enough, to reading these canonical texts in their entirety. Instead, scholars have cherry-picked selectively: certain works and certain passages are cited over and over again, to the exclusion of others. As a result of this repetition compulsion, traditional readings of canonical texts have calcified over time. We think we know these texts, but we don't. To take but one striking example of this disciplinary blindness: the surface anti-Semitism of the Grimm Brothers' famous fairy tale "The Jew in Thorns" has long been recognized, yet the iconography announced in the text's title remains curiously unread. Scholars have missed the blatant allusion to the Crucifixion, and the full import of the text's programmatic anti-Semitism has not been analyzed correctly.[2] In short, the unreflected perpetuation of traditional reading practices has led to critical stasis, a problem compounded by contemporary cultural studies, which has made important critical advances, yet for the most part has moved away from canonical literature and largely abandoned sustained textual analysis.

My methodology, informed by reading strategies derived from deconstruction and feminist studies, opens up a new approach to interrogating the canon, to exposing blind spots in our understanding of the genealogy of modern anti-Semitism in the Austro-German context. Literature matters: as an expression of the cultural imaginary, it is an important indicator of how an educated population thought about Jews, as real people and as literary constructs, during a crucial period of the Jewish emancipation debate. Precisely because it sets up a tension between the real and the imaginary, literature provides a privileged sphere in which authors could explore the potentials and pitfalls of "the Jew" in German society in the era of emancipation and assimilation.

The authors under consideration in this study consciously experimented with the protean nature of "the Jew" as signifier. These authors *knew* that the rhetoric of anti-Semitism derives potency from its amorphousness, its intangibility; they intentionally used its inchoate language to effect critique in a multitude of contexts: religious, social, political, aesthetic, ethical, metaphysical. Hidden on the surface of the texts analyzed in this study is a *theory* of literary anti-Semitism, a self-reflexive discourse about the structure and function of anti-Semitism in literature. *The Word Unheard* aims to articulate this theory on the metatextual level: through rigorous close readings it presents a method for analyzing how latent discourses of anti-Semitism construct meaning in the literary text.

But what is latency in a literary text? How do we recognize or determine latent content?[3] And how can a text communicate latent content self-reflexively? For the purposes of this study, I understand "latent literary anti-Semitism" to be anti-Semitism in a literary text that historically has not been recognized, or is not readily evident, on first reading. Almost ironically, the latent anti-Semitism in question here is not deeply concealed in dark, cavernous recesses of a literary crypt. It is, rather, like Poe's purloined letter, hidden all too obviously out in the open and hence overlooked by most readers, yet it subtly and deliberately draws attention to itself and demands to be read. Learning to recognize this latent content is a matter of shifting perspectives, of asking new types of questions, of paying close attention to prejudices in our own readings practices and in the texts themselves.

As a graphic illustration of how a work can hide a latent subtext conspicuously in plain view, a latent subtext that deliberately draws attention to itself and demands to be read, consider Paul Klee's *Once Emerged from the Gray of Night . . . (Einst dem Grau der Nacht enttaucht . . .*, 1918). The painting, reproduced here and in color on the book jacket, is visually stunning. With its robust interplay of colors and forms, the painting attracts the viewer's gaze; the eye lingers on the dynamic beauty of this visual image. So much so, in fact, that it is very easy to miss a seminal feature of the artwork: embedded in this complex visual

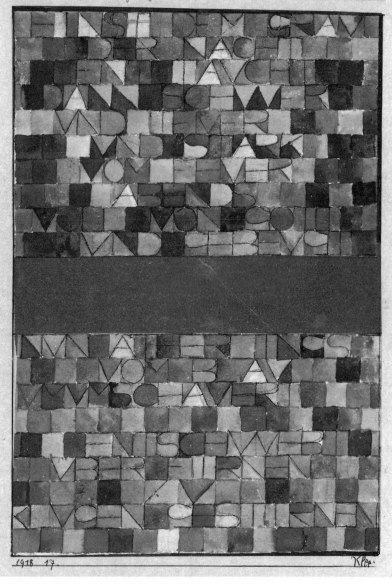

Paul Klee, *Once Emerged from the Gray of Night . . .*
(*Einst dem Grau der Nacht enttaucht . . .* , 1918);
watercolor, pen, and pencil on paper on cardboard; 22.6 x 15.8 cm.

image is a poem. Its words—segmented into letters inscribed individually in geometric blocks distinguished by both shape and color—are difficult to read. Yet the poem is very clearly there, and very clearly an integral part of this artwork. It announces its presence deliberately: it appears a second time, in careful, legible handwriting, at the top of the painting, as its epigraph. The handwritten poem serves as a guide, a program, for reading the text of the painting—the text in the painting—in its visual and verbal coherence.[4]

Klee's painting is not related thematically to the topic of this book, but it elegantly demonstrates how an artwork can contain an embedded subtext that is easy to overlook yet essential to its meaning, a subtext that calls attention to itself and provides a program, a theory, for understanding the work in its representational complexity.

This is precisely the nature of the latent anti-Semitism under consideration in *The Word Unheard*. The texts analyzed here all announce, in one form or another, that they take anti-Semitism as a major theme. As the following chapters demonstrate, many of the texts overtly state that they are theorizing the discursive construction of the figure of "the Jew"; others contain subtle clues that point to subtexts or semantic networks that reflect on, that implicitly or explicitly comment on, the structure and function of "the Jew" or of anti-Semitism in the text. This is what I mean when I say that the texts communicate their latent anti-Semitism self-reflexively, that they contain a *theory* of latent anti-Semitism. This latent content draws attention to itself through a variety of means: deployment of anti-Semitic stereotypes; contradictions between the text's surface message and the language used to convey this message; mention of a theme that then disappears; plots that don't make sense or have obvious lacunae; narrators that cannot be trusted; and so on. The history of a text's reception also can provide indicators of latent anti-Semitism. Secondary literature that cites select passages out of context, or that glosses over significant portions of a text, can draw attention to what is repressed, excluded, or latent: in this case, discourses of anti-Semitism. Finally, situating a work within certain historical contexts sometimes brings latent anti-Semitism to the fore. These assertions will be explicated in much greater detail in the course of this study using specific examples; I offer them here as general signposts for identifying latent anti-Semitism in literature.

I began this project intending to develop a new definition of literary anti-Semitism, and perhaps also a new theoretical vocabulary for the study of literary anti-Semitism. Gradually, and to my own increasing surprise,

I came to the conclusion that such an endeavor is misguided, indeed impossible, that it would be a mistake to try to formulate an exact definition of "literary anti-Semitism." This sense of impossibility was at first frustrating, yet proved to be unexpectedly productive. I realized that the rhetoric of anti-Semitism is by nature slippery and amorphous, that I was trying to define an "object" that is not one, whose force derives from its very elusiveness. I am well aware of the irony here: in a book about the language of anti-Semitism—a book that insists on close readings and argues for the power of words—I am declining to define the most basic of terms. This linguistic imprecision is a core strength, rather than a weakness, of the current project. It recognizes that a key feature of the rhetoric of anti-Semitism is its indeterminacy. It allows for flexibility and openness in examining a textual corpus. And it encourages intellectual curiosity. There is a danger to insisting on rigid definitions or inventing new theoretical terms to formalize the study of literary anti-Semitism. We risk obscuring the source material with over-intellectualized terminology, where the object of analysis becomes the terminology itself, rather than the literary text, and we risk forcing literature, which by its very nature is creative and often subversive, into predetermined categories.

This risk is particularly acute in studies of literary anti-Semitism, precisely because of the amorphous nature of the rhetoric of anti-Semitism. The problem is akin to Nietzsche's famous example about scientifically constructed definitions of "truth" in the essay "On Truth and Lie in an Extramoral Sense." If you put something behind a bush and then go back later and say, "Look! I found it!" of course you found it, Nietzsche says: you put it there in the first place. The discovery has some truth value, but only in a very limited way. Likewise, approaching a literary text with a preconceived notion of what you're looking for as "literary anti-Semitism" predetermines the types of questions you will ask and hence the outcome of the investigation. Incongruous though the turn to Nietzsche may seem in this context, the comparison is instructive. Just as Nietzsche argues for the importance of recognizing that our thought patterns have rigidified and that we need to recognize "truth" as a linguistic construct grounded in constantly shifting metaphors, metonymies, and anthropomorphisms, *The Word Unheard* seeks to move beyond inflexible definitions and preconceptions to expose and interpret the dynamically fluid linguistic structures on which literary anti-Semitism is predicated.

The pitfalls of formulating even a broad definition of literary anti-Semitism are readily apparent in one of the standards in the field, Mark Gelber's "What Is Literary Antisemitism?" In a cogent and thoughtful analysis Gelber argues that a working definition of literary anti-Semitism must proceed from literature itself, and must also take into account how readers perceive a text's anti-Semitic aspects over time.[5] Extrapolating from a careful survey of early manifestations of anti-Semitism in literature, Gelber defines literary anti-Semitism as "*the potential or capacity of a text to encourage or positively evaluate antisemitic attitudes or behaviors,* in accordance, generally, with a delineation of such attitudes and behaviors by social scientists and historians."[6] On the surface, this is a straightforward, pragmatic definition. Yet the definition is recursive: literary anti-Semitism is literature that promotes anti-Semitism, and Gelber does not define "anti-Semitism" but defers to social scientists and historians to delineate "antisemitic attitudes or behaviors." I will return to the difficult question of defining "anti-Semitism" shortly. For now, I want only to note that Gelber's definition assumes that literature is "generally" in sync with history and the social sciences; that historians and social scientists can come to some agreement about what anti-Semitism actually is; and that history and the social sciences are the disciplines that provide the primary basis for defining anti-Semitism. These assumptions are perhaps necessary, yet nonetheless problematic. First, literature by nature is creative and inventive, and does not necessarily or even generally reflect the "reality" of history or the social sciences. Second, historians and social scientists have not come to any consensus on what anti-Semitism actually is. Finally, the "reality" of history and the social sciences is grounded in a reading of texts and other data, a process that entails subjective selection and interpretation.[7] Indeed, historians often use literature as source material. In this sense, Gelber's turn to history and the social sciences to corroborate the findings of literary historians also involves an element of circular reasoning. My study challenges traditional methods of identifying and evaluating anti-Semitism, demonstrating that such methods have overlooked essential dimensions of these documents, and arguing that we need new strategies for reading primary texts—be they literary or historical—that move beyond manifest meaning to latency. In so doing, as I hope to show in the following chapters, we gain a more complete understanding of the structure and function of anti-Semitism in a textual corpus.

I want to turn briefly to the complex questions of defining and using the term "anti-Semitism." The scholarship on anti-Semitism is vast, and there is little critical agreement on what anti-Semitism is; when it is appropriate to use the terms "anti-Semitic" and "anti-Semitism" as opposed to other locutions like "anti-Jewish," "Jew-hatred," or "Judeophobia"; or even how to write the word. For the purposes of this book, I will use the

New Shorter Oxford English Dictionary definition of "anti-Semitism": "hostility or opposition to Jews."[8] This is the sense in which the word is used in everyday English, and I wish to preserve this straightforward meaning throughout my study. Some scholars maintain that the emergence of the word "anti-Semitism" around 1870 marks a decisive new form of anti-Jewish thought and behavior, and that it is therefore both anachronous and incorrect to use the term "anti-Semitism" to discuss earlier time periods. I find this argument highly problematic. First, distinctly modern forms of anti-Semitism are clearly evident in the eighteenth- and nineteenth-century literature under consideration here.[9] Second, it flies in the face of reason to deny the word the meaning it has for most speakers of English today. It's worth noting that words like "anti-Jewish" are also fraught with terminological imprecision. What is a Jew? What is Jewishness? What is Judaism? What does the "anti" in "anti-Jewish" mean? Is being "against" Jews the same as hating or fearing Jews, as the terms "Judeophobia" or "Jew-hatred" suggest? What to make of the fact that the Nazis tried unsuccessfully to replace the word "anti-Semitic" with "anti-Jewish" in the Third Reich, precisely because the term "Semite" did not mean "Jew"?[10]

Faced with this terminological quagmire, I at one point vaguely entertained the notion of inventing an entirely new vocabulary for analyzing literary anti-Semitism, a theoretical nomenclature that did not involve the words "Jew," "Judaism," "Jewishness," or "anti-Semitism." I quickly discarded this idea as absurd, as a linguistic innovation that itself borders on anti-Semitism: to do so would obscure the fact that we are talking about real people, Jews, and about a real historical phenomenon that has come to be known as "anti-Semitism," however problematic the term may be. Rather than trying to invent new vocabulary or formulate precise definitions where none are possible, we would do well to recognize that indeterminacy is a key feature of the rhetoric of anti-Semitism. Accordingly, I have opted to use the term "anti-Semitism" in its everyday meaning of "hostility or opposition to Jews," and will use "anti-Semitic" and "anti-Jewish" as synonyms.

In recent years many scholars and publishers have dropped the hyphen from the word "anti-Semitism," arguing that the hyphen buys into the ideology of anti-Semitism itself.[11] The reasoning is this. Wilhelm Marr, generally—albeit erroneously—credited with inventing the term in the 1870s,[12] introduced "anti-Semitism" to denote a modern, political, race-based opposition to Jews. But the word "Semitic" in fact does not denote a race or a people; it originally referred to a language group that includes both Hebrew and Arabic. There are no "Semites," only Jews. Hyphenating the term therefore gives credence to the ideology of anti-Semitism, in that it recognizes "Semitism" as referring to a race, the Jews: this racial definition is the basis of modern anti-Semitism. While I appreciate and respect the merits of this argument, it seems to me that its consequential conclusion is not to drop the hyphen, but to drop the word entirely. Hyphenated or not, "anti-Semitism" is comprised of two terms, "anti" and "Semitism." Graphic emendation cannot alter or elide this etymology. I find it inappropriate to drop the word, given its current widespread usage and its historical significance. I also think there may be some merit to using a term that inscribes its own problematic history. Finally, I personally find it difficult to drop the hyphen and to write "semitism" without capitalizing the term. To me this is tantamount to writing "jew" instead of "Jew"—not in the postmodern sense that Lyotard invoked, but in the derogatory sense the lowercase typography traditionally signifies. For these reasons I have chosen to write "anti-Semitism."

The Word Unheard covers the years 1749 to 1850, the period of the Jewish emancipation debate in Germany and Austria that saw the most intense public discussion of the "Jewish Question" in the print media. The authors selected are major writers representative of major literary movements: the Enlightenment, Storm and Stress, Classicism, Romanticism, Biedermeier, and poetic Realism. The book is programmatically *not* a survey of "Jews in German literature," and it makes no claims to comprehensiveness. The texts analyzed focus on key nodal points in the Jewish emancipation debate. They have been selected precisely because they participate in a larger sociopolitical debate, and precisely because they reflect on the function of the aesthetic in this debate.

There were four main phases in the development of Jewish emancipation in Germany.[13] The first, which extended from 1781 to 1815, began with a debate in the print media initiated by the publication of Christian Wilhelm von Dohm's *On the Civic Improvement of the Jews* in 1781, and was fueled in large part by the French Revolution and the Napoleonic era. As a direct result of the Revolution, Jews in France were granted full civic equality in 1791–1792, a right extended to Jews in the French-occupied territories of Germany under Napoleon's reign. At the Congress of Vienna in 1815 the civil rights of most Jews in Germany were rescinded. The second phase of the emancipation process, the period from 1815 to 1847, was characterized by an intense public debate about the "Jewish Question." Some two thousand five hundred books, pamphlets, and essays devoted to this topic were published between 1815 and 1850. The third phase was marked by the 1848 revolutions, during which the "Jewish Question" was hotly contested; the fourth extended from 1850 to 1871, when, with the creation of the Reich under Bismarck, Jews throughout Germany were granted full civic equality.

The emancipation debate in Austria differed somewhat from its German counterpart.[14] With Joseph II's Edict of Toleration of 1782, Austria had been the first European country to grant Jews the right to become naturalized subjects, but the government did not pursue the issue of legal rights for its Jewish subjects further until forced to do so by the 1848 revolutions. (This stasis in emancipation legislation in Austria stands in marked contrast to other European countries: in France, Holland, Prussia, and many other German states, Jews made decisive advances toward full legal integration in the wake of the French Revolution and the Napoleonic era.) The Austrian government retreated from enacting emancipation legislation once the 1848 uprisings were quelled; Jews in Austria received full legal rights in 1868.

Conceptually, and to a large extent chronologically, *The Word Unheard* describes a trajectory from the beginning to the end of the debate. It takes as its starting point the great Enlightenment playwright and critic Gotthold Ephraim Lessing, whose writings on Jews and Judaism, published at the inception of the debate, constitute the de facto benchmark of philo-Semitic discourse in German letters. It concludes with Austria's leading nineteenth-century dramatist Franz Grillparzer, who was carried from his sickbed to vote in support of the 1868 referendum that finally granted Jews in Austria full legal and civic rights. The chapters analyze texts dating from or reflecting on pivotal points in the emancipation debate: its inception, the French Revolution and the Napoleonic era, the intense discussion of the "Jewish Question" in Germany and Austria from the Congress of Vienna through the 1840s, and the 1848 revolutions.

Chapter 1, "Lessing and the Limits of Enlightenment," demonstrates that the three major works Lessing wrote promoting tolerance toward Jews and Judaism, *The Jews* (1749), *The Education of the Human Race* (1780), and *Nathan the Wise* (1779), all question their pro-Jewish and anti-anti-Semitic Enlightenment messages to a far greater degree than has been recognized in the scholarship to date. Lessing uses aesthetic experimentation to educate his readers about prejudice: these texts articulate a self-reflexive, self-critical theory of the discursive construction of "the Jew." Lessing's writings hence constitute a pivotal juncture in the formation of the rhetoric of anti-Semitism in German letters.

Chapter 2, "Questioning Origins," challenges the common conception that Friedrich von Schiller, the "poet of freedom" and one of the pillars of German Classicism, was a pro-Jewish writer in the spirit of Lessing. I interpret *The Legation of Moses* (1790) as political theory, and demonstrate the centrality of this often-marginalized essay to Schiller's aesthetic theory and praxis. The text, part of the series of lectures on "universal history" Schiller presented at the University of Jena, intentionally fictionalizes history to call into question the origins of the Judeo-Christian tradition. In Schiller's rewriting of the Exodus account, Moses is a shrewd charlatan who steals the secret of monotheism from the Egyptians and invents Judaism for his own political gain. Divested of its divine Jewishness, the Mosaic state provides a prototype for modern European state building in Schiller's theory. Directly linking his analysis to the contemporary debate about the "Jewish Question," Schiller argues that numerous negative traits are inherent in Jews and Judaism from the start. Rhetorically, religiously, racially, politically, ethically, and culturally, *The Legation of Moses* presents a historical justification for anti-Semitism.

Chapter 3, "Germany Under the Sign of the Jew," reads Achim von Arnim's Romantic novella *Isabella of Egypt* (1811) in tandem with his overtly anti-Semitic political speech "On the Distinguishing Signs of Jewishness," and argues that Arnim develops an incisive semiotic theory of "Jewishness" as a signifier of all that threatens German society; at the same time, the sign of "the Jew" also constitutes the condition of possibility for the construction of a unified Germany. The sociopolitical agenda articulated in these early nineteenth-century Romantic texts arguably anticipates what Shulamit Volkov identifies as the hallmark of anti-Semitism at the end of the nineteenth century in Germany: anti-Semitism becomes a cultural code.

Chapter 4, "Reading Blood," interprets Annette von Droste-Hülshoff's *The Jews' Beech Tree* (1842), one of Germany's most popular and beloved Biedermeier novellas, arguing that its protagonist is a hidden Jew according to a racial or "blood" definition, and that the novella narrates a subtextual story about the danger of concealed Jewish identity in Germany after the French Revolution. This anti-Semitic subtext is encoded on the linguistic level: the narrator specifically exhorts the reader to read each word and its roots, that is, to read etymologically, to see how language becomes the "secret soul-thief" of prejudice. The novella hence presents a self-reflexive theory of the structure and function of the rhetoric of anti-Semitism in literature.

Chapter 5, "Natural Anti-Semitism," analyzes the discursive construction of "the Jew" in conjunction with nature metaphors in Adalbert

Stifter's poetic Realist novella *Abdias* (1842), and demonstrates that this serenely beautiful narrative casts anti-Semitism as a natural phenomenon and inscribes an anti-assimilationist political agenda. Read as a document in the debate about the "Jewish Question," *Abdias* is a cautionary text about the Judaizing of Austrian society: its nature, its economy, and its art. The text stages this cautionary message self-reflexively. It deliberately and self-consciously derives its narrative force from shiftiness, slipperiness, and moral ambivalence—all quintessential stereotypical "Jewish" traits. At the same time, the novella presents a hermeneutic theory of literary anti-Semitism: the reader is asked to judge the image of the Jew as it is presented in the text, a text that takes "Jewishness" as its own narrative principle.

Chapter 6, "Framing the Jew," demonstrates that Franz Grillparzer's grand historical tragedy *The Jewess of Toledo* (completed in 1851 and published posthumously in 1872) pits philo-Semitism against anti-Semitism repeatedly and programmatically, thereby foregrounding one of its central themes: the representation of the Jew. After situating the text historically and thematically within the context of the Jewish emancipation debate at the time of the 1848 revolutions and showing how Grillparzer draws on a contemporaneous political event, the Lola Montez affair, to cast the "Jewish Question" as a discursive issue, the chapter offers an extensive analysis of how the figure of the Jew is framed in the text. In this "historical tragedy," a beautiful Jewess seduces a king who has pro-Jewish political sympathies, and causes the downfall of his realm: this is a play about the consequences of the state's love affair with "the Jew." Thematically and structurally, *The Jewess of Toledo* effects a trenchant critique of the dangers of philo-Semitism in the era of emancipation and assimilation.

Taken individually, the analyses developed in these chapters present fundamentally new readings of canonical texts. Taken together, they expose systematic blind spots around which and over which portions of the German canon have been constructed, and in so doing constitute an important critical intervention in our understanding of the nature and structure of anti-Semitism in general. In demonstrating the thoroughgoing extent to which the anti-Jewish discourse inflected in mainstream literature has remained undetected in the scholarship to date, *The Word Unheard* challenges traditional methods of identifying and evaluating anti-Semitism, arguing that we need to learn how to read primary texts—be they literary or historical—more carefully than has been the case in the past. The conclusion considers the risks of *not* reading this latent anti-Semitism, of not understanding how anti-Semitic thought patterns can subtly infuse literature.

"The Word unheard" is a phrase from T. S. Eliot's *Ash Wednesday*. It encapsulates this book's agenda precisely and poetically. The following chapters listen attentively to words that are there, words that have been unheard, giving voice to silent words that resonate strongly in our cultural consciousness today.

THE WORD UNHEARD

CHAPTER ONE

~

Lessing and the Limits of Enlightenment

This book begins with a necessary provocation: Lessing and latent anti-Semitism. The great Enlightenment playwright and critic Gotthold Ephraim Lessing was unequivocally a pro-Jewish author and political activist. Lessing was very likely the sponsor of the first published document calling for the full emancipation of the Jews in Germany,[1] and his theological and dramatic writings on Jews and Judaism form the de facto benchmark of pro-Jewish discourse in German letters. Lessing's influence on German literature and culture is profound. Just as every Jewish character in Western literature in some sense references Shakespeare's Shylock, every Jewish character in German literature in some sense references Lessing's Nathan the Wise.[2] Lessing's merchant Nathan is a good Jew, a wise Jew, the embodiment of Enlightenment who famously advocates tolerance for the three great monotheistic religions, Judaism, Christianity, and Islam. Lessing's Nathan is so good, so wise, and Lessing's reputation as a pro-Jewish German cultural icon so strong that the Nazis peremptorily prohibited the production of the play at the beginning of the Third Reich in 1933. After the war, in 1945, many German theaters reopened with *Nathan the Wise,* the symbol of tolerance and Enlightenment humanism, and the play is still one of the most frequently performed on the German stage today.[3]

And yet I begin—and must begin—this study of latent anti-Semitism with Lessing, the paragon of pro-Jewish thought in German literature and culture. I begin with Lessing not only because of his influence on subsequent authors and on German culture in general, but also because of systemic tensions inherent in Lessing's texts themselves. The three major works Lessing wrote promoting tolerance toward Jews and Judaism[4]—the theological treatise on *The Education of the Human Race* and the two plays *The Jews* and *Nathan the Wise*—all question their pro-Jewish and anti-anti-Semitic Enlightenment messages, and hence constitute a pivotal juncture in the formation of the rhetoric of anti-Semitism in German letters.

I want to make very clear from the start that I am *not* arguing that either Lessing or his texts are anti-Semitic. My argument is rather this: Lessing's pro-Jewish agenda turns back on itself and subtly and programmatically questions its own basic premises in true Enlightenment fashion. This is Enlightenment criticism pure and simple, and it is operative in Lessing's works in general. As Friedrich Schlegel incisively noted, Lessing's entire life and oeuvre are defined by criticism.[5] In both form and content, Lessing's writings enact a thoroughgoing questioning of established concepts, definitions, and thought patterns. The goal of Lessing's criticism is to combat dogma, to combat prejudice in the true sense of the word, pre-judging that does not examine its own basic premises. This constant calling into question informs Lessing's writing: it is self-reflexive, self-critical, internally contradictory, intentionally polemical, dialectical, multi-perspectival, and dynamically fluid in nature. The *process* of looking for truth, not truth itself, is at stake in Lessing's epistemology and in his poetic production.[6] This is why it is notoriously difficult to establish Lessing's own views in a given text, and this is why it would be folly to argue that there is only one possible reading of a given Lessing text. The following discussion analyzes the language and structure of Lessing's three major works on Jews and Judaism, and demonstrates that these texts by design set up a dialectical relationship between the rhetoric of philo-Semitism and the rhetoric of anti-Semitism, and hence articulate a self-reflexive, self-critical theory of the discursive construction of the Jew.

We begin somewhat anachronistically with *The Education of the Human Race* (*Die Erziehung des Menschengeschlechts*, 1777–1780), since this theological essay in many ways functions as a blueprint for the discursive construction of Jewishness evident in the earlier play *The Jews* (*Die Juden*, 1749) and the roughly contemporaneous play *Nathan the Wise* (*Nathan der Weise*, 1779).[7] In *The Education of the Human Race*, Lessing, writing from a Protestant theological vantage, sets out to account for the evolution of Christianity from Judaism; or, more precisely, to explain why, in his view, Christianity must necessarily supersede Judaism, and why Christianity as it is currently practiced likewise must give way to a more Enlightened version of Christianity, to a Christian religion of reason.[8] Lessing's essay, importantly, is cast as a response to Reimarus and Warburton debating the roles of reason versus revelation in recognizing eternal truths, and in fact intends to defend Judaism as a valid religion, as the historical predecessor to Christianity.[9] Neatly, if somewhat arbitrarily, divided into one hundred paragraphs, the essay's rational form reflects its rational Enlightenment agenda, and here, as in Kant's contemporaneous essay "What Is Enlightenment?" of 1783, Enlightenment is inextricably tied to the written word. Using a logical argument motored by metaphors and internal inconsistencies,[10] Lessing presents a history of theology—a theology of history—divided into four distinct stages. According to Lessing's fanciful historical schema, the religious development of the human race from polytheism through Judaism and Christianity to an Enlightened Christian "Gospel of Reason" parallels the physical stages of human development from birth through childhood and adolescence to manhood.[11] This phylogenetic maturation metaphor implies that the evolution of Christianity from Judaism is both a theological and a biological necessity. Moreover, Lessing equates religious maturation with sexual maturation, and he explicitly genders this Enlightenment maturation process as male: Jews are unsexed children ("Kinder"); present-day Christians are lads or male adolescents ("Knaben"); and practitioners of Lessing's new Enlightened "Gospel of Reason" are men ("Männer"). According to the metaphoric logic of Lessing's argument, Jews are less than men. Ex negativo, and likely unintentionally, Lessing invokes the stock anti-Semitic stereotype of the Jews as an effeminate people in the very framework of his argument.

Disturbingly, Lessing relies on many other anti-Semitic stereotypes and anti-Semitic rhetorical gestures to develop his theological history of the education of the human race. The story Lessing tells is this. In the beginning there was polytheism. The human race, Lessing implies, without actually using the metaphor, was in its baby stage at this earliest phase of its development. Then God selected the Jews, "the crudest and wildest of all peoples" ("das ungeschliffenste, das verwildertste" [§8: 76]), to reveal Himself to, so as to begin His educational plan with a clean slate, as it were. The Israelites, a people still in its childhood, raw, and clumsily incapable of abstract thought, had to be educated as one educates children, using a doctrine of immediate punishment and reward (§16: 78). The Old Testament, a primer for children ("ein Elementarbuch für Kinder" [§26: 81]), guided the Jews' pedagogical development. In Persian captivity the Jews began to compare "their Jehovah" to the Being of all Beings, a more rational and more moral being than they themselves had envisioned. The Jews then turned to their long-abandoned Old Testament to blame their own immaturity on the word of God, but had to admit to themselves, ashamed, that they themselves bore the guilt for not having recognized the true nature of God and for not having lived their lives accordingly (§38: 85). Remarkably, the Jews themselves are "guilty" of being Jews—children—in Lessing's schema, and the Jews—who must be "ashamed" of their own behavior—need an outside guiding force to set them straight. Using the Persian model as an example, the Jews then became "a completely different people" (§40: 85), and scoured their Bible for evidence of the truths they had seen in other religions. (In particular, Lessing is concerned here with the doctrine of the immortality of the soul.) But for all its richness and its hints at truth, its allegorical allusions to truth, Lessing argues, the Jews' Bible had its limits: "A better pedagogue had to come to tear this tired, worn-out primer from the children's hands: Christ came" (§53: 88). Under the tutelage of Jesus, "the first reliable, practical teacher of the doctrine of the immortality of the soul" (§58: 89), the "better teacher," the Israelites began to mature. The Jews became Christians; the children became young men ("Knaben" [§58: 89]). The New Testament, "the second, better primer" ("das zweite, beßre Elementarbuch" [§64: 91]), now directs their development. Guided by a "better" teacher and a "better" primer, the Christians are clearly "better" than the Jews in Lessing's view, but their education is as yet incomplete. The Christian ethos still is motivated by a reward system: the doctrine of eternal salvation. The youths will become men when they act in a moral way not because of a promise of salvation or a fear of damnation, but simply because it's the right thing to do. Goodness for the sake of goodness is the new Gospel of Reason, "the highest stage of Enlightenment and purity" ("diese höchste Stufen der Aufklärung und Reinigkeit" [§81: 96]). The metaphors Lessing uses here jarringly introduce an implied impurity, an implied dirtiness, into earlier stages of development: rhetorically, Lessing casts the Jews as an unclean, impure people, excluded from the highest stages of Enlightenment. Lessing reasons that it cannot be fair that those people who were born at the early phases of humankind's development should miss out on this highest level of human perfection. Hence he concludes his essay by speculating on metempsychosis, the transmigration of souls.[12] According to the logic of Lessing's Enlightenment agenda, Jews can and should become—literally—born-again Christians.

Just as each earlier stage of Enlightenment is tied to the written word in Lessing's model—the childlike Jews are guided by the Old Testament, the lad-like Christians by the New Testament—the last stage of Enlightenment, the new "Gospel of Reason" for mature Christian men, is inaugurated by a text: Lessing's own *The Education of the Human Race*. In a telling self-reflexive rhetorical gesture located at the precise center of the essay's one hundred paragraphs, Lessing draws a pronounced parallel between his own writing and the "clothing" and "style" of the Jews' *Elementarbuch,* the Jews' "primer."[13] With its allegories and instructive examples, its presentation that is at times plain, at times poetic, and full of polyvalent tautologies designed to sharpen its reader's acumen, *The Education of the Human Race* is explicitly patterned after the Old Testament (§§48–51: 87–88). In drawing this bold connection between the Jews' "primer" and his own, Lessing emphasizes the like education that Jews and Christians must undergo, an education that is to take place in and through language, through the written word: here, through the very text of *The Education of the Human Race* itself.

This is why the essay's anti-Jewish rhetoric is so important. On the one hand, Lessing clearly intends to portray Judaism in a positive light, defending Judaism as a necessary predecessor to Christianity, as a developmentally early stage of Christianity. And of course, historically, this is the case: Jesus was a Jew, and Christianity is an outgrowth of Judaism. On the other hand, Lessing clearly criticizes the Jews in his rhetoric throughout the essay. To be sure, from a Protestant theological perspective Lessing *must* criticize the Jews. To justify the later stages of this religion—the religion of reason, as well as the prevailing state religion of the time—Lessing *must* explain why Judaism, in this view, is superseded by Christianity. Lessing arguably softens his critique of Judaism by casting present-day Christians as likewise immature: the new Gospel of Reason is still to come. Yet there is no sense in which the essay should be read *only* as a critique of present-day Christianity, no sense in which Lessing uses the Jews *only* as a cipher for his critique of present-day Christians.[14] Both the form and the rhetoric of Lessing's essay belie the real object of his critique. Structurally, the bulk of the essay—almost half of the one hundred paragraphs—addresses the Jews as a crude, raw, wild people clumsily incapable of abstract thought who are themselves to blame for their own ignorance, as children at an immature developmental stage that must be superseded. Fewer than twenty paragraphs are addressed to the present-day Christians, who have yet to develop into mature adult practitioners of Lessing's new Gospel of Reason. Nowhere does Lessing characterize present-day Christians as "crude," "raw," "wild," "clumsy," or "guilty," as he does the Jews. Importantly, the essay contains no recognition of present-day Jews as practicing a reasonable or defensible religion.[15] Unsurprisingly, Lessing's close friend and collaborator Moses Mendelssohn, the great German Jewish Enlightenment philosopher famous for his piercing intellect, blasted Lessing for basing his entire argument on an invalid metaphor: the human race does not undergo a phylogenetic maturation process through religious stages of development as a baby progresses from childhood through adolescence to adulthood.[16] The motivation for Mendelssohn's critique is clear. There is no place for "grown-up Jews" in Lessing's new Gospel of Reason: "adult" Jews must become Christian. Despite his pro-Jewish intentions, in *The Education of the Human Race* Lessing scripts Enlightenment in its highest form, the new "Gospel of Reason," as anti-Jewish.

A similar dialectic informs *The Jews* of 1749, a comedy (*Lustspiel*) Lessing identified in the preface to the 1754 edition of his works as a serious reflection on the disgraceful repression of the Jewish people, intended to give its Christian audience pause. Irony figures prominently in the play's design: Lessing states that he tried to show virtue on the stage where the audience never would have suspected it, in the figure of the Jew.[17] Yet ironically, and perhaps intentionally, Lessing's Enlightenment defense of the Jews simultaneously contains a veiled but devastating critique of the Jews. Significantly, both form and content of the play turn back on themselves and question their own basic premises: in true Enlightenment fashion, the play stages a self-reflexive critique. On the formal level, the level of genre, Lessing's experimental *Lustspiel* defies the then-current comedic convention of making a mockery of its title figure(s).[18] The play likewise defies comedic convention in that it does not end with the requisite marriage, thereby challenging the entire genre of comedy, itself included, with its lack of a clear resolution. This self-reflexive critique—the challenge to comedic conventions and the lack of a clear resolution—also is evident in the play's content. In short, in both form and content the text programmatically and self-consciously calls its surface pro-Jewish stance into question.

   The Jews picks up on two interrelated social issues current at the time of the play's writing concerning the moral character and the physical identity of Jews in Germany. The first was the popular belief, reflected in published pamphlets and police reports, that Jewish swindlers and bands of Jewish robbers were terrorizing the mainstream Christian population, at times shaving their beards and otherwise disguising themselves so as not to be recognized as Jews. There are also records of Christian thieves disguising themselves as Jews. To be sure, there were isolated crimes that had Jewish perpetrators, yet these single cases grew in the public's eyes to a general characterization about the Jews as a people.[19] According to this line of thinking, a dangerous—and at times disguised or hidden—Jewish element threatened Christian society.

   A cognate concern for marking the Jew as "Jew"—for outing the disguised or otherwise unrecognizable, and hence dangerous, Jew in

Christian society—is at stake in the second sociohistorical event motivating Lessing's play. In August 1748, Frederick the Great of Prussia issued a decree prohibiting Jews from shaving their beards completely, precisely so that they would be readily identifiable as Jews. The decree opens with a statement that numerous investigations ("Inquisitionen") have shown that most robberies are either committed or organized by Jews; that Jews are shaving their beards "in order not to pass as Jews" and then slinking into houses and carrying out their plans with great success; that accordingly the king hereby orders Jews not to shave their beards completely, so that they can be identified as Jews.[20] (Frederick the Great, noted in historical annals for his tolerance toward religious minorities, harbored a pronounced animosity toward the Jews. In eighteenth-century Prussia some Jewish men, in an effort to acculturate into the mainstream population, had started to shave their traditional beards. Fear of the unmarked Jew "passing" in Christian society no doubt prompted Frederick's legislation.)[21] Lessing's *The Jews,* first published in 1754 but prominently dated in its subtitle as having been completed in 1749, arguably references the 1748 beard decree. The play's plot, set in motion by "Jew beard" disguises, clearly addresses the public's fears about bands of Jewish criminals terrorizing the Christian population, and its central theme resonates strongly with the unspoken fears motivating the 1748 beard decree: how to recognize the Jew, to read the Jew, to identify the unmarked Jew in German society.

The play's pedestrian plot revolves around a good-hearted, upright, clean-shaven traveler who saves a baron from two murderous robbers wearing "Jew beard" disguises. The robbers in fact are not Jews, but the baron's own servants. The good-hearted traveler discovers their true identity when one of the servants stupidly dumps the "Jew beard" disguises out of his bag. The traveler warns the baron that his servants have turned against him and intend to kill him. As a reward, the baron wants to give the good man his daughter's hand in marriage. But the good-hearted traveler must decline, since he himself, it turns out, is a Jew.

On its most basic plot level, then, the play is about the discovery and exposure of Jewish identity. Now, the good-hearted, clean-shaven traveler's Jewish identity and the beard-clad murderous robbers' non-Jewish identity are clearly evident from the start of the play. In the first lines of the play Martin Krumm and Michel Stich are introduced into the play as the "dumb" robbers whose plot has failed. Their "speaking names," *Krumm* ("crooked") and *Stich* ("stab"), draw attention to their criminal nature, and alert the play's readers and viewers to focus on names in this text. In the second scene the "Jewish" robber Krumm condemns the Jews

as a godless, murderous people, as deceivers, thieves, and highway robbers who deserve to be poisoned en masse, clearly identifying himself as
a non-Jew. Conversely, the good-hearted traveler's protestation of this
characterization strongly suggests that he is a Jew. The traveler exclaims
that he simply cannot understand how Jews possibly can be making the
streets unsafe, since there are so few Jews allowed ("geduldet," "tolerated") in Germany (2: 452).[22] When Krumm warns the traveler to protect
himself against the Jews more vigilantly than against the plague, thereby
rhetorically linking the Jews *to* the plague, the traveler remarks that he
wishes this were only the voice of commoners speaking. Lest there be
any doubt that the traveler is a Jew at this early point in the play, Lessing heavy-handedly reinforces this identification in the next scenes of the
text. The traveler's Enlightenment defense of the Jews in the third scene,
and his impassioned reaction to the slew of anti-Jewish comments the
baron makes in the sixth scene, unequivocally identify the traveler as
a Jew. In the third scene, immediately following the robber's comments
that the Jews are a godless, thieving people, the traveler protests that
when Jews are deceivers, most of the time it is because Christians have
driven them to such behavior, and Christians then wonder that Jews
react badly when they have been treated badly. If the two peoples are
to treat each other with respect and trust, the traveler continues, both
parties must act accordingly. But what if one religion considers the persecution of the other to be virtually a calling ("ein verdienstliches Werk"),
the traveler muses, and then breaks off his comments (3: 454). With his
strong condemnation of "Christian" behavior that is not Christian, as
well as his critique of Christian behavior that *is* Christian, the traveler
again implicitly identifies himself as a Jew. In the sixth scene the identification is overt. The traveler, crestfallen when the baron exclaims that
the Jews are the most malicious, despicable people of all, conspicuously
averts his face when the baron states that the Jews' negative character is
said to be evident in their physiognomy.[23] At this early point in the text
the good-hearted traveler is definitively marked as a Jew, and the bulk of
the play works to reinforce his virtuous nature. The play's conclusion,
in which the traveler reveals his Jewish identity, may come as a surprise
to the other characters, but it comes as no surprise to the text's attentive
readers.[24]

   The most obvious way to interpret this play about the discovery
and exposure of Jewish identity, then, is as a sledgehammer approach
to combating anti-Semitic stereotypes: the murderous, deceiving Christian robbers are the "Jews" in this text, and the real Jew in the text,
the traveler, is a good-hearted person. According to this reading, *The*

Jews is a play that challenges stock anti-Semitic stereotypes and portrays real Jews as virtuous, good people. The deep-rooted prejudice Lessing was attempting to combat is evident in one of the few reviews the play received when it was first published in 1754. The Protestant theologian Johann David Michaelis attacked *The Jews* on the grounds that it presented the entirely improbable characterization of a Jew who was completely good, completely noble, completely concerned for the well-being of others: even a middling virtue and probity are exceedingly rare among Jews, Michaelis argued. Lessing countered this critique by publishing an indignant anonymous letter, authored by Moses Mendelssohn, responding to Michaelis's attack.[25] Lessing clearly had cause to want to educate people about the nature of prejudice, and explicitly set out to portray a virtuous Jew in his play. The play is called *The Jews,* it would seem, precisely to underscore that it is a play about characterizing the Jews as a good people.

Strikingly, however, there is only one real Jew identified as such in this text, a Jew who says he is no fan of general characterizations like "Jews are thieves," or "Jews are good people" (6: 461). Given that this is a play about the discovery and exposure of Jewish identity, the very fact that the good-hearted traveler's Jewish identity is evident from the start suggests that the point of the play is not merely to combat anti-Semitism and to characterize the Jews as good people. This we know from the opening scenes; so what is the play really about? The play's title in its plural form, *The Jews,* suggests another possible reading: there is another Jewish identity, a hidden Jew, to be discovered and exposed in this text.[26] And in fact the Jew's servant—named, ironically, *Christ*oph— is subtly but repeatedly characterized as being, very possibly, a Jew. The very possibility of this concealed Jewish identity profoundly problematizes the play's surface pro-Jewish and anti-anti-Semitic messages.

Christoph's "speaking name" marks him as a Christian, yet the text is almost overdetermined in calling this Christian identity into question. Christoph is introduced into the play as a character not in his place, as a character found nowhere and everywhere (4:455).[27] He is repeatedly asked about his employer's identity, but the question put to him— "Wer mein Herr ist?" ("who my master is?" / "who my Lord is?" [14: 473])—obliquely asks after Christoph's own religious identity. Significantly, Christoph is characterized as an accomplished, smooth schemer who invents stories and lies to get what he wants: material goods and a woman. Christoph protests bitterly—perhaps too bitterly—when he discovers that he, "an honest Christian" (22: 487), has been serving a Jew, the good-hearted traveler. Since the play has established Christoph as anything but an honest Christian, his ensuing harangue against the traveler is suspect. Proclaiming that the Jew has insulted all of Christendom by taking a Christian into his service, and that this is why he had not understood why the traveler did not want to eat pork and did "a hundred" other "silly things" ("Alfanzereien" [22: 487], a noun that derives from "Alfanz," a foreign rogue or deceiver),[28] Christoph threatens the traveler with legal action.

This scene subtly illustrates *in nuce* the point of the entire play. Christoph's comment about why he did not understand the Jew's avoidance of pork and his "foolish" behavior does much more than simply mock the traveler's religious practices. Christoph in fact suggests the traveler duped him into not recognizing the signs of Jewishness in his character. This accusation—that the Jew was passing unmarked and had injured all of Christendom by his deceptive actions—resonates with the sociohistorical context motivating the play: the widespread belief that a "hidden" criminal Jewish element threatened Christian society to its very core, and Frederick the Great's beard edict designed to distinguish Jews from Christians. In short, Christoph's rant against the traveler underscores that this is a text about learning to "read" the Jew, the Jew passing unmarked in Christian society. Ironically, of course, the text has *marked* the good-hearted traveler as a Jew from the start. At the same time, Christoph is typecast in the role of "the Jew." This is why it is significant that Christoph, marked by name but not by behavior as Christian, begins his rant with the words: "But now I return from my astonishment back to myself again!" ("Nun komme ich erst von meinem Erstaunen wieder zu mir selber!" [22: 487]). Again the text suggests we should read self-reflexively, that we too should return to Christoph again.

As if to underscore the fundamental question surrounding Christoph's identity, the traveler responds to Christoph's harangue in a predictably good-hearted manner, yet intimates that Christoph himself has a shady background. Noting the wretched circumstances from which he had saved Christoph in Hamburg, the traveler dismisses Christoph from his service and gives him his coveted silver tobacco can. In a dramatic volte-face Christoph then praises the traveler's generosity, remarking: "It seems there are also Jews who aren't Jews" ("Es gibt doch wohl auch Juden, die keine Juden sind" [scene 22]).[29] Christoph's words can be interpreted two ways. First, the good-hearted traveler isn't a "Jew" because he would willingly give away the valuable silver tobacco can—something a "Jew" never would do—and the traveler is hence a good person.[30] This reading is substantiated by Christoph's subsequent remark that a Christian, in contrast, would have kicked him in the ribs, and by the baron's ensuing exclamation that all Jews would be worthy of respect if only they were like the traveler. The traveler's rejoinder that all Christians likewise would be worthy of love if they had the baron's traits would seem to suggest that *The Jews* is a simple morality play: not all Jews are bad; not all Christians are good. According to this reading the play ends where it began, with an attack on common prejudices, with a plea for universalism.

Yet Lessing is an author known for nuance and irony, and the very fact that Christoph is the character marked by name as Christian perforce draws attention to his religious identity, especially in a play titled *The Jews,* a play about the discovery and exposure of Jewish identity. Importantly, there is a second way to interpret Christoph's remark that "It seems there are also Jews who aren't Jews" ("Es gibt doch wohl auch Juden, die keine Juden sind"): there are in fact Jews who are not identified as Jews. The conclusion of the play supports this latter reading. In the final scene, which immediately follows Christoph's comment about Jews who aren't Jews, the servant woman Lisette pointedly asks Christoph a question laden with innuendo: "Are you perhaps also a Jew? You're constantly misrepresenting yourself / you're constantly putting yourself in the wrong place!" ("Ist Er wohl gar auch ein Jude, so sehr Er sich verstellt?" [23: 488]). Christoph laughs off Lisette's question with a flip retort: this is too curious a question for a maiden to be asking—that is, a virtuous woman should not be asking him whether he is circumcised. The play ends on a comic note, but Lisette's question—"Are you perhaps also a Jew?"—hangs, unanswered, over the play's resolution.

Subtly, but significantly, in the very last lines of the play Christoph references that ultimate "hidden" sign of the Jew—circumcision—the sign the Jews take as the mark of the covenant between God and the Jews, "the supreme obligatory sign of loyalty and adherence to Judaism."[31] Of course this is no proof that Christoph *is* circumcised, and even if he were circumcised, this would not prove that he is a Jew. The point is rather this: the text underscores the *possibility* that Christoph is perhaps also a Jew. And the very possibility that Christoph, the slippery operator who lies and misrepresents himself to get what he wants—material goods and a woman—is indeed perhaps also a Jew severely compromises the play's surface pro-Jewish message. While the good-hearted Jewish traveler is a virtuous person, Christoph is the stereotypical "Jew" who poses as a Christian but in fact may be a Jew. The implications of this conclusion extend far beyond a simple statement of the play's universalist theme that there are good Christians and bad Christians, good Jews and bad Jews. In scripting Christoph as very possibly a hidden Jew who displays stereotypical "Jewish" traits, Lessing reinforces popular anti-Semitic suspicions about a concealed, dangerous Jewish element that threatens mainstream Christian German society: precisely the threat addressed by Frederick the Great's 1748 beard decree. No wonder, then, that the good-hearted Jewish traveler's library consists of comedies that move one to tears and tragedies that make one laugh ("besteht aus Lustspielen, die zum Weinen, aus Trauerspielen, die zum Lachen bewegen" [10: 467]). Again the play marks itself with a self-reflexive gesture. Lessing's pro-Jewish comedy *The Jews*—the comedy that is not really a comedy because it programmatically does not end with the requisite marriage and because it would not seem to mock its title figures—Lessing's pro-Jewish comedy that is not really pro-Jewish and does mock one of its title figures, this too is a comedy that moves one to tears.

The pro-Jewish tolerance message of Lessing's great masterpiece *Nathan the Wise* likewise programmatically calls itself into question, but here the text's self-reflexive Enlightenment critique is much more subtle and much more refined than in *The Jews* or *The Education of the Human Race*. Here, as in the earlier pieces, both form and content underscore the text's self-reflexive criticism, its constantly calling itself into question in true Enlightenment fashion. On the formal level, Lessing identifies the play as a "dramatic poem." This innovative genre aims to call traditional categories into question: it breaks down established boundaries and fuses together disparate genres or categories, ironically creating a new norm, a new standard, a new genre. This aesthetic program is reflected in the play's content. The plot aims to break down established boundaries between the three great monotheistic religions—Judaism, Christianity, and Islam—and to create a new Enlightened Gospel of Reason, as it were.

Set in the holy city of Jerusalem in the twelfth century during a pause in fighting in the Third Crusade, the play revolves around a wise Jewish merchant Nathan, who is cast as *the* Enlightenment figure in the text. One day Nathan returns home from a business trip to find that his house has burned down, and that his adoptive daughter Recha has been rescued from the flames by a Christian crusader, the Templar. Predictably, Recha and the Templar fall in love, although the Templar tries to resist the burning desire he feels for Recha, since he assumes—incorrectly—that she is Jewish. Fortuitously, the Templar's own life has been spared by the Sultan Saladin because the Templar looks like Saladin's brother. Following some convoluted plot twists, Recha and the Templar improbably turn out to be brother and sister, niece and nephew to the Sultan

Saladin. The play ends with the construction of a natural family that conjoins Christian, Muslim, and Jew: the play ends with the construction of an Enlightened Gospel of Reason in which Christian, Muslim, and Jew are united in one big happy family.

Like *The Education of the Human Race, Nathan the Wise* stages a critique of both Judaism and Christianity as it labors to construct this Enlightened Gospel of Reason. (Islam is bracketed from this self-reflexive critique, presumably because there were very few Muslims in Lessing's target audience in eighteenth-century Germany.) The Jews are criticized for being the first to maintain that they are "the chosen people," the first to maintain that their God is "the right God," and for passing on this false pride to their heirs, the Christians and Muslims (II, 5: 532).[32] The Christians—Daja, the Templar, and especially the Patriarch of Jerusalem—are taken to task for their belief in being "Christian" at the expense of all else, a belief that frequently leads them to act in an unchristian, inhuman way. The most extreme example of this inhuman "Christian" behavior is the Patriarch's repeated insistence that Nathan (or, more precisely, "the Jew") should be burned at the stake for raising a Christian girl. This self-reflexive critique of Christianity and Judaism would seem to culminate in act 4 when the Lay Brother ("der Klosterbruder")—who *is* a good Christian—exclaims that Nathan is Christian, that there never was a better Christian, and Nathan replies that precisely those traits that make him a good Christian make the Lay Brother a good Jew (IV, 7: 597). With this statement the border between Christianity and Judaism is broken down, paving the way for the play's conclusion, the construction of an Enlightened Gospel of Reason in which Christian, Muslim, and Jew are united in one big happy family.

Unsettlingly, however, the staying power of this universalist vision is called into question from the start of the text. The play is set in a pause in fighting during the Third Crusade: Lessing's eighteenth-century audience knows that the religious wars will continue, that this happy end will not last. The play begins with Nathan the Wise, Nathan the Jew, agreeing with his Christian servant Daja that the harmonious conjoining of Jew, Christian, and Muslim is a "sweet illusion" or "sweet delusion" ("ein süßer Wahn") that is sweet to him too, but at the same time Nathan argues that sweet delusions must make way for "sweeter truth" (I, 1: 490). With this statement the text underscores its self-reflexive, self-critical, realist agenda. And indeed, the plot's neat resolution is programmatically called into question by a number of troubling details that threaten to undermine the text's central Enlightenment tolerance message.

First, the natural family constructed in the last scene of the play faces a profound Freudian challenge: incest. Throughout the text both Recha and the Templar have been "burning" for each other, and now discover they are brother and sister. On hearing the news of their sibling relationship Recha seemingly transforms her ardent passion for the Templar into familial love, saying "my brother? [. . .] Oh! my brother!" and moves toward him, while the Templar says "I? her brother? [. . .] her brother?" and steps away. Giving voice to the true nature of the burning desire she and the Templar both still feel for each other, Recha then exclaims: "This cannot be! This cannot be! His heart / knows nothing of this!—We're deceivers! God!" (V, 8: 625). Needless to say, this smoldering sexuality does not bode well for the future of this natural family.

The "blood" problematic also threatens the play's Enlightenment resolution on a second level: religion. Throughout the play Nathan has been worried that Recha will disown him because he has not told her she is adopted and has not told her she is Christian. But Recha repeatedly insists that "blood" does not define families: Nathan is her father because he has raised her, not because of biological circumstances. Ironically, however, "blood" does define the natural family constructed at the end of the drama. The play's happy end depends precisely on genealogy, on bloodlines. As if to underscore the fact that the play's resolution is grounded in blood, the Templar exclaims to the Sultan in the play's penultimate lines: "I am of your blood" ("Ich deines Bluts!" [V, 8: 627]). Given that the play aims at the construction of a natural family that conjoins the three great monotheistic religions in one big happy family, it is significant that Nathan—the Jew—is not related by blood to any of the other characters.[33] At the end of the play, "Nathan der Weise"—Nathan the Wise—becomes "Nathan die Waise"—Nathan the orphan.

The Jew's problematic status in this Enlightenment family is further accentuated in the so-called Ring Parable, which forms the structural and thematic core of the text. Here, too, "blood" is the driving force that motivates the text's central religious disquisition. Saladin, in dire financial straits, summons Nathan, but rather than asking the Jew for money decides to trick him by posing a probing religious question. Only one of the three religions—Judaism, Christianity, and Islam—can be the true religion, and a wise man like Nathan would not stay where the accident of birth, of blood, had thrown him; if he does stay, it must be because of insight, principles, choice of "the better," Saladin asks, so how does Nathan justify his faith? Nathan hesitates before answering, aware that Saladin wants money and is trying to trick him, to "Jew" him: "Who's the Jew here," Nathan asks, "me or him?" ("Wer ist denn hier der Jude? / Ich oder er?" [III, 6: 554]). The suspicion that the potentate Saladin may be using "truth" as a trap, Nathan reasons, forces him to proceed cautiously in answering the question.

(It is worth noting parenthetically that Nathan is faced here with the same dilemma that tormented his real-life model Moses Mendelssohn, who in 1769 was challenged by the Swiss clergyman Johann Caspar Lavater to defend his Judaism publicly or convert to Christianity.[34] Given the dangers inherent in offending the ruling authorities and the mainstream population, the Jew clearly must proceed cautiously in defending his faith. Likewise, in Lessing's source for the Ring Parable, Boccaccio's *Decameron,* the Jew Melchisedech, by recounting the Tale of the Three Rings to the Sultan Saladin, prevents a great danger that had been prepared for him. It is also worth noting that in Lessing's play Saladin is correct that Nathan has *chosen* to retain his Judaism: following the murder of his wife and seven sons by Christians, Nathan, at wit's end in a Job-like state of despair, had questioned God and vowed irreconcilable hatred toward all Christians, but then reason returned, and with it his equanimity and his faith in God [IV, 7: 596–97].)

Nathan, by birth and by choice a Jew, is now forced to justify his religion. Aware that Saladin may be trying to trick him, he then considers what kind of Jew he should present himself as, and concludes he should answer Saladin's "Jewing" with "Jewing." Nathan decides to "fob off" a fairy tale on Saladin in lieu of an answer, thereby opting to present himself as an upright Jew who nonetheless engages in stereotypical crafty "Jewish" behavior, deception:

> Being a Jew through and through, won't work.—
> And not being a Jew at all is even worse.
> Since—if not a Jew, he might ask,
> Why not a Muslim?—That's it! That can
> Save me!—It's not just children to whom one feeds
> Fairy tales [one fobs off fairy tales on].

>   So ganz
> Stockjude sein zu wollen, geht schon nicht.—
> Und ganz und gar nicht Jude, geht noch minder.
> Denn, wenn kein Jude, dürft' er mich fragen,
> Warum kein Muselmann?—Das war's! Das kann
> Mich retten!—Nicht die Kinder bloß, speist man
> Mit Märchen ab. (III, 6: 554)

Nathan identifies his story as both a "Märchen"—a fairy tale—and a "Geschichtchen"—a little story or a little history, a history in miniature that he wishes to tell Saladin *before* he answers his question in complete trust, in complete confidence (III, 7: 555). Nonetheless, scholars and readers almost uniformly interpret Nathan's tale as *the* answer to Saladin's question, an answer that takes the form of a parable illustrating the equal truth value of the three great monotheistic religions.[35] Certainly there is a great deal of validity to this standard interpretation. Read from a different perspective, however, Nathan's tale tells a very different story: Nathan the Jew in fact defends Judaism as the originary religion.

Structurally, the ring tale is divided into two distinct parts. In the first, Nathan tells of a ring with magic powers that made its bearer beloved in the eyes of God and his fellow men. The ring was passed on from one generation to the next, from father to son, until one day a father cannot decide which of his three beloved sons should receive the ring. In "pious weakness" he promises each son his ring (III, 7: 556). On his deathbed, "in embarrassment" (III, 7: 556), the father devises an aesthetic solution to his problem. He has an artist make two copies of the ring, gives each of his sons a ring, and dies. Now there are three rings, an original ring and two artistic reproductions indistinguishable from the original. If the rings do indeed represent the three great monotheistic religions in this little historical story ("Geschichtchen"), the original would represent Judaism; the reproductions, Christianity and Islam. (Historically, Christianity and Islam are derived from Judaism; elsewhere in the play Lessing pointedly underscores this genealogy by having the good Christian Lay Brother exclaim emphatically that all of Christianity builds on Judaism and that Jesus was a Jew [IV, 7: 595], and by having the Templar identify Christianity and Islam as Judaism's heirs [II, 5: 532].) According to Nathan's tale the original "Jewish" ring still exists (or perhaps was lost— but not destroyed), and this indistinguishable "Jewish" ring threatens the integrity of Christian and Islamic societies by virtue of the fact that it *is* the original. As Nathan puts it: "the true ring was not / Demonstrable;— *(Nathan pauses, waiting for Saladin's answer) Almost* as indemonstrable as / The true religion is to us now" ("der rechte Ring war nicht / Erweislich;—*(nach einer Pause, in welcher er des Sultans Antwort erwartet) Fast* so unerweislich, als / Uns itzt—der rechte Glaube" [III, 7: 557, emphasis mine]). The stage directions dictating Nathan's dramatic pause emphasize the enormity of the conclusion he is about to draw: the adverb "*almost,*" "*fast,*" suggests the true faith—presumably Judaism—is indeed distinguishable to us today. And at this point, Nathan notes, his story is over (III, 7: 557).

Nathan, criticized at the start of the scene for being repeatedly "so proudly modest" (III, 7: 555), carefully does not draw any conclusion from his little historical story. He humbly asserts that the story is not meant as an answer to Saladin's question about the single true religion; it is only meant to excuse him if he does not feel he can distinguish what the father intentionally designed to be indistinguishable. Saladin, taken aback, responds that there are distinct differences among the religions. Nathan replies that the differences are discernible only in the religions' practices, but not in their foundations, since each religion is grounded in history, be it written or oral, and history must be accepted on the basis of loyalty and faith. And are we not least likely to question the word of the father, whose blood we share, Nathan asks, are we not least likely to question the father who tests our love, the father who never deceives us except when deception is more healing than truth? (III, 7: 557–58). The irony here is profound. Nathan has just related a story in which the father—"in pious weakness" and "in embarrassment," but with every good intention—deceives his sons, calling "each especially" to him, giving each son his ring and giving "each especially" his blessing (III, 7: 557). If this deception is more healing than truth, as Nathan suggests, then truth itself has been jeopardized in the father's well-intentioned act. In short, in Nathan's story there *is* reason to doubt the word of the father, to question the history that grounds each son's faith. (In a doubly ironic gesture the status of "the father" is repeatedly called into question in the main body of the play: Nathan's standing as Recha's father, the crucial question of the Templar's paternity, and the distressingly bigoted Patriarch of Jerusalem. The issue of literary paternity, of Lessing's indebtedness to Boccaccio, comes into play on the metatextual level here as well.)

The question of historical legitimacy, of testing the word of the father, forms the core of the second part of Nathan's tale. Following the death of the father, Nathan relates, all three sons claim to have the true ring, given by the father. Predictably, the sons begin to fight. They go to a judge, who states that the value of each ring is to be proven by the behavior of its bearer. If none of the rings works with its original intent, then all three sons have been deceived: presumably the real ring was lost, and the father made three copies to hide the loss of the original. But, the judge continues, if each son believes he has received the original ring from his father, each should strive to prove its validity through his behavior, and in a thousand years a wiser judge than he might be able to identify the true ring. This suggests, of course, that the adherents of each faith must prove their religion's worth through their actions. If all three rings can prove their worth, the judge continues, perhaps the father no longer wished to tolerate the "tyranny" of a single ring in his own house. This pragmatic proof surely establishes the practical validity of all three rings, of all three religions, but it does not change the fact that there *is* an original ring in Nathan's historical account—a ring that might be identified in a thousand years. And the existence of this original Jewish ring constitutes a challenge to the other two religions. This is why Nathan is left out of the natural family constructed at the end of the play. The Jew, by virtue of his originary status, represents a threat to the integrity of Christian and Muslim societies, and hence is excluded from the natural family's bloodline at the drama's conclusion.

As if to confirm this reading, the ring tale ends with a subtle anti-Jewish gesture presented in an entirely positive light. Nathan, aware that Saladin's real motivation in asking him to justify his faith is financial, offers the Sultan money. His magnanimous gesture notwithstanding, the truth of Nathan's tale is thus "Judaized" by that quintessential "Jewish" trait: money. Nathan's ring tale is framed by money: it is introduced by money; it concludes with money; it is grounded in money. "As if truth were a coin," Nathan says in introducing his tale (III, 6: 554).[36] And indeed, truth *is* a coin in the ring tale, an object presented as having truth value, as having exchange value, when in fact it has none: the tale is presented in lieu of an answer.

The truth of Nathan's tale is Judaized on a second level as well. The tale—introduced as an excuse not to tell the truth, as a deception—tells a "Jewish" truth that is, ironically, the truth of the Jew. The smart Jew Nathan uses stock anti-Semitic stereotypes, craftiness and subterfuge, to defend his own Judaism as the originary religion. And it is precisely this defense of Judaism—the Jews' insistence that they are "the chosen people"—for which the Jews are criticized in the text. It is no accident that Nathan is introduced into the play, in a structurally prominent position in the last lines of act 1, scene 1, as being "so good, and at the same time so bad!" ("Ihr seid so gut, und seid zugleich so schlimm!" [I, 1: 490]). For all his wisdom, for all his goodness, Nathan remains "the Jew"—with all its stereotypical associations—at the end of the play. In true Enlightenment fashion *Nathan the Wise*, like *The Education of the Human Race* and *The Jews*, turns back on itself and calls its own pro-Jewish message into question.

This self-reflexive gesture is entirely in keeping with the spirit of Enlightenment criticism, and I do not believe that either Lessing or his writings should be characterized as anti-Semitic. In comparison to the unambiguous anti-Semitism evident elsewhere in Enlightenment letters—Kant's call for the euthanasia of Judaism, Voltaire's attack on the Jews as a barbarous, contemptible people who nonetheless should not be burned, or Fichte's proposal to decapitate the Jews and replace their Jewish heads with Christian ones, to cite but a few famous examples—Lessing clearly intends to promote a pro-Jewish Enlightenment tolerance agenda. It is also the case, I believe, that we simply cannot read Lessing's writings on Jews and Judaism as they were read in the eighteenth century. Our post-Holocaust eyes perforce read the anti-Jewish moments in these texts more critically, and perhaps with an ineluctable implied teleology. Still, these anti-Jewish moments in Lessing's writings must be read, and not simply read over or excused away as not existing. This is precisely the point of the three close readings I have offered here: to demonstrate a structural homology that *must* be accounted for in any study of "Lessing and the Jews." At the limits of his Enlightenment discourse, Lessing's pro-Jewish writings turn back on themselves programmatically and self-critically. Whether Lessing *intentionally* wrote this critique into his texts—as I have proposed—ultimately is a matter of little consequence. Intentional or not, the anti-Jewish moments in these texts constitute an important juncture in the history of the formation of the rhetoric of anti-Semitism.

This chapter has exposed systematic blind spots on which our critical understanding of the pro-Jewish author and activist Lessing has been predicated for over two hundred years. It has opened up new dimensions of three foundational works by paying close attention to their language and structure, by pausing to consider troubling features of these works that do not fit neatly into the image of the "pro-Jewish Lessing" that has been the unassailable basis of most scholarship to date. The method-ological framework used here has focused instead on structural tensions inherent in Lessing's writing, thereby allowing formative, and heretofore unnoticed, aspects of these texts to come into view. Reading synthetically across these texts, this chapter has argued for a new way of analyzing Lessing's discursive construction of "the Jew" in its complexity. In so doing, it has presented a fundamental reevaluation of Lessing's writ-ings on Jews and Judaism. Situating these works within the context of Lessing's entire oeuvre, an oeuvre *defined* by criticism, by a constant call-ing into question, the preceding analysis has unraveled the myth of the staunchly pro-Jewish Lessing, not so much to discredit it, but rather to complicate it, as Lessing's texts themselves programmatically do. These results are important not only for our critical understanding of Lessing per se, but also because the tensions inherent in Lessing's writings on Jews and Judaism lay the groundwork for, and to some extent inform, the discursive construction of Jewishness in subsequent German letters.

CHAPTER TWO

~

Questioning Origins

Friedrich von Schiller's *The Legation of Moses*

In *The Legation of Moses* (*Die Sendung Moses,* 1790), Schiller the historian presents a remarkable revisionist thesis: Moses used reason to invent the Jewish faith, and he did so for expressly political purposes—to establish himself as the legitimate leader of his people. In effect, Schiller maintains, Moses was a shrewd charlatan who cobbled together Judaism from beliefs he took from indigenous Egyptian religions, and then used this invented faith to dupe the Hebrews into following him out of Egypt. The establishment of the Jewish state, grounded in a fabricated "religion of reason" ("Vernunftreligion"),[1] has profound consequences for world history in Schiller's account: the two major religions that "rule" most of the world, Christianity and Islam, "support themselves" on "the Hebrew religion"; indeed, neither Christendom nor the Koran would exist without it; and the "Mosaic religion" forms the cornerstone of the Enlightenment (451).[2]

Despite its momentous rewriting of the Mosaic tradition, Schiller's *The Legation of Moses* is little known and has received scant attention in the secondary literature to date. Indeed, I would hazard to say that many Germanists have not read the essay, and do not even know of its existence. Most surveys of Schiller's historiography mention the essay only cursorily, if at all.[3] The few significant interpretations of *The Legation of Moses* have focused primarily on Schiller's sources, and to a lesser extent on his historical methodology.[4] One recent study argues cogently for a synthetic reading within the context of Schiller's oeuvre as a whole, correctly asserting that the literary dimension of the essay has not been adequately analyzed.[5]

This limited reception history deserves explanation. As Otto Dann has noted, Schiller attached special significance to *The Legation of Moses,* publishing it as the lead essay in his journal *Thalia* in 1790 and again as the opening piece in his *Shorter Prose Works (Kleinere prosaische Schriften)* of 1792.[6] Schiller's decision to place the essay at the start, at the beginning, of two published volumes reflects his agenda in *The Legation of Moses:* precisely the issue of origins, of originality, is at stake here. This is a text about the origins of monotheism, about the origins of the Jews as "the chosen people," and about the origins of the presumed author of the Torah, the Five Books of Moses: Moses as "author" is under scrutiny in this text.

Ironically, precisely the issue of origins, of originality, has led in part to the essay's limited reception history. Many—if not most—of the ideas expressed in *The Legation of Moses* are not new, and Schiller himself raises the question of the originality of his own authorship. Yet the essay's limited critical reception is too easily explained away by the fact that it is to some extent derivative of a text published pseudonymously by Karl Leonhard Reinhold. By the same token, Schiller's famous lecture on "universal history," *What Is Universal History and What Is the Goal of Studying It? (Was heißt und zu welchem Ende studiert man Universalgeschichte?)*, is heavily indebted to August Ludwig Schlözer, Immanuel Kant, and Johann Gottfried Herder, yet this essay is widely celebrated both in the scholarship and in the German cultural tradition. It is also too easy to dismiss *The Legation of Moses* as a minor and not particularly original contribution to the eighteenth century's burgeoning discourse on Moses, when Schiller accorded the piece significance, twice publishing it as the opening work in collections of his writings. The dearth of recent scholarship on the essay is all the more surprising in light of its influence on *Moses and Monotheism,* although Freud, characteristically, does not explicitly acknowledge Schiller as a source.[7] The reason, I suspect, that *Germanistik* as a discipline has largely ignored, conveniently forgotten, or tersely glossed over *The Legation of Moses* is quite simply this: the German poet, philosopher, historian, and playwright Friedrich von Schiller is a cultural icon, one of the pillars of German Classicism, and the essay's treatment of Jews is highly problematic, a fact at best acknowledged in most scholarship to date with an embarrassed nod to the prevalent prejudices of Schiller's day.[8]

The following analysis examines the structure and function of the figure of "the Jew" in *The Legation of Moses* and interprets Schiller's text as an important document in the history of the formation of the rhetoric of modern anti-Semitism. The first section briefly discusses the status of "the Jew" in Schiller's thought in general and then contextualizes *The Legation of Moses* with respect to Schiller's theory of "universal history" and his *Aesthetic Letters.* The second considers the provenance of *The*

Legation of Moses and examines Schiller's pseudo-plagiarist methodology. The third section offers a close reading of the title and opening
two paragraphs of the essay and establishes the text as political theory: Moses provides a prototype for modern European state building,
yet Schiller must divest the Mosaic state of its Jewishness for it to be
a viable model for contemporary Europe. This Schiller does by arguing
that Moses' political and religious genius is fundamentally Egyptian in
origin; Schiller directly relates this political theory to the contemporaneous debate about the "Jewish Question," the debate about the Jews'
civil and legal status in Germany. The final two sections explicate this
thesis, demonstrating that Schiller grounds his critique of contemporary
Jewish emancipation in a "universal historical" reading of the *Urtext* of
Jewish emancipation, the biblical Exodus account.[9] In his universal historical analysis Schiller inscribes the rhetoric of anti-Semitism into the
very inception of "the Mosaic religion," arguing that numerous negative
traits are inherent in Jews and Judaism from the start. *The Legation of
Moses* thereby offers a historical justification for anti-Semitism.

My reading of *The Legation of Moses* challenges the common conception that—with the possible exception of the play *The Robbers* (*Die
Räuber*, 1781)—Schiller largely ignored Jews and the "Jewish Question,"
and that what he did have to say about Jews and the "Jewish Question" in *The Legation of Moses* was largely positive, a concerted effort
in the spirit of Lessing to justify Judaism historically and to promote
tolerance toward the Jews.[10] Apart from these two texts, sparse evidence
documents Schiller's actual thinking on issues related to Jews. To briefly
summarize previous research: Schiller had a long-standing interest in
Moses, and during his student days apparently penned a Moses ode,
perhaps influenced by Klopstock, that has not been preserved; Schiller's
father encouraged him to write a history of the Jews; Schiller staged and
popularized Lessing's *Nathan the Wise*; Schiller had a few business transactions and professional contacts with Jews; Schiller quotes and alludes
to the Old Testament in his writings.[11] This paucity of evidence notwithstanding, *The Legation of Moses* indicates Schiller's deep engagement
with the "Jewish Question," an engagement also clearly evident in his
first play, from almost a decade earlier, *The Robbers*.

In *The Robbers*, Schiller articulates a disquieting view of Jewish emancipation in the figure of Moritz Spiegelberg, a member of the robber
band who is implicitly identified as a Jew. Spiegelberg is driven by unbridled ambition: he wants to take control of the robber band; he wants
to wrest Jerusalem from Turkish control; and he wants to dominate the

world. Spiegelberg leads some of the robbers in an assault on Christianity pure and simple: he pillages a convent, rapes nuns, and then gloats about this heinous crime.[12] While scholars have long disputed whether the calculating, power-driven, morally degenerate Spiegelberg actually is a Jew, the text strongly suggests he is.[13] Spiegelberg repeatedly is linked to Jewish themes and to anti-Semitic stereotypes: his name either is Jewish or sounds Jewish; and he is identified with sorcery, circumcision, Jerusalem, and the Jewish historian Josephus. Spiegelberg proposes to his fellow robber Karl Moor that they "become Jews" and carry out a grand plan to send out a manifesto to all four corners of the world to call to Palestine "whatever doesn't eat pork" (I, 2: l. 5–7, p. 33).[14] This proposal—introduced by a humorous repartee that indicates that Spiegelberg is circumcised and wants to make circumcision "fashionable" for all men (I, 2: l. 1–3, p. 33)—unequivocally identifies Spiegelberg with "the Jewish," and also gives voice to the anti-Semitic fear of the Jews as castrators.[15] Spiegelberg's grand plan to call all Jews to Palestine might be read as proto-Zionist or anti-Jewish, or both: it envisions a world where Jews are separated from the rest of society. To the best of my knowledge, scholars have not recognized that another crucial character, introduced into the text in close proximity to Spiegelberg, arguably is depicted as a "Jew" from the start of the play as well. In act 1, scene 1, the scheming Franz, burdened by "ugliness" and fighting for the birthright nature has denied him, claims to have cast hexes on his brother. With his thick, flattened "Lappland nose," his "Moorish maw" and his "Hottentott eyes" (I, 1: l. 13–14, p. 28), Franz may well be cast as a "Jew": Negroid features are an anti-Semitic stereotype common in eighteenth- and nineteenth-century literature,[16] and the identification of Franz with scheming and sorcery, likewise stock anti-Semitic stereotypes, reinforces this "Jewish" characterization. Again, as with Spiegelberg, the point is not to prove that Franz actually *is* a Jew, but merely to indicate that he is depicted as having "Jewish" traits. This is significant, in that Franz's machinations set the entire tragic plot into motion. In light of these "Jewish" characterizations, the play's very title invokes the popular eighteenth-century anti-Semitic belief discussed in the previous chapter in connection with Lessing's *The Jews,* another "robber play" that constitutes a cultural intertext to Schiller's: that robber bands roaming the German countryside and terrorizing the German population were Jewish. Whereas *The Jews* works to dispel popular anti-Jewish sentiments, *The Robbers* caricatures and reinforces them.

This brief discussion of *The Robbers,* which will mesh with my analysis of *The Legation of Moses,* points to a profound irony in Schiller reception in the nineteenth century.[17] Many German Jews regarded Schiller, the poet of freedom, as their champion in the fight for emancipation, and in works like *Wilhelm Tell* and *Don Carlos* saw important parallels to their own cause. This idealized picture of Schiller was grounded in wishful thinking and analogy, rather than in concrete evidence that Schiller actually supported Jewish emancipation. Faced with concrete evidence to the contrary—the negative depictions of the Hebrews in *The Legation of Moses*—some Jews dismissed the essay as not the "real" Schiller, but rather Schiller under the misguided sway of Goethe. Schiller was a true hero and a beloved author for many Jews: his works were read with enormous enthusiasm and were translated into Hebrew and Yiddish. In the Third Reich the Nazis tried to impose an abrupt end to the "Jewish Schiller": from 1933 onward Jews were forbidden to perform Schiller's plays, to publish Schiller, to interpret Schiller, and to read Schiller. Disturbingly, the Nazis claimed "the German Schiller" as one of their own. In 1934, at a festival honoring Schiller's 175th birthday, Josef Goebbels celebrated Schiller as the forerunner of Hitler; and Schiller's writings were considered a precursor to National Socialism and to National Socialist anti-Semitism.[18] As we will see, Schiller does use highly offensive language to describe the Hebrews, and he does raise the specter of the complete annihilation of the Jews in *The Legation of Moses,* but he does so within the context of the biblical Exodus story, in considering what would have happened if Pharaoh's barbaric command to murder all Hebrew male infants had been heeded. However, Schiller *strongly* condemns this state action. This is important. Much as I will be arguing that we need to read—and not read over—the programmatically ambivalent statements about Jews in *The Legation of Moses,* and much as I will be arguing that we need to confront the anti-Semitism in the essay for what it is, I am not arguing for a teleological reading that perverts Schiller's text and ends in the Holocaust.

Before turning to *The Legation of Moses* I would like to broach a fundamental methodological question: the validity of isolating the theme of "the Jew" in Schiller's thought. This question might well be raised on two levels. First, one might argue that Schiller's critique of Judaism is an expression of his general skepticism of religion in general, and that it would be shortsighted to focus solely on "the Jew" in his writings; indeed, one might argue that Schiller used Judaism as a safe vehicle to voice his critique of aspects of Christianity.[19] This may well be true, but it does not change the fact that *The Legation of Moses* by design participates in a larger discourse on Jews and the "Jewish Question" in

eighteenth-century Germany, and must be analyzed in this context. At
the same time, we should bear in mind that Schiller is far from unique in
the views he expresses in this essay. Schiller's critique of revelation and
his critique of Moses are very much in keeping with mainstream Enlightenment philosophy. At stake in the following analysis are the rhetorical
strategies Schiller uses to construct his argument, not the novelty of his
ideas per se.

The second level on which the question of the methodological validity of isolating "the Jew" might be raised is that of proportion: given
the relative infrequency of the topic in Schiller's oeuvre, a focus on Jews
and the "Jewish Question" might seem to skew Schiller's thought as a
whole. One important answer to this is that *The Legation of Moses* is
an integral component of Schiller's philosophical and aesthetic theory:
it offers a prime example of Schiller's theory of "universal history" and
anticipates his *Aesthetic Letters* in fundamental ways.

Schiller lays out his theory of "universal history" in *What Is Universal History and What Is the Goal of Studying It?*, the inaugural lecture
celebrating his appointment as professor of history at the University of
Jena, delivered in 1789, a few weeks before he presented *The Legation
of Moses* as part of the same lecture series.[20] In the inaugural lecture,
Schiller identifies history as a fundamentally ethical endeavor: the entire
moral world lies in its province (411). The universal historian uses philosophical acumen to construct an *aesthetic* interpretation of history,
with the goal of presenting truth as a harmonious whole. Not content to regard knowledge or history as an assemblage of disconnected
fragments, the universal historian aims to "manufacture" connections
among disciplines (414). Historical events in and of themselves may
appear isolated and lacking an intrinsic connection to other contemporaneous events: Schiller cites the origin of Christianity and of Christian
morality as an example (427), arguably laying the groundwork for his
subsequent analysis of the origins of Judaism and of Jewish morality and drawing an implicit parallel between the two religions. Starting
from his own standpoint and working backward, the universal historian
selects those events that have an essential, incontestable, easily trace-
able influence on the present generation (425–26), and constructs, by
artificial means, an *artistic* narrative that presents a coherent, cohesive
totality: "by conjoining these fragments through *artificial* [*"künstlich,"*
also: *artistic*] connections, he elevates the aggregate to the system, to a
rational, coherent whole" ("indem er diese Bruchstücke durch *künstliche*
Bindungsglieder verkettet, erhebt er das Aggregat zum System, zu einem
vernunftmäßig zusammenhängenden Ganzen" [427, emphasis mine]). As

universal history, *The Legation of Moses* is an *artistic* narrative, replete with manufactured connections, metaphoric language, poetic imagery, and a calculated mix of past and present tenses: by design, Schiller's version of the Exodus account is both history and fiction.

Universal history also functions as contemporary cultural criticism. In his inaugural lecture, Schiller argues that the universal historian takes his harmonious principle from his own spirit, and transplants it into the external world, into "the order of things." In so doing, he introduces a rational goal into world events, and a teleological principle into world history (428). Importantly, since the universal historian starts from the present and works backward, projecting his own spirit onto past events, the universal historical analysis is perforce both subjective and dialectical, a simultaneous critique of past and present. Accordingly, Schiller's universal historical analysis of the Hebrews in Egypt in *The Legation of Moses* directly bears on his views of Jews in his present-day European society, and his analysis of Moses as statesman directly bears on his views of contemporary European politics.

Schiller's theory of universal history finds its mature articulation in his *On the Aesthetic Education of Man in a Series of Letters* (*Über die aesthetische Erziehung des Menschen in einer Reihe von Briefen,* 1795). In the *Aesthetic Letters,* the political artist rewrites history by means of a necessary fiction, and uses deception to guide his audience toward truth, with the goal of constructing a moral state.[21] Schiller's Moses, I will suggest, is the prototype for the Enlightenment political artist, for Schiller himself, and this is precisely why the question of the origins of Moses' political praxis is so important to Schiller.

The history of the provenance of *The Legation of Moses* indicates its strong, if oblique, grounding in the transcendental idealist tradition.[22] The essay, presented in lecture form in the summer semester of 1789 and published in the journal *Thalia* in 1790, was to some extent cribbed from a Freemason text published pseudonymously by a certain "Brother Decius" in 1788 titled *The Hebrew Mysteries, or The Oldest Religious Freemasonry* (*Die Hebräischen Mysterien, oder die älteste religiöse Freymaurerey*). Brother Decius was none other than Karl Leonhard Reinhold, whose *Letters on the Kantian Philosophy* (*Briefe über die kantische Philosophie*) had popularized the critical philosophy in a way that Kant himself had been unable to do, and had earned Reinhold the first chair in transcendental idealism at the University of Jena. On the surface, Reinhold's text has little to do with transcendental idealism. Reinhold, a Freemason, had originally intended to present this work in the form of a series of lectures at a Freemason lodge; the lodge's meetings were, of course, secret. Circumstances intervened in that the lodge was closed, and Reinhold never delivered the lectures, but published them instead for a limited Freemason readership.[23] The lectures deal with the putative Hebrew origins of many of the Freemason mysteries, which Reinhold maintains are actually Egyptian in foundation. This topic at first glance seems far removed from the critical philosophy. However, I would argue that the text is strongly inscribed in transcendental idealist discourse, albeit in a historical-theological Freemasonic register: one of Reinhold's main concerns in this text—as it is in his Elementary Philosophy—is that of first principles; here, of the origins of monotheism. As Jan Assmann has pointed out, the fact that The Hebrew Mysteries is largely ignored in the scholarship on Reinhold's life and work is symptomatic of a disciplinary divide that separates philosophy from theology today, and very problematically overlooks how intertwined the two disciplines were in the eighteenth century.[24] Written for an exclusively Freemason audience and published pseudonymously in a journal with limited circulation, Reinhold's treatise likely would not have received much attention were it not for the fact that Schiller, whom Reinhold had strongly supported for a professorship in universal history at Jena, used it as the basis of his own lecture on The Legation of Moses.

Schiller acknowledges this scholarly debt in an obscure footnote situated at the very end of his essay. The placement of the footnote at the end of the essay is significant. In contrast, in another of his lectures on "universal history" Schiller declares right from the beginning, in a footnote to the title of his lecture, that his ideas derive from Kant.[25] Here, in The Legation of Moses, almost as an afterthought, but in a structurally prominent position as the last words of the text, Schiller announces to his readers that he has taken many of the foundational ideas and data for his lecture from a work "of similar content," On the Oldest Hebrew Mysteries by Brother Decius, whom Schiller, perhaps heeding the secret code of the Freemasons, identifies only as "a famous and meritorious writer" (474).[26] Schiller's footnote is understated: in addition to taking foundational ideas and data, he lifts entire passages and wording from Reinhold, with no indication that he has done so.[27]

Schiller's pseudo-plagiarist methodology deserves consideration.[28] On the one hand, we might speculate that the harried young Professor Schiller, who had been on the job only a few months, was pressed for time in writing his lecture[29]—a perennial problem in academia—and resorted to an expeditious solution by presenting Reinhold's ideas in a different format and then covering his scholarly back with that all-important footnote. Given that Reinhold himself had built his own reputation and his academic career popularizing the work of another "famous and meritorious writer," Immanuel Kant, Schiller's plagiarist gesture seems strangely fitting. On the other hand, and perhaps more accurately, we might speculate that Schiller intended to thank Reinhold for his support in helping him secure the professorship at Jena, and did so using that highest form of academic respect and flattery: citation. Or perhaps it is the case, as Wolf-Daniel Hartwich has suggested, that Schiller was trying to deflect potential criticism for his essay's "bold speculations" by referencing Reinhold.[30] But I think there is a much more profound and subtle motivation behind Schiller's decision to crib Reinhold's text—a text, we recall, that originally was intended for limited circulation in the secret Freemason society. In co-opting this secret Freemason text and exploiting it for his own purposes, Schiller tacitly, and perhaps subconsciously, aligns himself with the Moses of his own essay, the calculating Hebrew who shrewdly appropriated and revealed the secrets of an Egyptian religious sect, claiming the Egyptian god Jao as the Jews' Yahweh for political gain. Just as Moses' mission is in essence Egyptian in *The Legation of Moses,* Schiller casts his own mission in this lecture as in essence Mosaic. Before considering the implications of this grandiose gesture, a review of Schiller's argument in *The Legation of Moses* is in order. Precisely the question of origins, of originality—programmatically staged in the essay's pseudo-plagiarist methodology—forms the crux of Schiller's analysis.

The opening paragraphs of the essay provide a key indication of Schiller's interest in the subject matter, of how he intends to appropriate Reinhold's work for his own political purposes. Here I depart from Jan Assmann, who maintains that Schiller "adds nothing to Reinhold's argument, merely highlighting those points which to his mind were most important."[31] This may be true from Assmann's perspective as an Egyptologist interested in Schiller's contributions to an analysis of the putative connections between Judaism and Egyptian religions. However, Assmann does not consider how Schiller shifts the focus of Reinhold's analysis from a religious discussion of the origins of the Hebrew mysteries to a distinctly political and legal register, using language that very clearly inscribes his essay in the contemporary debate about the "Jewish Question." Reinhold begins his study by pointing out that the word "mystery" has become as devoid of meaning as the vapid terminology of contemporary philosophical discourse, but he then expressly distances himself from a critique of Enlightenment—a modish critique of

Enlightenment that is increasingly popular in Freemason texts, Reinhold writes—and proceeds directly to his subject matter, the origins of the Hebrew mysteries.[32]

In contrast, Schiller begins his essay by pointedly *linking* Moses' founding of the Jewish state with contemporary history, contemporary religion, and contemporary philosophy, that is to to say, *with* the Enlightenment, thereby explicitly identifying his essay as contemporary cultural critique. From the very start of the essay, Schiller's precise focus is on political policy, on the founding of a state. Recall that Schiller is writing in 1789, on the brink of the French Revolution, at a time when the building of a German state is very much on his mind, and when nation building is very much on the minds of the European intelligentsia. In this context, it is highly significant that Schiller explicitly links his analysis of Moses' founding of the "Jewish state" to the Enlightenment. In *The Legation of Moses* Schiller patterns modern state building on the Mosaic model, and at the same time strips the Mosaic model of its divine provenance, of its divinely ordained Jewishness.

Schiller lays out this agenda very precisely in the title and in the opening two paragraphs of the essay. It is worth reading this introductory section both very carefully and in its entirety. In the past scholars have cited select passages from the first two paragraphs out of context, skewing and misrepresenting Schiller's argument. Moreover, few scholars have recognized the full significance of the essay's title, which introduces Schiller's entire agenda *in nuce*.

The German title of the essay, *Die Sendung Moses,* is most often translated as "The Mission of Moses" or "Moses' Mission." This translation is accurate, but misses a crucial point: the title is a gloss on William Warburton's influential *The Divine Legation of Moses, Demonstrated on the Principles of a Religious Deist* (1738–1741). Warburton's treatise had a strong reception in Germany: Lessing's *On the Education of the Human Race,* which builds on and takes issue with Warburton's analysis, is a famous case in point. Warburton's *Divine Legation* was translated into German as *Die Göttliche Sendung Mosis, aus den Grundsätzen der Deisten bewiesen* (1751–1753). As Klaus Weimar has noted, the German title was so widely cited that "die göttliche Sendung Moses" ("the divine legation of Moses") was a fixed turn of phrase, a technical term, in the second half of the eighteenth century. Schiller's omission of the word "göttlich," "divine," in his own title, *Die Sendung Moses,* was thus clearly a provocation.[33] Schiller thereby declares his opposition to Warburton's argument from the start. Warburton's study, one of the major sources for Reinhold's *Hebrew Mysteries,* aimed to refute the deists' evaluation of the Mosaic institutions. The deists maintained that the Hebrew Bible contained no evidence of the immortality of the soul and of a future state of reward and punishment. Warburton agreed with this thesis, but contested the deists' conclusions: "that these ideas were indispensable for every institution of religion coming from God and that consequently the Mosaic institutions could necessarily be nothing but a fabrication, if not an imposture. Instead, Warburton saw in the very absence of these ideas the proof of the divine origin of Moses' legislation!" Jan Assmann, whom I cite here, has traced the genealogy of "The Moses Discourse in the Eighteenth Century" from the deists through Warburton to Reinhold and Schiller.[34] Assmann draws a direct connection between Warburton and Schiller when he translates the title of Schiller's essay as *The Legation of Moses.* Yet he either does not recognize, or more likely simply does not comment on, the significance of this connection. Schiller sets *The Legation of Moses* in direct juxtaposition to *The Divine Legation of Moses,* thereby announcing his essay's agenda: Schiller, following Reinhold, dismisses Warburton's thesis about the *divine* origin of Moses' legislation and sides with the deists in arguing that the Mosaic institutions are a fabrication, an imposture. Schiller goes beyond Reinhold in seeing this Mosaic fabrication as tremendously positive, as directly relevant to contemporary political theory. This is precisely the aim of his essay: to celebrate the genius of Moses, the founder of the first political state based on reason, and, at the same time, to debunk the divine Jewishness of the Mosaic state. True to his essay's title, Schiller argues against the *divine* legation of Moses, thereby stripping Judaism of its claim to be the original divinely ordained monotheistic religion. In Schiller's reading Moses is the consummate plagiarist, a supremely skilled politician who co-opts Egyptian state secrets and invents Judaism for his own political gain: religiously and politically, the Jewish state Moses founds is in essence Egyptian. Divested of its Jewishness, the Mosaic state forms the cornerstone for the construction of a modern European state in Schiller's political theory.

Schiller formulates this political agenda in the opening two paragraphs of the essay. In the first sentences of the text Schiller introduces his topic, Moses' founding of the Jewish state, and establishes its importance to contemporary cultural criticism. Close attention to his wording is crucial here. The English translation follows the original text as precisely as possible:

> The founding of the Jewish state by Moses is one of the events most worthy of thought that history has preserved, important because of

the power of the intellect through which it was implemented, even more important because of its consequences for the world, which continue to last up until this moment. Two religions, which rule the largest part of the inhabited world, Christianity and Islam, both support themselves on the religion of the Hebrews, and without the religion of the Hebrews there never would have been either a Christianity or a Koran.

Die Gründung des Jüdischen Staats durch Moses ist eine der denk-würdigsten Begebenheiten, welche die Geschichte aufbewahrt hat, wichtig durch die Stärke des Verstandes, wodurch sie ins Werk geri-chtet worden, wichtiger noch durch ihre Folgen auf die Welt, die noch bis auf diesen Augenblick fortdauern. Zwei Religionen, welche den größten Teil der bewohnten Erde beherrschen, das Christentum und der Islamismus, stützen sich beide auf die Religion der Hebräer, und ohne diese würde es niemals weder ein Christentum noch einen Koran gegeben haben. (451)

Schiller begins his essay on a seemingly strong note, celebrating Moses' founding of the Jewish state as a momentous event in world history, as a world historical event most worthy of *thought*. This event is important first, Schiller says, expanding the reflective "thought" register, for the power of the intellect that set it into motion. One might easily read over this detail, but it is of central importance to Schiller's analysis: Schiller praises Moses as a keen political thinker and, I would argue, patterns himself after Moses from the start of the text. Recall that this is pre-cisely the project of "universal history": for the universal historian, here Schiller, to *think*, to analyze past history for the patterns it offers, for its relevance to modernity. Schiller specifically praises Moses' keen politi-cal *intellect*, an intellect Schiller will emulate in his own construction of modern political theory in the course of the essay. Moses' founding of the Jewish state, Schiller then asserts, is even more important for its profound consequences on the world, which continue to last into the present: both Christianity and Islam "support themselves"("stützen sich") on "the religion of the Hebrews," and without this "religion of the Hebrews" neither Christianity nor the Koran would exist. Schil-ler's rhetoric here is remarkable in both what it does and does not say. Importantly, Schiller does not say that Christianity and Islam *derive* from Judaism, are an outgrowth of Judaism, as Lessing repeatedly had emphasized a decade earlier in both *Nathan the Wise* and *The Educa-tion of the Human Race*, and as Schiller himself had indicated in his inaugural essay on "universal history," where he acknowledges Christianity's provenance from Judaism: "this religion [Christianity] had to arise from Judaism" ("mußte diese Religion [Christianity] aus dem Judentum hervorgehen"[422]). Here Schiller states that Christianity and Islam "support themselves" on "the religion of the Hebrews." Rhetorically, Schiller thereby indirectly denies—or at the very least does not accord—Judaism its historical status as the original of the three great monotheistic religions. Significantly, Schiller chooses the circumlocution "the religion of the Hebrews," rather than the term "Judaism" in describing this relationship. While one might easily read both instances of word choice as simple turns of phrase common in eighteenth-century discourse, there is much more at stake in Schiller's diction than mere poetic license. The bulk of the essay is devoted to proving that the "religion of the Hebrews" is Egyptian, that Judaism is, in effect, a farce. This is why Schiller avoids stating that Christianity and Islam derive from Judaism, while simultaneously acknowledging that the two later religions "support themselves" on the Hebrew religion and would not exist without it. The point of the entire essay is to deny a *divine* derivation, to strip Judaism of the *divine* provenance accorded it in the Old Testament.[35] The context in which this denial occurs is key. This is an essay about state building using the Mosaic paradigm: the denial divests the Mosaic model of its divinely ordained Jewishness. At the same time, Schiller launches a polemic against Jewish emancipation in the modern European state.

Schiller lays out his stance on the "Jewish Question" in the second paragraph of the essay using remarkably ambivalent language. Schiller begins the paragraph by drawing a direct connection between the "Mosaic religion" and the Enlightenment:

> Indeed, in a certain sense it is irrefutably true that we have the Mosaic religion to thank for a large part of the *Enlightenment* we enjoy today. For through the Mosaic religion a precious truth, which reason left to itself would have found only after a slow development, the doctrine of monotheism, was provisionally spread among the people, and preserved as an object of blind faith among them until it eventually could mature into a concept of reason in the brighter minds. Through this a large portion of humanity was spared the sad erring paths to which the belief in polytheism must necessarily lead, and the Hebrew constitution had the exclusive advantage that the religion of the sages did not stand in direct conflict with the popular religion, as was the case with the *enlightened* heathens. (emphasis mine)

Ja in einem gewissen Sinne ist es unwiderleglich wahr, daß wir der
Mosaischen Religion einen großen Teil der *Aufklärung* danken,
deren wir uns heute erfreuen. Denn durch sie wurde eine kostbare
Wahrheit, welche die sich selbst überlassene Vernunft erst nach einer
langsamen Entwicklung gefunden haben, die Lehre von dem Eini-
gen Gott, vorläufig unter dem Volke verbreitet, und als ein Gegenstand des blinden Glaubens so lange unter demselben erhalten, bis
sie endlich in den helleren Köpfen zu einem Vernunftbegriff rei-
fen konnte. Dadurch wurden einem großen Teil des Menschenge-
schlechtes alle die traurigen Irrwege erspart, worauf der Glaube an
Vielgötterei führen muß, und die Hebräische Verfassung erhielt den
ausschließenden Vorzug, daß die Religion der Weisen mit der Volks-
religion nicht in direktem Widerspruche stand, wie es doch bei den
aufgeklärten Heiden der Fall war. (451, emphasis mine)

Significantly, the paragraph begins with a qualification. "Indeed, in
a certain sense," Schiller states, "it is irrefutably true that we have the
Mosaic religion to thank for a large part of the Enlightenment we enjoy
today." Schiller again does not use the term "Judaism" here, nor will he
throughout the essay. Linguistic conventions of the day notwithstanding,
Schiller's word choice is intentional. The focus here is on *Moses,* on the
religion Moses *invented.*[36] "*Through* the Mosaic religion"—not *in* the
Mosaic religion—Schiller continues, "a precious truth" was transmitted,
the doctrine of a monotheistic God. Borrowing a line of argumentation
from Lessing's *The Education of the Human Race,* Schiller explains that
human reason would eventually have come to the "truth" of monotheism
by itself, but that the Hebrews spread the word, as it were, and kept the
faith blindly, until monotheism could mature into a concept of reason in
"brighter minds." In contrast to Lessing, who characterizes the Jews as
immature thinkers because they are the "children" of the human race,
Schiller suggests that the Hebrews "blindly" followed their faith because
they were stupid. (Schiller arguably mitigates his source material here:
Reinhold calls the Hebrews "the stupidest and evilest rabble that ancient
and modern history has known."[37] However, as we will see, Schiller
picks up on and amplifies Reinhold's damning description later in the
text.) Taking a central idea about the Hebrew constitution from Reinhold, Schiller then draws a political conclusion from his discussion of
monotheism: "This spared a large part of humanity from straying down
the sorry erring paths to which polytheism must ultimately lead, and the
Hebrew constitution had the exclusive advantage that the religion of the
sages was not in direct contradiction to the popular religion, as was the

case with the enlightened heathens."[38] What Schiller particularly values here is not the doctrine of monotheism as a religious doctrine or as a concept of reason *per se,* but that the Hebrews—specifically, Moses—turned this doctrine into sound political practice. Recall that Schiller opens the essay with the statement that "Moses' founding of the Jewish state is one of the most notable events preserved in history." *The Legation of Moses* is first and foremost political theory.

Schiller subtly introduces his own contribution to Mosaic political theory on the lexical level of the text. Twice repeating the signifier "Enlightenment" in the space of two sentences, Schiller draws a direct connection between the "enlightened heathens" ("den aufgeklärten Heiden") of biblical Egypt and contemporary Enlightenment Europe, "die Aufklärung," the topic introduced in the first sentence of the paragraph. In so doing, he argues for the relevance of his universal historical critique for Enlightenment Europe: just as Moses provided a religious corrective to the civil constitution of the "enlightened heathens" for the Hebrews, Schiller proposes a religious corrective to Moses' civil constitution for modernity. The "Mosaic religion" is the precise target of his critique.

In the second part of the paragraph Schiller contextualizes his political analysis within the discourse of the contemporary debate about the "Jewish Question." Having just argued that the Hebrews transmitted the doctrine of monotheism and turned this doctrine into sound political practice, Schiller then lauds the Hebrew nation as an important "universal historical people," again muting his praise with an introductory qualification:

> From this perspective, the Hebrew nation must appear to us as an important universal historical people, and everything evil one is accustomed to impute to this people, all efforts of witty minds to belittle this people, will not prevent us from doing it justice. The unworthiness and depravity of the nation cannot extinguish the sublime achievement of its lawgiver, and can just as little nullify the great influence that this nation rightly claims in world history. We must value it as an impure base vessel in which something precious was stored; we must honor it as the channel which, as impure as it was, Providence chose to transmit to us the noblest of all goods, the truth, the channel Providence then shattered as soon as it had accomplished what it was intended to do. In this way we will be equally far from forcing on the Hebrew people a value it never had and of robbing it of a merit that cannot be contested.

Aus diesem Standpunkte betrachtet, muß uns die Nation der
Hebräer als ein wichtiges universalhistorisches Volk erscheinen, und
alles Böse, welches man diesem Volke nachzusagen gewohnt ist, die
Bemühungen witziger Köpfe, es zu verkleinern, werden uns nicht
hindern, gerecht gegen dasselbe zu sein. Die Unwürdigkeit und Ver-
worfenheit der Nation kann das erhabene Verdienst ihres Gesetzge-
bers nicht vertilgen, und eben so wenig den großen Einfluß vernich-
ten, den diese Nation mit Recht in der Weltgeschichte behauptet.
Als ein unreines und gemeines Gefäß, worin aber etwas sehr kost-
bahres aufbewahrt worden, müssen wir sie schätzen; wir müssen
in ihr den Kanal verehren, den, so unrein er auch war, die Vorsicht
erwählte, uns das edelste aller Güter, die Wahrheit zuzuführen; den
sie aber zerbrach, sobald er geleistet hatte, was er sollte. Auf diese
Art werden wir gleich entfernt sein, dem Ebräischen Volk einen
Wert aufzudringen, den es nie gehabt hat, und ihm ein Verdienst
zu rauben, das ihm nicht streitig gemacht werden kann. (451–52)

In a remarkable display of rhetorical ambivalence Schiller celebrates "the
Hebrew people," yet again and again qualifies this praise to the point
of condemnation. "From this perspective," Schiller begins, referencing
the Hebrews' transmittal of the doctrine of monotheism and their introduction of a sound state constitution, "the Hebrew nation must appear
to us as an important universal people, and everything evil that one is
accustomed to impute to this people, all efforts of witty minds to belit-
tle this people, will not prevent us from doing it justice." Schiller starts
with a strong Enlightenment defense of the "Hebrew nation" worthy of
Lessing, yet his idea of doing "justice" to the Hebrews shines through in
the next sentence of the text: "The unworthiness and depravity of the
nation cannot extinguish the sublime achievement of its lawgiver, and
can just as little nullify the great influence that this nation rightly claims
in world history." Lest there be any doubt about his characterization of
the Hebrew people, his careful separation of the "unworthy," "depraved"
Hebrews from their "sublime" lawgiver Moses, Schiller again distinguishes between the "unclean" Hebrews and their "noble" influence in
the following sentence: "We must value it [the Hebrew nation] as an
impure base vessel in which something precious was stored; we must
honor it as the channel which, as impure as it was, Providence chose to
transmit to us the noblest of all goods, the truth, the channel Providence
then shattered as soon as it had accomplished what it was intended to
do." Ambivalent diction notwithstanding, the metaphors and adjec-
tives Schiller uses to describe the Hebrews leave no doubt about his

meaning here. The Hebrews are "unworthy," "depraved," "impure," a "base vessel" in which truth was stored, the "impure channel" Providence selected to transmit the truth, but then "shattered" ("zerbrach": smashed to pieces) as soon as it had accomplished its mission.[39] In no way can this text be understood as an Enlightenment defense of the biblical Hebrews or of contemporary Jews. Quite the opposite: in Schiller's view the biblical Hebrews only served as a morally reprehensible *repository* for storing the truth, as an impure *conduit* for transmitting the truth. This is "the merit that cannot be contested." But importantly, as Schiller will explicate in the remainder of the essay, the Hebrews were not the *originators* of the truth of monotheism, did not receive the *divine revelation* of monotheism. This is "the value the Hebrews never had." Likewise, Schiller does not defend Jews in contemporary Enlightenment Europe: he argues that Providence irreparably "shattered" ("zerbrach") the impure Hebrew channel as soon as it had done its job. This is why Schiller avoids the words "Jews" and "Judaism" throughout his essay: there is no place in the world today for Jews or Judaism. Read within the context of the contemporary Jewish emancipation debate, the debate about the "Jewish Question," *The Legation of Moses* inscribes a very disconcerting cultural agenda.

Schiller grounds his critique of the contemporary "Jewish Question" in a critical "universal historical" reading of the *Urtext* of Jewish emancipation, the biblical Exodus account. In keeping with the project of universal history, of constructing history as a coherent, rational, moral whole, of reading past history philosophically for its relevance to modernity, Schiller's universal historical analysis is simultaneously contemporary cultural criticism. Using rhetoric designed to invoke the contemporary emancipation debate, Schiller redacts the biblical Exodus story into a pseudo-historical Exodus story, an Exodus story without God. Again, close attention to the structure and language of Schiller's argument is key. My English summary of Schiller's account below follows his own wording. The wording of the interspersed commentary is of course my own.

According to Schiller's version of events, the Hebrews, a small nomadic family of no more than seventy souls, settled in Egypt, where they first became a people. This identification of the origin of the Hebrew "people" in Egypt is important: Schiller, following Reinhold, grounds the origins of the Hebrew people in the Book of Exodus, and has excised Genesis from their history.[40] Socially, politically, and, as he will later argue, religiously, Schiller asserts that the Hebrews are, in effect, Egyptian. In Egypt, Schiller continues, the Hebrews multiplied rapidly, indeed exponentially: in a time span of four hundred years the initial population of seventy burgeoned to some two million people, of which six hundred thousand were battle-ready men (452).[41] By choice the Hebrews kept apart from the general population both in their living quarters and in their nomadic traditions:

> During this long stay they lived *segregated* from the Egyptians, *segregated* both in their choice of living quarters and in their nomadic status, which made them the abhorrence of the native inhabitants of the country and excluded them from all participation in the civil rights of the Egyptians. (emphasis mine)

> Während dieses langen Aufenthalts lebten sie *abgesondert* von den Egyptern, *abgesondert* sowohl durch den eigenen Wohnplatz, den sie einnahmen, als durch ihren nomadischen Stand, der sie allen Eingebornen des Landes zum Abscheu machte, und von allem Anteil an den bürgerlichen Rechten der Egypter ausschloß. (452, emphasis mine)

Schiller's argument resonates with the contemporary emancipation debate both conceptually and linguistically. Twice repeating the word "abgesondert" ("segregated" or "separated") for emphasis, Schiller asserts that the Hebrews *wanted* to keep apart from the Egyptians, both in living quarters and in lifestyle. This intentional isolationism—which was very much a target of criticism in the contemporary debate about the "Jewish Question"—made the Hebrews into an object of loathing and completely excluded them from all participation in the civil rights of Egyptians. Socially and politically, Schiller maintains, the Hebrews brought their own pariah status onto themselves. (As we will see, Schiller draws an explicit connection between the Jews and the Hindu pariahs later in the text [455], thereby anticipating Max Weber.)

Schiller then argues that the Hebrews' insistence on autonomy proved dangerous to the weal of the state that harbored them. Using language that again squarely identifies his analysis as contemporary cultural criticism, Schiller asserts that the isolated Hebrew community eventually developed into a "state within the state." The "state within a state" argument—that the Jews formed a dangerous nation living within the German state—was an anti-Semitic slogan that came into vogue in the 1780s and was repeatedly raised in the debate about the "Jewish Question."[42] Schiller's universal historical analysis clearly fuels this contention. In the Egyptian context, Schiller continues, the population of this autonomous "state within a state" then increased prodigiously, indeed colossally, until the Hebrew state eventually raised the Egyptian king's concern because of its "monstrous proliferation" ("durch seine ungeheure Vermehrung"):

> They [the Hebrews] continued to rule themselves in this manner, the patriarch ruling the family, the prince the tribes, and eventually developed into a state within the state, which, with its monstrous proliferation, eventually awakened the king's concern.

> Sie [the Hebrews] regierten sich nach dieser Art fort, der Hausvater die Familie, der Stammfurst die Stämme, und machten auf diese Art einen Staat im Staat aus, der endlich durch seine ungeheure Vermehrung die Besorgnis der König erweckte. (452)

Schiller ends the paragraph here, structurally emphasizing the danger of this rapidly expanding Kafkaesque Hebrew monstrosity.

Heightening this rhetorical effect, Schiller then details the imminent danger the "segregated" Hebrews pose to the state that harbors them, again stressing their intentional isolationism in the opening sentence of the next paragraph:

> Such a *segregated* mass of people at the heart of the realm, made idle by its nomadic lifestyle, *who kept to themselves very precisely and had no common interest whatsoever with the state,* could be dangerous in an enemy attack, and could easily be tempted to avail themselves of the state's weaknesses, which she [the Hebrew "mass"] had idly observed. (emphasis mine)

> Eine solche *abgesonderte* Menschenmenge im Herzen des Reichs, durch ihre nomadische Lebensart müßig, *die unter sich sehr genau zusammenhielt, mit dem Staat aber gar kein Interesse gemein hatte,* konnte bei einem feindlichen Einfall gefährlich werden, und leicht in Versuchung geraten, die Schwäche des Staats, deren müßige Zuschauerin sie war, zu benutzen. (452, emphasis mine)

Invoking a series of stock anti-Semitic stereotypes, Schiller characterizes the isolationist Hebrews as an unproductive, calculating, potentially traitorous, effeminate "human horde" that jeopardized the state. This was not a potential threat, Schiller argues, but a real danger: Schiller uses the indicative mood, rather than the subjunctive, in his rhetoric ("konnte . . . gefährlich werden"). Importantly, this is precisely what Moses will do later in Schiller's account: the Hebrew will co-opt Egyptian state secrets, which he had idly and shrewdly observed from within, for his own political purposes. Schiller lays the groundwork for a carefully structured, subtle argument here.

At this point, Schiller asserts, the Egyptians responded in a very reasoned manner to the threat posed by the Hebrews, but this reasoned response soon went awry. Faced with a dangerous, burgeoning Hebrew population, the Egyptian elders devised methods to keep a sharp eye on the idle Hebrews, to keep them busy, and to reduce their population. Hence the Egyptians imposed hard labor on the Hebrews for the good of the state.[43] In this way, the Egyptians learned that the Hebrews could even become useful to the state. (This argument about the Jews' usefulness to the state was a major theme in the contemporary debate about the "Jewish Question.") Politics combined with self-interest, however, and the Egyptians increased the Hebrews' labors, enslaved them, and abused them, a move Schiller clearly condemns: in his words, the Egyptian bondage is both "inhuman" and "barbaric." Yet this barbaric, inhuman treatment still did not reduce, much less control, the Hebrew population. On the contrary, the Hebrews expanded with ever-increasing strength (453).[44]

At this juncture, a few paragraphs into the opening gambit of the essay—into the argument connecting Enlightenment Europe with Moses' founding of the Jewish state—Schiller introduces a political proposal that unequivocally identifies the essay as a contribution to the contemporary debate about the "Jewish Question." Schiller remarks that a "healthy politics" in biblical Egypt could have dealt productively with the issue of a worrisome, burgeoning Hebrew population—the Hebrew "Menschen-menge" ("human mass"), to use Schiller's term (452)—by integrating the Hebrews into the general population and giving them equal civil rights. "A healthy politics would naturally have led to dispersing them among the other inhabitants and giving them equal rights" ("Eine gesunde Politik würde also natürlich darauf geführt haben, sie unter den übrigen Einwohnern zu verteilen und ihnen gleiche Rechte mit diesen zu geben" [453]). But the Egyptians were prevented from enacting this "healthy" political agenda, Schiller continues in the same sentence, because "the general abhorrence they harbored against the Hebrews did not allow this" ("aber dieses erlaubte der allgemeine Abscheu nicht, den die Egypter gegen sie hegten" [453]). Recall that Schiller had argued in the preceding paragraph that the root of the Egyptians' "universal aversion" to the Hebrews lies in the Hebrews themselves. The Hebrews' desire to live apart from the Egyptians, to perpetuate their own nomadic lifestyle, made them an object of loathing and excluded them from Egyptian civil rights (452): the Hebrews themselves opposed assimilation, and this isolationism made them abhorrent to the Egyptians.

Schiller then offers a biological explanation for the etiology of the Hebrews' "otherness," for their increasingly entrenched status as "outsiders" in Egyptian society: they contracted leprosy, "der Aussatz" (literally: that which sets apart from).[45] Again, careful attention to Schiller's language indicates the programmatic relevance of his argument to the contemporary debate about the "Jewish Question." The "general abhorrence" that prevented the Egyptians from enacting the "healthy politics" of integrating the Hebrews into the general population and giving them equal civil rights was amplified, Schiller continues, expanding and explicating the health metaphor, by the fact that the Hebrews were a diseased people. They "quite naturally" become leprous as a result of their living circumstances. The original parcel of land they were given was "generous enough" (453), but the Hebrews' rapidly expanding population was increasingly crammed into this allotted space. These crowded living conditions then naturally promoted abject squalor and illness:

> What was more natural than that precisely those consequences developed that are unavoidable in such circumstances?—the highest degree of uncleanness and contagious diseases ["die höchste Unreinlichkeit und ansteckende Seuchen"]. Here the first ground was laid already for the disease ["Übel"] that has remained exclusive to this nation up until today.

> Was war natürlicher, als daß sich nun eben die Folgen einstellten, welche in einem solchen Falle unausbleiblich sind?—die höchste Unreinlichkeit und ansteckende Seuchen. Hier also wurde schon der erste Grund zu dem Übel gelegt, welches dieser Nation bis auf die heutigen Zeiten eigen geblieben ist. (453)

Borrowing a line of argument from Christian Wilhelm von Dohm's *On the Civic Improvement of the Jews* (1781), Schiller asserts that the Hebrews' supreme uncleanness ["Unreinlichkeit," also: impurity] and disease ["Übel," also: evil, degeneracy] were a direct consequence of the poor conditions under which they were forced to live. Unlike Dohm, who maintains the Jews can reform their moral character if the causal circumstances leading to their degeneracy are removed, Schiller argues the degeneracy is everlasting. In Schiller's analysis, the Hebrews become permanently unclean, permanently diseased:

The most horrible plague of the region, leprosy ["der Aussatz"] tore
into them and was inherited for many generations. The source of life
and of procreation was slowly poisoned by it, and from a fortuitous
ill ["Übel"] there eventually arose an inherited tribal constitution.

Die schrecklichste Plage dieses Himmelstrichs, der Aussatz, riß
unter ihnen ein, und erbte sich durch viele Generationen hinunter.
Die Quelle des Lebens und der Zeugung wurden langsam durch ihn
vergiftet, und aus einem zufälligen Übel enstand endlich eine erbli-
che Stammeskonstitution. (453–54)

Inverting, and at the same time invoking, a potent stock anti-Semitic
stereotype—the Jews poisoning Christian wells—Schiller argues that
leprosy ("der Aussatz": "that which sets apart") "poisoned" the "source
of life" and eventually became part of the Hebrews' hereditary makeup.
With this argument Schiller implicitly underscores the threat the poisoned
and poisoning Jews still pose to the general population today: the Jews
are the genetic carriers of the most horrible and most highly contagious
of diseases. At this point Schiller cites numerous ancient historians who
attest to widespread leprosy among the Jews, who univocally identify
leprosy as the Jews' signal characteristic, their sole characteristic (454).[46]
Schiller ends the paragraph here, emphasizing the Hebrews' leprosy on
the structural level of the text. To cite Heinrich Heine's poignantly wry
formulation, Judaism hence becomes "the thousand-year-old family disease / the plague the Jews schlepped with themselves from the Nile valley, /
the unhealthy faith of ancient Egypt."[47]

Schiller then concludes his discussion of the leprous Hebrews by
returning to a Dohmian line of argument. To summarize, following
Schiller's wording precisely: the Hebrews' sickness was a natural consequence of the poor living conditions the Egyptians imposed on the
Hebrews, their poor living quarters, their poor food, their mistreatment,
yet the sickness now became the new cause of further mistreatment.
Where they had once simply scorned the Hebrews for being shepherds,
avoided them because they were foreigners, because they were aliens
("Fremdlinge"), the Egyptians now became increasingly disgusted and
profoundly repulsed by the leprous Hebrews: "The fear and repugnance
which the Egyptians had always harbored toward the Hebrews was
now compounded by loathing and a deep repulsing contempt" ("Zu der
Furcht und Widerwillen also, welche man in Egypten von jeher gegen
sie gehegt, gesellte sich noch Ekel und eine tiefe zurückstoßende Verach-
tung" [454]). Reading their sickness as a legible sign of the gods' wrath,

the Egyptians then revoked the Hebrews' "most holy human rights" and ordered the slaughter of their male infants.[48] The Egyptian government's plan to annihilate the nation of Jews completely would have succeeded in a few generations, Schiller notes, were a savior not to have come (455).[49] Using language concordant with Christian salvation history, *Heilsgeschichte,* Schiller then introduces Moses into his universal historical account.

Before turning to the Moses portion of Schiller's narrative, let us review his argument thus far. In short, Schiller offers a reasoned historical explanation, grounded in biology, to explain how the Hebrews—by their own making—became the infectious "other." The Hebrews insisted on their own separateness from the start; their prodigious rate of reproduction caused them to outgrow the living space that had been "generously enough" allotted them; overcrowding naturally led to disease; this disease became hereditary, indeed became their defining characteristic. From the beginning, the Hebrews' own actions made them into an object of loathing in their host nation. This prevented the Egyptians from initiating a "healthy" political agenda for controlling the "monstrously expanding" Hebrew population, a "healthy" political agenda that became impossible once the Hebrews became congenitally diseased. The Egyptians hosting this "state within a state" very understandably feared the Hebrews and tried to control the increasing threat they posed both politically and biologically to the native population. Importantly, Schiller strongly condemns the Egyptians for their "bad" political solution (454) to the Hebrew problem, for inhumanly, barbarically, mistakenly enslaving the Hebrews, and then attempting to annihilate them.

With this background information Schiller thus sets the stage for the birth of Moses, the sublime champion of Jewish emancipation. At the same time Schiller precisely and forcefully articulates his own stance on the contemporary Jewish emancipation debate, using diction and argumentation designed to resonate with the contemporary discourse on the "Jewish Question." Keep in mind the trajectory of Schiller's argument up until this point, just five paragraphs into the text. In drawing a connection between present and past, between Enlightenment Europe and biblical Egypt, and then offering a "healthy" political solution for dealing with the segregated Hebrew masses living in the heart of the Egyptian realm who had no common interest with the state, who threatened the security and the health of the state, Schiller clearly identifies his "universal historical" analysis as a contribution to the contemporary debate about the "Jewish Question," to the question of the Jews' civil and legal status in Germany.

But I think it would be a mistake to overlook or excuse Schiller's rhetoric and to conclude, as does Alfred Low, that Schiller supports a pro-Jewish assimilationist political agenda.[50] Schiller's proposal to spread out the Hebrew horde ("Menschenmenge") and to give the dispersed Hebrews equal rights so as to weaken the threat they pose to the state is hardly a *pro-Jewish* emancipation argument, even if it is an emancipation argument of sorts, and we should not ignore the fact that Schiller argues the Egyptians were *prevented* from enacting this "healthy" political agenda because of the "general disgust" they felt against the Hebrews, a disgust that derived from the circumstance that the Hebrews by choice kept to themselves and that intensified as the Hebrews became increasingly and then permanently diseased. Schiller's essay does little to dispel this "general disgust" in his contemporary readers. On the contrary, Schiller's programmatically ambivalent language throughout the essay actively *promotes* in his fellow Germans the same loathing against the now genetically leprous Jews—so Schiller—that the Egyptians had harbored against the dangerous, diseased Hebrew "aliens" living in their midst.

To put it very pointedly, the story of emancipation Schiller tells in *The Legation of Moses* is a story of emancipation *from* the Jews, not *of* the Jews. The bulk of the essay is devoted to proving that the origins of both the "Mosaic religion" and the "Jewish state" are not Jewish at all, but fundamentally Egyptian. Moses in effect steals the truth of monotheism from the Egyptians, and then uses this purloined knowledge to fabricate the "Mosaic religion" and betray Egyptian state secrets for his own political gain. The implications of Schiller's argument are profound. In its inception the "Mosaic religion" is grounded in craftiness, theft, betrayal, guileful ambition, deception, and, as we will see, murder: Schiller inscribes the rhetoric of anti-Semitism into the very foundation of Judaism, and implicitly identifies Judaism as the *source* of anti-Semitism itself.

Rhetorically, Schiller's analysis of the genesis of the "Mosaic religion" parallels his analysis of the genesis of Egyptian hatred toward the Hebrews: Schiller sets into play an extensive array of anti-Semitic descriptors and argues that these stereotypes are in fact a historically accurate portrayal of the Hebrews and the "Mosaic religion." In contrast to the overtly negative language Schiller uses to characterize the Hebrews, his descriptions of Moses are modulated by praise for "the sublime achievements" of the Hebrew lawgiver (452). But careful attention to Schiller's rhetoric reveals that a subtle, strong, increasingly sophisticated anti-Semitic register infuses the Moses portion of Schiller's universal historical analysis as well.

Schiller begins the Moses portion of the account by drawing a stark contrast between the degenerate Hebrews and their savior. Recall that Schiller has just strongly condemned the Egyptians' barbaric, inhuman order to slaughter all Hebrew male babies. This mistaken political agenda would have wiped out the "nation of Jews" in a few generations, Schiller writes, were a savior not to have come. Of course this savior could not come from the Egyptians, who lacked the necessary "national interest" for the Hebrews (456). And how could the savior come from the Hebrews? Three hundred years of inhuman, brutal mistreatment had made the Hebrews the most despicable people on the face of the earth:

> The coarsest, most malicious, most depraved people on earth, made savage by three hundred years of neglect, made despondent and embittered by their slavish oppression, debased in their own eyes by an inherited infamy that clung to them, enervated and lamed to all heroic decisions, through such a long-standing dumbness finally cast down almost to the level of the animal.

> Das roheste, das bösartigste, das verworfenste Volk der Erde, durch eine dreihundertjährige Vernachlässigung verwildert, durch einen so langen knechtischen Druck verzagt gemacht und erbittert, durch eine erblich auf ihm haftende Infamie vor sich selbst erniedrigt, entnervt und gelähmt zu allen heroischen Entschlüssen, durch eine so lange anhaltende Dummheit endlich fast bis zum Tier herunter gestoßen. (455)

Using language derived from his source material, Schiller offers a Dohmian argument to justify, and indeed amplify, Reinhold's characterization of the Hebrews as "the stupidest and evilest rabble that ancient and modern history has known."[51] A "bold and heroic spirit" could just as little have arisen from the Hebrews of yore, Schiller writes, as from the depraved caste of the pariahs among the Hindus (455). Here "the great hand of Providence," "destiny," intervenes—God is not completely absent from Schiller's account—and finds a simple solution to the savior problem. Enter Moses, born Hebrew but raised Egyptian, the basket in the bulrushes having done its job. Moses, adopted by Pharaoh's daughter, leads a life of privilege befitting a king's child. He is educated by Egyptian priests and becomes privy to all their secret knowledge (457), including what was with "the utmost probability" "the very first idea of the unity of the most supreme Being" ("die erste Idee von der Einheit des höchsten Wesens" [458]).

Schiller, following Reinhold, devotes a great deal of narrative space to detailing the secret knowledge Moses gleaned from the Egyptians, and, like Reinhold, notes a "remarkable similarity" between the Egyptian mysteries and "what Moses later did, what he later instituted" (457). Moses, educated by Egyptian priests, was privy to all their secrets; so much so, Schiller observes, that the Egyptian historian Manetho even makes Moses into an apostate Egyptian priest (457). Schiller does not follow Manetho's line of argument, although his universal historical method certainly would allow for an Egyptian Moses. Schiller needs Moses to be a Jew precisely so that he can prove the "Mosaic religion" is a sham, albeit based on essential Egyptian truths.

At this point, numerous stereotypical "Jewish" attributes creep into Schiller's characterization of Moses. These descriptors might not seem anti-Semitic on first reading, but they resonate with increasing forcefulness when considered within the fabric of the text as a whole. Subtly invoking the stereotypical association of Jews with money, Schiller maintains that Moses gathers from the Egyptian priests a veritable "treasure trove" ("Schatz") of hieroglyphs, mystical images, and ceremonies, which his creative mind would subsequently make use of: everything from the rite of circumcision to an advanced knowledge of physics, which he would later draw on to stage his "miracles" (464). In addition to taking both the trappings and truth of his religion from the Egyptians, Moses also appropriates their political theory. Indirectly invoking yet another anti-Semitic trope—the Wandering Jew—Schiller summarizes Moses' "peregrinations" through the entire field of Egyptian knowledge, and at the same time highlights Moses' intellect, his careful consideration of the strengths and weaknesses of the Egyptian political system:

> He *wandered through* the entire field of Egyptian knowledge, thought through the whole system of priests, weighed its shortcomings and merits, its strengths and weaknesses, and gained important great insights into this people's art of governing ["Regierungskunst"]. (emphasis mine)

> Er hatte das ganze Gebiet egyptischer Weisheit *durchwandert,* das ganze System der Priester durchdacht, sein Gebrechen und Vorzüge, seine Stärke und Schwäche gegen einander abgewogen, und große wichtige Blicke in die Regierungskunst dieses Volks getan. (464, emphasis mine)

Moses thus actualizes the Egyptians' fears about harboring Hebrews in their midst that Schiller had outlined at the beginning of the essay (452): he shrewdly observes Egyptian state secrets from within, and will later exploit the Egyptian state's strengths and weaknesses for his own political gain.

In so doing, Moses boldly corrects a shortcoming in the Egyptian political system when he founds the Jewish state. The Egyptian priests, the "enlightened" epopts (460), Schiller argues, knew the fundamental truth of monotheism, but recognized the dangers of translating this truth into political praxis. The popular religion upon which the entire civil constitution was based was polytheistic. Were the priests to overthrow polytheism, they would perforce overthrow the civil constitution, and they did not know whether the new monotheistic religion would be strong enough to carry the "entire state building" from the start (458–59). Accordingly, they decided to keep the truth of monotheism to themselves, but devised a plan to expose the general population to monotheism indirectly, hinting at the truth through hieroglyphs, secret mysteries, and the like. Gradually, however, the priestly institute lost its bearing. Rather than guarding the truth of monotheism through their secret mysteries, the priests came to take the mysteries themselves *as* the truth. Moses astutely corrects this failed Egyptian religious and political praxis: he will betray the priestly secret of monotheism and make it the basis of the Jewish state constitution. In addition to taking the fundamental truth of monotheism, Moses also "borrows" ("abborgen") many of the institute's "frivolities" ("Spielereien") and lesser-known "special effects" ("Kunstgriffe") for his new religion (463).

Schiller's use of anti-Semitic language becomes increasingly penetrating in his analysis of how Moses came to invent the "Mosaic religion." Throughout his extensive Egyptian education, Schiller recounts, Moses still has contact with his own people, and his own sense of "national feeling" ("Nationalgefühl" [464]) for the Hebrews remains intact. One day he sees an Egyptian brutally mistreat a Hebrew slave. Outraged, Moses smites down the Egyptian. Schiller accurately follows the Old Testament account here, but intensifies the biblical rhetoric in the verb he selects to describe this action. In Exodus 2:12, Moses "looked this way and that and when he saw there was no one around he *struck down* the Egyptian and hid him in the sand." The Luther translation, which Schiller would have consulted, is concordant with the English, as well as with the original Hebrew: "Da schaute er sich nach allen Seiten um, und als er sah, daß kein Mensch da war, *erschlug* er den Ägypter und verscharrte ihn im Sande." The Hebrew verb derives from the root *nun-kaf-he*, which has a wide range of meanings; its basic sense is "hit, strike."[52] In Schiller's account, Moses does not simply "strike down" the Egyptian: "he *murdered* the Egyptian" ("er *ermordete* den Egypter" [464, emphasis mine]), and is forced to leave Egypt and flee into the Arabian desert. Schiller's identification of Moses as a murderer is a stunning distortion of the biblical Exodus account: all the more so in that this murderous act eventually drives Moses to invent Judaism in Schiller's universal historical analysis.

Moses' Arabian exile marks a new epoch in his life, Schiller asserts, at the same time emphasizing that Moses' murderous nature remains intact. Schiller reports that Moses carries a "bloody hatred" with him into the desert, along with all the knowledge he had appropriated from the Egyptian priests. Syntactically, Schiller adds special stress to Moses' "bloody hatred" by positioning the phrase at the start of the sentence:

> A bloody hatred against the oppressors of his nation, and all the knowledge he had obtained from the mysteries, he carried with him into the Arabian desert. His mind was full of ideas and plans, his heart was full of bitterness, and nothing distracted him in this unpopulated desert.

> Einen blutigen Haß gegen die Unterdrücker seiner Nation, und alle Kenntnisse, die er in den Mysterien geschöpft hatte, trug er mit sich in die Arabische Wüste. Sein Geist war voll von Ideen und Entwürfen, sein Herz voll Erbitterung, und nichts zerstreute ihn in dieser menschenleere Wüste. (465)

Having just characterized Moses as a murderer who carries his "bloody hatred" and his Egyptian learning into the desert, Schiller then emphasizes Moses' scheming, bitter nature: his mind is "full of ideas and plans"; his heart "full of bitterness." When Moses becomes a shepherd in a nomad's employ, this "steep fall" from his previous ambitions to become a leader of men must have "deeply wounded his soul," Schiller muses (465).

Schiller then transforms his statement about Moses' dashed plans to become a leader of men into a cutting characterization of the future leader of the Hebrews in the first sentence of the next paragraph, in a position of structural prominence. Careful attention to the original German underscores the pervasive anti-Semitic stereotyping Schiller uses to depict Moses:

> In a shepherd's cloak he carries a fiery regent's-spirit, a restless ambition, around with himself.

> In dem Kleid eines Hirten trägt er einen feurigen Regenten-Geist, einen rastlosen Ehrgeiz mit sich herum. (465)

In the original German the sentence is poetic in cadence and imagery; this poetic import is further intensified by the mention of the "romantic desert" in the next sentence of the text (465). Just as the simple shepherd's garb cloaks the fiery spirit of its wearer, the simple poetic language of the text cloaks its own fiery spirit, its intense anti-Semitism. (Schiller explicitly uses the same clothing metaphor to describe poetic production later in the text, in his description of Moses as author: Moses "wraps" the true God in a "heathen cloak" [472–73] and "dresses" his story about his divine mission in all the requisite props to make the Hebrews believe him [472].) Here, in this striking poetic description, Moses, who had previously "wandered through" the entire field of Egyptian knowledge (464), becomes the prototypical Wandering Jew, "carrying around with himself" a "fiery regent's-spirit" and "restless ambition." Syntactically, the phrases "fiery regent's-spirit" and "restless ambition" are set in apposition to each other, suggesting parallelism, if not equivalence. This parallelism is accentuated on the linguistic level of the text. In German the phrases "fiery regent's-spirit" and "restless ambition" ("feurigen Regenten-Geist," "rastlosen Ehrgeiz") are set in paradigmatic opposition. First, graphically: the unusual hyphenated compound noun "Regenten-Geist" (regent's-spirit) perforce draws attention to itself, and by extension, to the other compound noun in the sentence, with which it rhymes, "Ehrgeiz" (ambition; literally, *Ehr-Geiz,* "honor-greed": greed of honor). Second, and more forcefully, the two phrases are set in paradigmatic opposition by alliteration, by the repetition of the letters *r, g,* and *n,* and by the internal rhyme of the words *Geist* (spirit) and *Geiz* (greed), linguistically identical save for their final phonemes, *st* and *z,* which mirror each other almost exactly in pronunciation. Syntactically and linguistically, Schiller indicates, Moses' "fiery regent's-spirit" and his "restless ambition" are mutually interdependent and share a cognate root: for Moses *Geist* (spirit) and *Geiz* (greed) are inherently interrelated, if not one and the same.[53] At the core of this poetic description of the man Moses, to use Freud's phrase, is an acute expression of anti-Semitism.

At this point Schiller's version of events diverges markedly from the Old Testament. In Schiller's account God does not reveal Himself to

Moses; God does not lead the Hebrews out of Egypt; and God most certainly does not select the Jews as "the chosen people": "The true God does not concern Himself with the Hebrews any more than any other people.—The true God could not fight for them, could not overthrow the law of nature for their sake" (468).[54] Moses invents this story out of desperation. In the desert, we recall, Moses becomes a simple shepherd for a Bedouin. Unwilling to accept this lowly wage laborer's position, unwilling to accept that his education is for naught, his "fiery soul" unwilling to give up his former grand plans to become a leader, motivated by wounded pride and a compelling drive to distinguish himself, and still outraged by his people's mistreatment (465–66), Moses looks for a way to get himself out of the desert, and decides to become a politician. Moses' decision to save his people from the horrendous treatment they suffered in Egyptian captivity is simply a convenient way to save himself. The people he aims to lead are neither capable nor worthy of redemption, Schiller notes, but Moses needs them for his "bold exploit" to be successful (466). Moses thus concludes that he needs to rehabilitate the Hebrews by restoring their human rights, by giving them the traits that had suffocated in their long savagery: hope, confidence, courage, enthusiasm (466).

Moses turns to his Egyptian education for help in figuring out how to proceed, and sets his rescue plan into motion by converting, in effect, from Egyptian to Hebrew, nationally, religiously, and militarily: "In Egypt he would have become an Egyptian, a hierophant, a general; in Arabia he becomes a Hebrew" ("In Egypten wäre er ein Egypter, ein Hierophant, ein Feldherr geworden; in Arabien wird er zum Ebräer" [466]). Resourcefully putting his knowledge of Egyptian religion and politics to good use, Moses recalls that a small group of priests succeeded in manipulating millions of people by cultivating their faith in supernatural powers (467). Accordingly, Moses fabricates the story about the burning bush, about God speaking to him, about God selecting the Hebrews as the chosen people, using military strategy—Schiller compares Moses' account of the revelation to a "general's call" (470)—with the express purpose of gaining political control over the Hebrews, to make the Hebrews "putty in his hands," to establish himself as their undisputed leader:

> If he can legitimate himself to his fellow brothers as this god's agent and emissary, they will be a ball in his hands; he can lead them as he will. But now the question arises: which god should he proclaim to them and how can he secure their faith in him?

> Kann er sich seinen Mitbrüdern als das Organ und den Gesandten
> dieses Gottes legitimieren, so sind sie ein Ball in seinen Händen, er
> kann sie leiten, wie er will. Aber nun fragt sichs: welchen Gott soll
> er ihnen verkündigen, und wodurch kann er ihm Glauben bei ihnen
> verschaffen? (467).

Too enlightened, too upright, too noble to build his plan to save the
Hebrews on deception, and with an eye to posterity (468), Moses decides
to ground his undertaking in the truth—the truth of the fundamental
essential unity of the most supreme Being, the true Egyptian God Jao,
whom Moses co-opts for the Hebrews.

In his description of the founding moment of the "Mosaic religion"
Schiller invokes the most virulent of anti-Semitic tropes: the singular
accusation of deicide that lies at the very core of Christian anti-Semitism.
(Jesus obviously does not enter into the Exodus account, but in keeping
with Schiller's universal historical method, of reading the past dialecti-
cally for its relevance to modernity, Moses' act of violence against "all
gods" [469] bears directly on Christianity. The identification of Moses
with the Wandering Jew, who according to legend taunted Jesus on the
way to the Crucifixion and now wanders the earth as punishment for
this crime, further solidifies this association.) In converting Jao to Yahweh, Schiller argues, Moses introduces a fundamentally new religious
paradigm: he makes Yahweh into the only God. Schiller identifies the
desire to "possess the godhead exclusively" as "conceited, childish pride"
which Moses exploits to appeal to his gullible Hebrew audience and to
advance his political agenda, merely replacing one false belief system
with another (469). This religious ethos—Moses' promotion of Yahweh
to the *only* God, the God of the Hebrews—reflects the Hebrews' exclu-
sionism that Schiller had carefully detailed earlier in the essay. Recall his
argument that the Hebrews intentionally kept to themselves, and then
contracted leprosy, *der Aussatz* (that which sets apart from), rendering
them a permanent lethal threat to their host community. The same holds
true for the religion Moses invents. At the time, Schiller notes, it was
fashionable for each people to have its own national godhead, and to
declare this godhead better than the others. Moses goes one step further,
and declares all other gods null and void. The language Schiller uses to
describe this foundational event picks up on his previous characterizations of the Wandering Jew Moses' fiery temperament, his murderous
nature, his greedy ambition, and his bloody hatred: "Not content to have
his national godhead merely mightier than all the others, Moses made
his God the only God, *and plunged all other gods around him back into*

their nothingness" ("Er begnügte sich nicht bloß, diesen Nationalgott zum mächtigsten aller Götter zu machen, sondern er machte ihn zum Einzigen, *und stürzte alle Götter um ihn her in ihr Nichts zurück*" [469, emphasis mine]). In the very act of founding Judaism, Moses the murderer commits deicide.

Schiller thereby inscribes a pernicious rhetoric of anti-Semitism into the very inception of "the Mosaic religion," and implicitly identifies "the Mosaic religion" as the *source* of anti-Semitism itself. Just as the genetically leprous Hebrews pose a mortal threat to their Egyptian host community, so too does Moses prove lethal to "all gods around him." In arguing that the "exclusionist" Hebrews are "unworthy," "depraved" and "impure" from the start, that the Hebrew "state within the state" presents a real danger to the nation that hosts it, that the murderous Moses, driven by unbridled ambition and bloody hatred, steals the truth of monotheism and then commits deicide in the very process of inventing the Hebrew faith, Schiller thoroughly debunks the "Mosaic religion" and asserts that Judaism has been superseded, indeed obliterated, by divine decree: the Hebrews are the "base vessel" in which truth was stored, the "impure channel" Providence selected to transmit the truth, but then smashed to pieces as soon as it had accomplished its mission. Rhetorically, religiously, racially, politically, ethically, and culturally, *The Legation of Moses* presents a universal historical justification for anti-Semitism.

What Schiller does value in the Exodus story is Moses the lawgiver: the Jewish nation Moses founded was the first in which the state religion and the religion of the people do not contradict each other (451). As a priest and as a statesman, Moses knew that the strongest and most indispensable support for a state's constitution is religion; he knew that he had to found his state based on the true God (473), the Egyptian God Jao. This the Egyptian priests had dared not do: they kept the truth to themselves, hidden from the general polytheistic population. Moses wanted to make his state last; he wanted his people to be free and happy. Moses was too great, too noble, to found his state on a lie, Schiller writes, and had to be satisfied in wrapping the true God in a "heathen cloak" to make Him comprehensible to the "weak heads" of the Hebrews (473–74). But in this Moses gains immeasurably, Schiller concludes: the foundation of his law is true, and a future reformer need not demolish the basic constitution when he corrects its false concepts (474). To be sure, the future reformer Schiller states in the last sentence of his essay, the Egyptian epopts, the enlightened high priests (460), had a tremendous advantage over the Hebrews: the Egyptians were able to recognize truth using reason; the Hebrews at best could believe only blindly in truth.[55] Schiller ends his essay as he had begun it, denigrating the Hebrews but celebrating Moses the lawgiver, Moses the great betrayer of the secrets of the Egyptian mysteries for the good of the world (474). And this is why Schiller, the betrayer, as it were, of Reinhold's *Hebrew Mysteries* for the good of the world, aligns himself with Moses. Moses, the shrewd politician who invented Judaism to dupe his people into following him out of Egypt, is the prototype for the political artist of Schiller's *Aesthetic Letters:* the political artist—here, Schiller himself—who rewrites history using necessary fictions and uses deception productively to correct the "Hebrew" failures of Enlightenment.

The preceding analysis has considered a relatively unknown essay by one of Germany's most celebrated authors, and asked why this text has not received the attention it deserves in the scholarship to date. Challenging the historical record that too easily dismisses *The Legation of Moses* as a minor work, I have argued that the essay has important implications for our understanding of Schiller's more canonical writings, *The Robbers,* the *Aesthetic Letters,* and his highly influential theory of universal history. Contextualized historically, the essay presents itself as political theory; its very rhetoric marks it as a document in the contemporaneous debate about the "Jewish Question." The surface universalistic pretensions of the essay not withstanding, Schiller invokes medieval calumnies to develop a trenchant genealogy of how the Jew has become the permanently degenerate, permanently diseased, murderous "other": the universal historical theory expressed in this essay anticipates racial anti-Semitism.

This chapter has proposed a new way of recognizing and interpreting the discourse of anti-Semitism in one particular historical document by questioning its reception history and by paying close attention to its rhetorical underpinnings, its internal logic, and its structure. Read in the context of the contemporaneous Jewish emancipation debate, the latent anti-Semitism of *The Legation of Moses* is in fact quite blatant. *That* the essay is anti-Semitic is of limited interest. What is really at stake in the preceding analysis is *how* the essay is anti-Semitic, and what this might mean for our critical understanding of Schiller's poetics and historiography in general. As I hope to have shown, re-reading the "major" Schiller through this "minor" essay, in concert with this "minor" essay, sheds a new and different light on both *The Legation of Moses* and on better-known portions of Schiller's oeuvre.

CHAPTER THREE

~

Germany Under the Sign of the Jew

Achim von Arnim's *Isabella of Egypt*

Achim von Arnim's *Isabella of Egypt* (*Isabella von Ägypten*, 1811) stages the Exodus of the Jews from Europe. In effect, Arnim pushes Schiller's political theory to an extreme. Whereas Schiller's Moses leads the Hebrews out of Egypt and converts them to Jews who are fundamentally Egyptian, Arnim makes the Jews into Egyptian Gypsies wandering in exile in Europe, converts them to Christianity, and then sends them back to Egypt. Confusingly, and intentionally, Arnim's Gypsies are Jews and they are not Jews: in this text "the Jew" is an amorphous signifier, found nowhere and everywhere. It is no accident that the Gypsy-Jews are introduced into the narrative as ghosts, as invisible specters haunting Christian society. The storyline works to expose a hidden "Jewish" danger that leads to the downfall of the Holy Roman Empire. At the same time, "the Jew"—or rather, the sign of "the Jew"—represents the condition of possibility for the construction of a unified German nation: but only in its absence.

Isabella of Egypt, written in 1811 and published in 1812 as the lead story in a novella collection dedicated to Jakob Grimm and Wilhelm Grimm, presents a theory of German nationalism grounded in the Jew and its exclusion. (In using the neuter form "its" to refer to "the Jew" I intentionally replicate the problematic logic of Arnim's ideology: "the Jew" is a concept that does not necessarily signify actual Jews or people.) Underlying this political agenda is a paradoxical dialectic: one *needs* "the Jew" to exclude it. Arnim was acutely aware of this paradox. In his contemporaneous essay "On the Distinguishing Signs of Jewishness" ("Ueber die Kennzeichen des Judenthums") Arnim inveighs against all things Jewish and presents numerous techniques for ridding Christian-German society of Jews and insidious Jewish influences, yet at the same time he formulates a scientific experiment for the construction of the pure Jew: in this text the Jew is the sine qua non of Arnim's nationalist agenda.

Arnim is notorious for his anti-Semitism, and Romantic anti-Semitism is a well-researched phenomenon. It is not without a certain irony, or chutzpah, even, that I broach the topic of this chapter: latent anti-Semitism in overtly anti-Semitic Romantic literature. Yet there is a danger to reading Romantic texts *only* for their manifest anti-Semitism. In not considering these texts in their complexity, we risk an incomplete understanding of a crucial period in the genealogy of modern anti-Semitism. The following analysis interprets *Isabella of Egypt* in conjunction with the essay "On the Distinguishing Signs of Jewishness," and argues that Arnim develops an incisive semiotic theory of "Jewishness" as a signifier of all that threatens German society; at the same time, the sign of "the Jew" also constitutes the condition of possibility for the construction of a unified Germany. Anti-Semitism thus functions as a positive, productive, and specifically German sociopolitical force for Arnim. The semiotic theory articulated in these early nineteenth-century Romantic texts arguably anticipates what Shulamit Volkov identifies as the hallmark of anti-Semitism at the end of the nineteenth century in Germany: anti-Semitism becomes a cultural code, the distinctive marker of a particular political philosophy and a particular worldview.[1]

Arnim's anti-Semitism is an expression of a new type of Jew-hatred that emerged in Berlin at the beginning of the nineteenth century. The watershed event that marked the inauguration of this era was the publication of Karl Wilhelm Grattenauer's 1803 pamphlet *Against the Jews: A Word of Warning to All Our Christian Fellow Citizens*. Grattenauer, a jurist, argued that the Jews were a distinct race, a "foreign Oriental people" whose character is a "mix of all the evils and failings that exist in humanity,"[2] and he warned that assimilated Jews, who were no longer outwardly marked as different from Christians, aimed for world domination. Although many of Grattenauer's ideas were not new, he promoted them with wit and erudition, and the pamphlet was a best seller: thirteen thousand copies were printed in six editions in 1803, along with an "explanation" and a "supplement." *Against the Jews* provoked a heated pamphlet war in Berlin: sixty different titles debating Grattenauer's views were published in 1803 alone. The public discussion grew so vociferous that the Prussian authorities, fearing public unrest, imposed a censorship decree.[3] Anti-Jewish sentiment intensified after Prussia's defeat by Napoleon in 1806. To some extent, hostility against the French was bound up with this anti-Semitism: the Jews became the "foreign" enemy living

on German soil when one could not openly attack the French occupy-
ing force. Yet, as Amos Elon notes, this new anti-Semitism was based
not on ignorance, but on increasing familiarity with Jews.[4] Berlin had a
sizable Jewish population, and assimilated middle-class Jews played an
important role in the economic and cultural life of the city. Arnim, well
connected in Berlin, interacted with Jews socially and studied aspects of
Judaism and Jewish culture; he was well acquainted with the charges
leveled against the Jews in the pamphlet war; and he was a great fan of
Eisenmenger's *Judaism Revealed*. Arnim's attitude toward Jews and the
"Jewish Question" is marked by some degree of ambivalence: a simultaneous attraction to and rejection of "the Jewish."[5] Despite complex,
contradictory, and at times relatively sympathetic portrayals of Jews
in some of his works, this ambivalence largely resolves in anti-Jewish
hostility. The essay that concerns us here, "On the Distinguishing Signs
of Jewishness," is overwhelmingly anti-Semitic, indeed shockingly anti-
Semitic, given Arnim's acquaintance with well-educated assimilated Jews
in Berlin. In this essay Arnim unequivocally makes anti-Semitism into a
political and cultural platform.

"On the Distinguishing Signs of Jewishness" was delivered before the
Christian-German Table Society, a tremendously popular eating club
Arnim cofounded in French-occupied Berlin in 1811, for "men of honor
and good morals, and born into the Christian religion."[6] With the phrase
"born into the Christian religion" Arnim indicated that membership was
not open to Jews or Jews who had converted to Christianity.[7] By design,
the Christian-German Table Society met for the first time on the anniversary of the Coronation Day of Friedrich I, the event that marked the
founding of the Kingdom of Prussia in 1701: the Table Society was to
serve as a political model for a future Prussian—and later, more generally, German—society.[8] I use the literal translation of the club's name,
the Christian-German Table Society—"die christlich-deutsche Tischgesellschaft"—to emphasize its importance as a *social* model.[9] Friedrich
I, not coincidentally, paid for the printing and distribution of Eisenmenger's *Judaism Revealed* in Prussia in 1711: the Prussian ruler Arnim
chose to celebrate at the kickoff event for the Table Society actively promoted anti-Semitism, and Arnim lauded this state action in his speech
"On the Distinguishing Signs of Jewishness." The Table Society defined
itself in its opposition to and its exclusion of "Philistines," women, and,
especially, Jews. In its exclusion of women and Jews, the Table Society explicitly countered the Berlin salons run by Jewish women that
had played a central role in Berlin's cultural life a few years before.[10]
The Table Society also countered the Berlin "Wednesday Society" ("die

Mittwochsgesellschaft"), a group of Enlightenment thinkers working to
further tolerance and Jewish emancipation.[11]

The Table Society was not a fringe group with radical views that
differed from mainstream educated Berlin society; it *was* mainstream
educated Berlin society, to a large degree.[12] Participants included many
of Berlin's leading non-Jewish male intellectuals, government, business,
and military officials, doctors, and artists; all disciplines of Berlin's new
university were well represented. Membership was open to the bour-
geoisie and the aristocracy, social conservatives and reformers alike.[13]
In a retrospective speech to the Table Society in 1815 Arnim articulated
its original goals precisely. In the face of the French occupation, the
Christian-German Table Society, a "mixed society" comprising men of
differing political persuasions and social backgrounds, aimed to secretly
formulate a constitution, agreed on by free debate and consensus, that
was to be a model for a future Christian German society, a unified Christian Germany that explicitly excluded Jews.[14]

The Table Society met every other week for lectures, discussions of
art, literature, and music, and, most importantly, for a communal meal:
in Arnim's words, it was a "Freßgesellschaft," a "pigging out" society.[15]
The metaphor that I use to translate "Freß"—"pigging out" (literally:
eating like an animal, glutton)—aptly captures the Table Society's overtly
anti-Semitic ideology: the founding speaker of the Society, Georg Beckedorff, called for a large ham to figure prominently at every meal as a
symbol that no Jews were allowed.[16]

This anti-Semitic agenda proved to be a strong selling point. As Beckedorff noted in his final speech to the Table Society in June 1811, the
upbeat, joyful atmosphere of the Table Society, its lively debates, its
constitutional character and its desire for laws, and, above all, the half-
joking, half-serious war it waged against Philistines and Jews led to such
an increase in membership that larger meeting venues twice had to be
arranged.[17] Anti-Jewish diatribes were popular forms of entertainment
at Table Society gatherings. Precisely what constituted a "Philistine,"
a crass, uncultured person, was the topic of a well-publicized address
delivered by Clemens Brentano at one of the early meetings of the Table
Society, in February 1811.[18] In a bantering and playful discussion of "The
Philistine Before, In, and After History"—which his audience found tremendously funny—Brentano defined the "Philistine" in opposition to
the Jew, but did so in an intentionally confusing way, such that "Philistine" and "Jew" became intertwined, and to some extent conflated,
as signifiers.[19] Arnim, not to be outdone by his friend's witty presentation, delivered his speech "On the Distinguishing Signs of Jewishness"

soon thereafter.[20] His audience presumably roared with laughter. Succinctly summarizing Brentano's and Arnim's speeches in his report to the Table Society in June 1811, Beckedorff proclaimed that the Table Society waged a "double war" against Philistines and Jews: "a superficial, joking and ironic war against Philistines"—although it is not clear "whether such a species ["Geschlecht"] really exists"—and "a profound, serious, and sincere war against Jews, a race ["Gezücht": breed, brood] [. . .] trying to insinuate itself, to force its way into, to penetrate into the state, into science, into art, into society, and into the knightly ranks of the duel."[21] In short, the Table Society made anti-Semitism into an explicit sociopolitical platform.

"On the Distinguishing Signs of Jewishness" holds the dubious distinction of being perhaps the most anti-Semitic text of the Romantic era.[22] Indeed, the speech is so anti-Semitic that it is easy to focus only on its overt anti-Jewish message and to read over its profound import: its systemic fusion of the anti-Semitic and the semiotic.[23] That the essay was originally presented in oral form, as a speech act, an illocutionary act, is significant: this is a text about how to do things with words.[24] True to its title, "On the Distinguishing Signs of Jewishness" casts "Jewishness" as a sign: it presents a self-reflexive theory of the structure and function of "Jewishness" as a signifier in the rhetoric of anti-Semitism. This point bears repeating. The speech is unabashedly anti-Semitic and aims to be provocative—even sexually seductive—in its anti-Semitism. And it is remarkably successful in this goal: the text is so outrageous that it lures its audience into focusing only on its manifest anti-Semitism. Yet at the same time, the speech presents a trenchant analysis of the rhetoric of anti-Semitism: it stages its own semiotic theory self-reflexively.

To tease out this semiotic theory I turn now to "On the Distinguishing Signs of Jewishness," yet I do so with a cautionary note. Precisely because the text is so anti-Semitic, it is cited only briefly in much of the secondary literature.[25] This select citation is understandable in light of the highly offensive material, and there is a danger to providing a platform for Arnim's extreme views by discussing them extensively. At the same time, analyzing the essay only cursorily has the effect of downplaying, if not effacing, the brunt of Arnim's argument, and there is a danger to this too. To the best of my knowledge, the essay is not available in English translation. For these reasons I offer a comprehensive summary of the opening paragraph of the speech, following the form, wording, and tone of Arnim's rhetoric, and will then consider the remainder of the essay more concisely. The following material—which comprises only a subset of Arnim's argument—may be uncomfortable to read.

The opening paragraph of the text clearly demonstrates how Arnim turns anti-Semitism into a speech act, into performance art, with distinctly political goals.[26] "On the Distinguishing Signs of Jewishness" is subtitled "Report of One of the Members of the Lawgiving Committee." The legal dimension of Arnim's argument is crucial here. Arnim begins his joking, vitriolic speech by exhorting his colleagues to pass a law expelling hidden Jews and those who have converted to Judaism from the Table Society. From the start, Arnim thereby establishes the Jews as a hidden threat, an invisible menace to the Table Society and to German society at large, and he proposes legal action against them. This proposed amendment, Arnim explains, derives from his Christian German conscientiousness and follows necessarily from the spirit of the Society's bylaws, but has yet to be codified. Arnim unequivocally identifies a legislative political, cultural, religious, and ethical anti-Semitism as the *Geist,* the animating spirit, of the German Table Society, and by extension, of German society at large. Given the extraordinary discussion of religion these days—Arnim refers to the contemporary debate about the "Jewish Question" and impending emancipation legislation slated to go into effect in early 1812 in Prussia as part of the Hardenberg reforms—the Table Society must address this pressing danger immediately: even a two-week delay in passing a law would be unthinkable. Arnim's emergency amendment to the Society's bylaws, modeled on its law against Philistines, would require the written affirmation of ten members to expel hidden Jews or those who have converted to Judaism. At stake in Arnim's amendment is the legal authority to identify and rout the "hidden" Jew from Christian German society.

Identifying the hidden Jew—defining that which is invisible, that which has no distinguishing features, as "Jewish"—forms the crux of the essay, and in a striking series of metonymic displacements Arnim then proceeds to construct "the Jew" rhetorically. "With the rapid expansion of our Society," Arnim continues, "news has reached the Caraibans and the cannibals—descendants of the Jews, according to some theologians—that we're Illuminati—since our founding song speaks of 'rays'" (108). The Illuminati, an Enlightenment secret society of Freemasons, was thought to be conspiring to overthrow the government in Bavaria and Austria, and had been outlawed in 1784–1785. Inverting this conspiracy theory, Arnim asserts that the wild, far-flung, cannibalistic Jews are secretly plotting to take control of the German Table Society. The Jews could smuggle themselves into the Society through disguise or dissimulation ("Verstellung," a common anti-Semitic attribute) or exchange ("Wechselverhältnisse," an economic term) and could then turn the law against us, Arnim warns, since they hate us. Arnim uses the verbs "einschmuggeln" and "einschwärzen" for "smuggle" (108): the latter locution renders the Jews "black."[27] On the linguistic level of the text, Arnim hence identifies the Jews as wild, cannibalistic, malicious, disingenuous black bigots who already control the economy and are intent on seizing control of the state legal system and harming the Christian German population.[28]

In a diatribe of pernicious slurs that make medieval anti-Semitic stereotypes into present-day realities, Arnim then details the dire consequences of a Jewish infiltration into the Table Society. This Jewish cabal will "convert our Christian eating club into a synagogue, replace our joyous Christian German song with Jewish cackling,[29] slaughter Christian children in place of pheasants [an image that resonates with Arnim's previous identification of the Jews as cannibals], stab the sacred Host with forks and knives instead of eating pudding, poison community wells instead of carrying out the philanthropic activities we Society members are planning, and carry out all kinds of other small misdeeds for which the Jews throughout all European countries have been teased to the blood" (108). However humorously Arnim may have intended this statement—and we should keep in mind that this *is* a speech, a performance, and Arnim was no doubt angling for a laugh—the charges he levels against the Jews here are deadly serious. In identifying these medieval anti-Semitic stereotypes as current realities, Arnim establishes the Jews as an ever-present pan-European threat transcending time and space. In detailing the severity of these "small misdeeds," Arnim tacitly indicates that "teasing" the Jews "to the blood" is just retribution for their crimes.

Arnim then provides concrete evidence that the Jews are involved in an international conspiracy, and at the same time establishes "Jewishness" as the universal signifier of all that menaces Christian society. "Gentlemen, how I rue the fact that I used to laugh at lawmakers who secretly plot to force a population to its happiness, but wipe out with one hand what the other hand has written," Arnim continues, alluding to ineffectual attempts to frame emancipation legislation that eventually resulted in the laws scheduled to go into effect in 1812, "until I read in the newspaper that secret societies of Jews in France and Vienna are causing all kinds of trouble" (108). Arnim's description of crafty lawmakers "secretly plotting" to pass emancipation legislation and force it on the population resonates with his description of the malicious Jews secretly plotting to seize control of the state legal system. Rhetorically,

Arnim casts the authors of emancipation legislation as "Jews." Arnim thereby illustrates the point of the entire essay self-reflexively: "Jewishness" becomes a signifier, grounded in, but not restricted to, actual Jews. Arnim underscores this point later in the essay, in explicating his "definition of the Jew." After noting that a litmus test designed to test for Jews does not yield the expected scientific results, i.e., that there is nothing essentially "Jewish" about the Jew, Arnim states: "I am firmly convinced that when a Christian does not like to smell roses, then all Jews smell of roses to him" (127). Importantly, Arnim defines "the Jew" as the universal signifier of whatever is disagreeable to Christians, and hence clearly articulates a projection theory of anti-Semitism.[30]

Ramping up to introduce the topic of his essay—the distinguishing signs of Jewishness—Arnim concludes the opening paragraph by contrasting the Enlightenment Christian Germans with the demonic Jews who threaten them. Given the secret societies of Jews in France and Vienna "who are responsible for all kinds of bad deeds," Arnim reports, "a veil lifted from my eyes" (108). Invoking a sight metaphor that resonates with the "rays" he had previously highlighted in the Table Society's founding song, Arnim "sees" the truth of the hidden Jew now, and will share it with his Enlightened Christian-German Table Society colleagues. "Unlike Philistines, who are easy to identify by the snail's shell they carry around with them" (108)—Arnim refers to Brentano's illustrious speech here—we have no way of recognizing these hidden Jews: their characteristics have in no way been scientifically determined yet. Driven by a "devilish" curiosity to be on the cutting edge of everything new and to besmirch all that is good, Arnim concludes, the Jews have perfected the art of secreting themselves in Christian society (109).

Before introducing his scientific methods for identifying Jews, Arnim offers an extensive discussion of the hidden Jewish menace that threatens Christian society. The Jews are very proud of their ability to insinuate themselves into Christian society, Arnim reports: in their books they boast of a Turkish kaiser, a pope, and a famous monk who all were Jews. Witness, too, the Marranos in Spain hiding from the Inquisition who secretly still practice their faith. Arnim suggests that allowing Jews to pass as Christians can be politically dangerous: the fact that Jews have mixed with the "first houses" of Portugal very likely resulted in Portugal having less feeling for "national honor" than Spain in their last war (109).

Arnim then details various techniques the Jews use to pass as Christians, arguing that "Jewishness" pervades Christian society as a result of this infiltration. The Jews deviously avoid practicing their own religious laws, flout German civil law and dress in Christian clothing, and pernicious Jewish traits and Jewish behavior like tobacco smoking have seeped into the Christian population such that it is impossible to distinguish Jew from Christian (113). Arnim regrets that the physical sign of the Jew, the physical marking of the Jew by clothing or by beard, has disappeared. Even circumcision, the somatic sign of the Jew, has been effaced: Arnim charges that rabbis are removing very little of the foreskin, or are only pretending to perform the rite. Arnim then explains how the Jews cunningly circumvent their own laws: they have sex and smoke tobacco on the Sabbath, and hairsplitting hermeneutics allow them to swear false oaths without damaging their honor. Arnim urges his audience to consult Eisenmenger's *Judaism Revealed* for more details, and laments the history of the suppression of the book's publication in Germany. Arnim goes on at great length in this vein, relating "historical" anecdotes about the Jews threatening Christians and Christian state policy, reciting an extensive and tedious rhymed poem that is supposed to be funny, and providing further "amusing" examples of the Jews' pernicious behavior. Arnim even uses scatological humor to promote his anti-Semitic agenda: he reports that an elegantly dressed Jewish youth repeatedly goes to concerts, slips Christian women cakes laced with laxatives, and boasts about this feat (112). Arnim hence makes anti-Semitism into performance art.

Arnim then formulates his call for action, his plan for recognizing the Jew, for reading "the Jewish" hidden in Christian society. Short of requiring the Jews to color their hands so that they'll glow phosphorescently when they count their money, or requiring Jewish women to uncover their heads to reveal their bushy Negroid hair (113), Arnim argues, we need to come up with a scientific way to recognize the distinguishing signs of Jews. Reasoning that language, politics, and nobility of spirit ("Edelmut") have become sham features precisely because of the invidious, invisible "Jewishness" that pervades Christian society (122), Arnim concentrates on analyzing the physical characteristics of Jews. He details innate Jewish behavior and traits specific to each of the twelve tribes of Israel, including inherited diseases like leprosy, spitting every time the name of Christ is mentioned, sweating excessively, lisping, and having abhorrent body odor (the *foeter judaicus*). These features provide important clues to a Jew's true identity, but the real key to recognizing the Jew lies in scientific analysis.

This scientific analysis grounds an overtly racial, politically motivated anti-Semitism. Arnim introduces a variety of scientific methods for identifying Jews: galvanic experiments, divining rods and magnets that would root out Jews by reacting to the money they have hidden on their bodies,

applying a caustic lye preparation that would render Jews' skin trans-
parent, skinning Jews and running litmus tests on them. This series of
scientific tests culminates in a gruesome chimerical experiment designed
to distill the pure Jewish essence, to construct the pure Jew. The experiment, based on Heinrich Martin Klaproth's method for chemical analysis,
consists in "the separation of components that are not alike" ("die Tren-
nung der ungleichartigen Bestandtheile" [124]). Arnim translates this
chemical analysis into racial terms: he proposes dismembering the Jew,
removing the four parts of Christian blood the Jew carries—which was
obtained secretly, through sinful miscegenation—replacing this Christian
blood with gold, and then reassembling the Jew in a smelting oven used
for purifying metals ("Kupellierofen": cupola furnace [125]). The Jew,
now 100 percent Jewish, profits from this experiment: the infusion of
new gold into his body animates the Jew, makes the Jew livelier, Arnim
reports. This horrifying imagined experiment—which perforce calls to
the present-day reader's mind the Nazis' very real brutal experimentation with and incineration of Jews—reveals an underlying motivation for
Arnim's anti-Semitism. This experiment does not—yet—aim to *eliminate*
the Jew, although Arnim will later broach this topic. Here, Arnim aims
to *construct* the pure Jew by "separating components that are not alike,"
by separating Jew from Christian. Arnim needs the pure Jew precisely so
that he can distinguish Christian from Jew; he needs the Jew precisely to
exclude "the Jewish" from Christian German society, to construct a pure
Christian German society.[31] Arnim accentuates this Prussian nationalist
agenda at the conclusion of the experiment. He tests his pure Jew by
asking him about two events that had recently devastated Prussia—the
Battle of Jena, at which Napoleon had resoundingly defeated Prussia in
1806, and the death of Prussia's beloved Queen Luise in 1810—and the
Jew merely laughs (124–25). Arnim hence offers scientific "proof" that
the Jews qua Jews are not Germans.

Arnim concludes the essay with a trenchant critique of anti-Semitism
that turns back on itself and proves to be all the more anti-Semitic as a
result. Throughout this final section Arnim uses a rhetorical technique
akin to apophasis, the raising of an issue by claiming not to mention it,
pretending to deny what is really affirmed.[32] Having just advocated that
Jews be skinned, dismembered, and put in ovens, Arnim recommends
these scientific tests be carried out with "humanity," given the innumer-
able horrors that have been committed against this "unfortunate people"
under the pretense of Christian faith, when in fact these atrocities were
merely an excuse to wipe out the debts Christians owed Jews (127).
Arnim—who had himself borrowed money from Jewish lenders—offers

an incisive analysis of the economic roots of anti-Semitism, but then goes on to suggest that this anti-Semitism is justified. Arnim carefully emphasizes that he does not want to harm the Jews, even though the entire wealth of nations has again fallen into Jewish hands, and notes that it would be rightly expected that horrible persecutions will again target "this rich race ["Geschlecht"] [...] that finds its prosperity in public misfortune, that is bound to no fatherland and siphons off the profits of every country" (127). Arnim then cites two historical examples of organized actions that aimed to exterminate or decimate the Jews: the infamous "King Armleder," Knight Arnold III of Uissigheim, who from 1336 to 1339 set out to destroy the Jews with an army of five hundred men and was revered for these massacres for hundreds of years afterward;[33] and the written opinion of Albrecht, Elector of Brandenburg, that proclaimed, with the full legal authority of Kaiser Friedrich III, that when a Roman kaiser or king is crowned, he has the right to kill all Jews at will, but must leave a few alive as "reminders" (128). Arnim states that he does not want to be accused of inciting such atrocities himself, and wishes the Jews the best of health: after all, some of his best friends are Jews, Arnim says. However much Arnim ostensibly distances himself from instigating organized violence against the Jews, rhetorically, he raises the proposal.

Arnim is fully cognizant of the rhetorical impact of his words: he wittingly turns anti-Semitism into a speech act. Having just denied that he is broaching the issue of murdering Jews, Arnim urges his fellow Society members to keep the truths transmitted here secret, as the start of a new type of Freemasonry. The call for secrecy is clearly tongue in cheek: Arnim knew full well that his speech would be the talk of the town, as was his friend Brentano's tremendously popular diatribe against Philistines and Jews, recently delivered before the same receptive audience. Ironically, and intentionally, with this call for secrecy and Freemasonry Arnim sets up an implicit parallel between the Jews who secretly sneak into the Society and the secret Table Society, a connection strengthened by the popular association of Jews and Freemasons.[34] With this connection Arnim harks back to the opening of his speech, where he had noted that the cannibalistic Jews have heard that the Table Society are Illuminati, Freemasons accused of plotting to take control of the government, and that the Jews are trying to sneak into this Enlightened Society to seize control of it and its conspiratorial action. Recall that the Table Society by design *did* constitute a secret model for a counter form of government during the French occupation, a secret model for a new Prussian nationalism. Arnim's call for a new type of Freemasonry, his rhetorical coupling of the "secret" truth of the Table Society and the Jews "secretly" trying to insinuate themselves into this Society, underscores his political agenda: Arnim links the Jew to the Table Society so that he can exclude the Jew from the Table Society. His call for a new type of Freemasonry is a model for a new Prussia that excludes Jews. Hence, Arnim concludes his speech as he had begun it, by urging the Table Society to take legal action against the Jews: Let's pass a law requiring members to guard against Jews infiltrating into our Society, and let's find a reliable chemical test to identify the distinguishing signs of the Jew (128), Arnim exhorts.

Arnim punctuates the end of his speech with two seemingly benign rhetorical flourishes that are incisively political in nature. The first sexualizes the rhetoric of anti-Semitism. We would be truly fortunate, Arnim asserts, if we could discover a sign that tests for Jewishness as reliably as the Jews test for virginity. An accused Jewish girl sits naked on the bunghole of a wine barrel. Kiss her after an hour and if she tastes of wine, then she's guilty; if there's no wine taste, then she's innocent (128). The impact of this raunchy, alcohol-imbued anecdote, designed to titillate his male audience, is profound: Arnim sexualizes his test for the sign of the pure Jew; he makes the politics of anti-Semitism powerfully, intoxicatingly, sexually attractive.

The second rhetorical flourish makes anti-Semitism into a religious necessity, a moral duty. Arnim again uses a rhetorical technique akin to apophasis, pretending to deny what is really affirmed. Immediately following the racy anecdote about the naked Jewish girl, Arnim asks: "But what can Spinoza, Mendelssohn, and my noble Jewish friends have in common with Judas Iscariot?" (128). On the surface this question appears to be a defense of the exceptional Jew—which in itself is a form of anti-Semitism—yet the question itself creates a connection between the exceptional Jew and Judas. Even in its implicit denial the very question suggests that exceptional Jews *do* have something in common with Judas: all Jews betrayed Jesus. Hence, Arnim ends his speech with a religious absolution, a religious exhortation: "The few noble Jews we're treating unjustly will think nothing of it, and the rest will receive their due. *Disci et salvavi animam!* [I have recognized the soul and saved it!]" (128). In the final lines of the speech, Arnim grounds the politics of anti-Semitism in the discourse of Christian redemption theology.

"On the Distinguishing Signs of Jewishness" stands as incontrovertible evidence of Arnim's appalling anti-Semitism, an anti-Semitism that until recently has been denied, dismissed, acknowledged only in passing, or glossed over completely in much of the secondary literature. In the face of its pervasive anti-Semitism, it is all too easy to read Arnim's essay only for its anti-Semitism, to conclude that the essay's interpretative significance lies solely in establishing that Arnim was anti-Semitic. Indeed, it is all too easy to read over the fundamental theory of "Jewishness" articulated in the text. "On the Distinguishing Signs of Jewishness" casts Jewishness as a semiotic event grounded primarily—but not exclusively—in the Jewish body. Not exclusively, since Arnim's theory also applies to converts to Judaism: Arnim's anti-Semitism is not just an anti-Semitism of the "blood."[35] Rather, as we have seen, Arnim clearly articulates a projection theory of anti-Semitism: "Jewishness" becomes the universal signifier of all that Christians dislike. "On the Distinguishing Signs of Jewishness" is an essay about how to read the distinguishing signs of Jewishness, how to read Jewishness as a sign, and how to read for the signs of Jewishness. More exactly, it is a profoundly political essay about how to read for the signs of the invisible Jewishness that has infiltrated Christian-German society, that pervades Christian-German society such that it is impossible to distinguish Christian from Jew, how to read for the signs of the invisible Jewishness that controls the economy of Christian-German society. The ultimate goal of this semiotic theory is to root out, proscribe, and rid Christian-German society of its invisible Jewishness.

Yet ironically, "the Jew" is both the bane and the condition of possibility of Arnim's nationalist agenda: his vision of a unified Germany is predicated on "the Jew" and its exclusion. In his 1815 speech Arnim rejoices that the Table Society can celebrate the victory over France with a second triumph: other like-minded societies—societies "that hate the French and shut out the Jews" (207)—have spread to numerous parts of Germany. "Our original Society has become Germany" (208), Arnim exults. At the same time, German society is still scattered, still fragmented ("zerstreut"), and Arnim calls for the construction of a unified Germany, a Germany that defines itself in its exclusion of Jews.

Precisely the same concerns motivate Arnim's most famous literary work, *Isabella of Egypt*, written contemporaneously to the speech "On the Distinguishing Signs of Jewishness" in 1811 and published in 1812. At first glance *Isabella of Egypt* would seem to have little to do with Jews and the "Jewish Question." It is, after all, a fantastic account of a failed love affair between the Gypsy princess Isabella of Egypt and the Holy Roman Emperor, Charles V. Yet, significantly, the novella was to have been introduced by a frame narrative that uses the failed love affair between a Jew and a Christian to expound one of its central themes, the undesirable assimilation of Jews into Christian-German society.[36] And like "On the

Distinguishing Signs of Jewishness," *Isabella of Egypt* is a text about reading the signs of Jewishness, and reading for the signs of Jewishness. This too is a text about eradicating the invisible Jewishness that pervades Christian-Germany society and threatens Christian-German society. Moreover, in this text the Jew represents the root cause of the failure to construct a unified Christian Germany. At the same time, the narrative presents a competing—and, on the surface, very surprising—argument. For all its invectives against all things Jewish, in this text the Jew—or rather, the sign of "the Jew"—also represents the condition of possibility for the construction of a unified Christian Germany: but only in its absence. *Isabella of Egypt* hence presents an aesthetic program for realizing the nationalist agenda articulated in "On the Distinguishing Signs of Jewishness."

Arnim announces the political goal of his writing in the dedicatory poem to Jakob Grimm and Wilhelm Grimm prefacing the *Novella Collection of 1812*, in which *Isabella of Egypt* was published as the lead story. In this poem Arnim laments the fact that Germany exists only in books, that the Germans are a divided people, and he indicates that he will distort truth and use legends to critique contemporary society and to construct a vision for the future (615–16).[37] Arnim's manipulation of history, truth, and legends was a bone of contention for the Brothers Grimm. In effect, however, Arnim articulates a political program reminiscent of Schiller's *Aesthetic Letters*. Like Schiller, Arnim stresses the Enlightenment provenance of his ideas, explicitly distancing himself from all "schools" of thought, but noting that his book was conceived and matured "in the light" (616). Like Schiller's political artist, Arnim rewrites history by fictional means and uses deception to heal the fragmentation of contemporary German society. Like Schiller's political artist, Arnim eschews popular opinion, claiming he courts no one's applause, no one's approval (616). In contradistinction to Schiller, however, Arnim does not aim to reproduce a formal totality, a totality of form, in his writing. Rather, as Goethe disapprovingly noted, *Isabella of Egypt* is like a barrel that overflows because the cooper forgot to hoop it. Similarly, Wilhelm Grimm compared the text to a picture that is framed on three sides, with the fourth side open, allowing the painter to constantly modify the canvas, creating an image that extends to infinity.[38]

Isabella of Egypt is first and foremost a text about the production of meaning, about creating new modes of signification and shaking up conventional semiotic systems. Its convoluted structure and plotline; its rambling language and dense syntax; its fusion of history, fact, fiction, legend, and fairy tale; its mixing of real, fantastic, magical, natural, and supernatural elements; the coexistence of living, dead, and undead characters; the doubling of characters and storylines; the narrator's interjections—all make for one bizarre, and very confusing, reading experience.[39] This confusion is both programmatic and thematic in nature. On the programmatic level, the text presents a hermeneutic crisis to the reader. It challenges the reader to construct meaning, to call into question what we know and how we know it. Importantly, the text resists linear interpretation, and constantly turns back on itself, intentionally creating confusion. On the thematic level, the text represents a key source of its own confusion as "Jewish" in nature.

The fundamental "Jewish" nature of this textual confusion is established at the start of the narrative. *Isabella of Egypt,* subtitled *Emperor Charles V's First Youthful Love,* is set in the first half of the sixteenth century in the Belgian Netherlands. The narrative opens with the old Gypsy woman Braka reciting the Lord's Prayer three times as a sign to her fellow Gypsies to gather to perform funeral rites for the Gypsy leader, Duke Michael. The recitation of the Lord's Prayer is important, in that it establishes the Gypsies as Christians. Despite his purported innocence, the Gypsy leader Michael has been charged with thievery and hanged, in accordance with strict laws to kill all Gypsies wherever they are found.[40] Significantly, the text never establishes beyond a reasonable doubt that Michael is in fact entirely innocent. He puts on a strongman show to earn money for two Gypsies newly arrived from France,[41] and one of these Gypsies steals roosters during the performance: intentionally or not, Michael creates a diversion for the thieving Gypsy, as charged. Here, and more overtly in the text's subsequent construction of Isabella, a systematic whitewashing of contradictory evidence casts the Gypsy leaders as good Christians. Heeding Braka's call, the Gypsies gather to cut Michael's corpse down and place it in the river Scheldt, so that Michael can return to "his people" in Egypt, the Gypsies' legendary homeland. Meanwhile, Michael's daughter Isabella, unaware of her father's death, has visions and dreams of her father on the Egyptian throne: Michael, the good, innocent leader who dies for the sins of others, Michael, the once and future king, clearly is a Christ figure. With Michael's death, it falls to the Gypsy princess Isabella to free her "coarse people" (624), the Gypsies scattered throughout Europe, and to lead them back to Egypt. The Gypsies are in exile in Europe as punishment for a tremendous religious transgression. They had refused the Holy Family refuge in Egypt because they did not look into the eyes of the Lord and hence did not recognize the divinity of the Holy Family, but thought they were Jews (624). In short, the Gypsies have been exiled from Egypt and have been sent on a pilgrimage as punishment for failing to recognize Jesus as Christ: to the Gypsies, Jesus was only a Jew.

At this point in the narrative—just two paragraphs into the text—the Gypsies are clearly identified as a stand-in for the Jews, and the narrative itself is clearly identified as an Exodus story *ex negativo*. The Gypsies' (Jews') crime: failing to recognize the divinity of Jesus. The Gypsies' (Jews') punishment: wandering endlessly in exile. In short, the Gypsies have become Wandering Jews. In contradistinction to the Jews, however, the Gypsies have atoned for their sin by becoming good Christians, and Isabella can now lead the Gypsies (now not Jews) back to Egypt. The standard reference work on Gypsies at the time, Grellmann's *The Gypsies,* which Arnim owned and used as source material for his narrative, flatly rejects the legend that the Gypsies originally came from Egypt and were wandering in exile as punishment for their refusal to offer the Holy Family refuge.[42] Arnim revives the spurious legend precisely because of the parallel it sets up between the Gypsies and the Jews. Arnim's interest in Gypsies in this narrative is not merely an interest in the Gypsies as an originary, innocent, romantic people, as some critics would have it, but an interest in the Gypsies as Jews.[43] As if to underscore the Jew-Gypsy equivalence, the text explicitly draws the connection and then pointedly denies it. (This narrative strategy is akin to the rhetorical technique of apophasis, claiming to deny what is really affirmed, operative in "On the Distinguishing Signs of Jewishness.") The narrator opens the second paragraph of the text by noting that the Gypsies are suffering extreme persecution in exile because the exiled Jews ("vertriebene Juden") have tried to pass themselves off as Gypsies in an effort to be tolerated. As a result of this Jewish infiltration the Gypsies have become "sinfully wild," "sinfully degenerate" ("sündlich verwildert" [624]). Moreover, the Jews have brought persecution to the Gypsies.[44] Recall Arnim's warning against hidden Jews infiltrating into Christian-German society. Here the Jews have infiltrated into Gypsy society and caused its moral depravation. Here the Gypsies are not Jews, yet they *are* Jews. Not only is it impossible to distinguish between Gypsy and Jew masquerading as Gypsy, but the Gypsies *themselves* also are troped as Jews. In this text "the Gypsy" as signifier clearly stands under the sign of "the Jew." Lest there be any doubt about this Gypsy-Jew connection, Arnim later drives the point home with a sledgehammer by making the Gypsy princess Isabella's double, Golem Bella, a Jew.

Following this opening passage, the Gypsies' "Jewishness" then goes underground—becomes "hidden"—in the text: Jews and Jewishness play no overt role, and indeed are not even mentioned, for the bulk of the narrative. At the same time that the Gypsies' "Jewishness" becomes hidden in the text, procuring money—that quintessentially "Jewish" trait—emerges as the driving force around which the plot revolves. Like the Jews living secretly in Gypsy society, the Gypsies are living hidden in Christian society, as invisible members of Christian society, as ghosts. (With their spectral status, the Gypsies clearly function as stand-ins for the Jews: from a Christian theological vantage, the Jews are living "ghosts" of a "dead" religion, the "dead letter" of the Old Testament.) Although the Gypsies now have received the right to live among Christians, this right was forced upon Christian society—as was the 1812 Jewish emancipation legislation—"under the sword of justice" (626). However, the Gypsies must stay hidden by day, and are allowed to emerge only at night. Isabella's guardian, the Gypsy woman Braka, exploits the Gypsies' "ghost" status to set into motion the conditions of possibility for fulfilling the prophecy that will lead to the Gypsies' salvation. Isabella is to become pregnant by a world leader, and her son is to lead the Gypsies back to Egypt.[45] Conveniently, Prince Charles, destined to become the Holy Roman Emperor, has decided to stay overnight in the house where the Gypsies are hiding, to dispel the rumor that the house is haunted. Braka arranges to have the scantily clad Isabella appear to Charles as a "ghost," and Isabella and Charles predictably fall in love. Charles, to be sure, is frightened out of his wits by his ghostly nocturnal visitor, and bolts from the house. Isabella, meanwhile, pines for Charles and seeks the means to wander about invisible in Christian society in search of her lover. Braka counsels her to get a lot of money, saying that wealth is the only way she knows of to pass undetected in Christian society. Isabella then sets out to acquire money so that she can enter into Christian society and seduce its most powerful leader.

Importantly, the pursuit of wealth is repeatedly characterized as "Jewish," but the signifiers of this "Jewishness" are not identified as such throughout much of the text: the sign of the Jew remains invisible, hidden, but obliquely legible nonetheless. To procure money Isabella—who as a Gypsy is troped as a Jew—turns to the occult arts, a narrative twist that invokes the stereotypical images of both the Gypsy and the Jew as sorcerers. Reading her father's book of "magical histories," Isabella learns that mandrake roots can take on human form, and that these mandrake root men relentlessly pursue gold and whatever else a "worldly heart" might desire, "with stealing, unfailing cunning" (635). Even before his appearance in the text the mandrake root man is hence defined by stock anti-Semitic attributes. Isabella then sacrifices the humanlike dog Simson, unearths the mandrake root, and calculatingly kills a kitten to provide nourishment for her mandrake root "child." The mandrake root man becomes increasingly "Jewish"—lustful, lying, cunning, opportunistic, and avaricious—and his incestuous relationship with Isabella becomes increasingly "Jewish"—perverse—in the course of the narrative. The text underscores the "Jewishness" of this unsavory figure repeatedly, using many of the same anti-Semitic stereotypes Arnim had used to characterize the twelve tribes of Israel in "On the Distinguishing Signs of Jewishness." The mandrake root man has no language of his own but excels in mimicking the rhetoric of others; he repeatedly gets drunk; he is ugly; he has kinky hair; he sweats excessively; he exudes a stink; he is a hypochondriac; he is associated with the plague; he aspires to power and grandeur; he glosses the Itzig affair, a notorious contretemps Arnim had had with a young Jewish man who had challenged Arnim to a duel;[46] he becomes increasingly demonic, and eventually dies in a cloud of sulfur. The mandrake root's pervasive "Jewish" characterization is all the more damning in that the text clearly casts this abhorrent, ridiculous creature as not human, as parading as human.

These signs of "Jewishness" are manifest in the other characters as well. Braka, who, as a Gypsy is troped as a Jew, is a manipulative, money-grubbing pander, thief, and liar, and she, like Isabella, proves to have magical powers: with her recounting of the legend of the bear skinner she raises the bear skinner from the dead. This repulsive legendary figure—who has fallen in love with his wealth during life and must stand guard over his treasure after death (656)—bears the curse of the Wandering Jew (728). Even the Christian woman Frau Nietken, to whom Braka turns for help in passing the "Jewish" Gypsies, the "Jewish" mandrake root man, and the "Jewish" bear skinner into Christian society, is marked by the sign of the Jew. Braka's old "sister in thievery" (660) Frau Nietken—"the good Frau Nietken" (662), "the excellent Frau Nietken" (663)—fences stolen goods and runs a whorehouse, and a chandelier, a "wonderfully fashioned brass crown" that once hung in the Ghent synagogue—a "Jewish" chandelier—now illuminates her "Christian" activities (661–62).[47] This sociopolitical religious image of the "Jewish" chandelier will recur at the text's conclusion, in the form of Queen Isabella, who, like Charles, renounces her earthly crown, dies, and appears as a guiding light in the heavens above. On the semiotic level of the text, Isabella's "Christian" star is inscribed as fundamentally "Jewish" in nature.

Strikingly, the hidden signs of "Jewishness" that subliminally animate the narrative coalesce around and become clearly legible in the figure of Golem Bella, Isabella's double. Golem Bella is expressly created as a deception. The mandrake root man has become smitten with his "mother," Isabella, and his lustful behavior prevents Isabella and Charles from realizing their love. Accordingly, one of Charles's aides commissions a Jew to create a golem, an ersatz-Isabella to distract the mandrake root man. Golem Bella looks almost exactly like Isabella, but is "Jewish" through and through: she has "a real Jew's heart" (701), "a mean Jewish disposition" (705), and "desired nothing of her own, except what had been in the thoughts of her Jewish creator: namely arrogance, lust, and greed" (688–89). Unlike Isabella, who is figuratively troped as a Jew, Golem Bella literally bears the sign of the Jew, reminiscent of the mark of Cain, on her body. Hidden on her forehead under her hair is the Hebrew word for "truth." (Note the irony: Isabella, glossed as the Virgin Mother and the redeemer of her people, stands for a Christian "truth," yet there is something essentially "Jewish" about Isabella too.) Now, Golem Bella, according to golem lore, can become too strong, too dangerous, and overpower human beings. The key to destroying Golem Bella lies in discovering and eradicating the Jewish "truth," the hidden sign of the Jew, inscribed on her body. And indeed, the lascivious Golem Bella becomes too strong, too dangerous, and must be destroyed. She succeeds in deceiving the mandrake root man into thinking she is Isabella, but she also succeeds in deceiving—and seducing—Charles, who experiences "an irresistible desire for the golem" (711).

This "Jewish" seduction proves disastrous to Charles, the most powerful leader of the Western world. The Holy Roman Emperor arguably takes on Golem Bella's "Jewish" traits, "arrogance, lust, and greed" (688–89): he is driven by dreams of richness and glory, and even tries to prostitute Isabella for financial gain by arranging a sham marriage between her and the mandrake root man. Not surprisingly, this "Jewish" seduction also leads to the downfall of Charles's relationship with Isabella and, more importantly, to the downfall of his empire. Charles eventually discovers the "truth" of Golem Bella and destroys her by eradicating the hidden sign of the Jew from her body. But Isabella is unable to forgive his transgression, and abandons Charles to lead her people—the Gypsies troped as Jews—back to Egypt. There she succeeds in unifying her people, but cannot prevent them from scattering again because of internal strife (740).[48] Even as converted Christians, the Gypsies remain Wandering Jews, and their customs simply do not belong, the narrator reports, in our European world (740). Charles, who has failed to unify his empire, becomes haunted by the demonic ghost of the mandrake root man, and becomes a Wandering Jew himself. He traverses the globe aimlessly, trying in vain to rid himself of this "money-bringing spirit" (737),[49] eventually abdicates, and spends the rest of his life in a monastery. Although separated in life, Charles and Isabella become conjoined in death: they die on the same day—Charles's birthday, also, importantly, the anniversary of the mandrake root man's entry into the world (738)—with Charles having a vision of his "first youthful love."

Isabella of Egypt is a profoundly political text that explores the possibility and presents the impossibility of a symbiotic union between Christian and "Gypsy," Christian and Jew. Even as converted Christians, Isabella and her Gypsies remain Jews.[50] And it is worth emphasizing that Isabella—for all her nobility of spirit—is a flawed character who shares many of Golem Bella's traits. In her single-minded pursuit of money, which she needs to seduce the world's most powerful leader, Isabella turns to the black arts, creates the mandrake root man, intentionally kills other creatures, and develops lustful feelings for her "child."[51] As the narrator tellingly reveals at the end of the text, he has *invented* "dear Isabella's innocence," and in the next sentence then asks why we should doubt the historical report of Isabella's death provided by the traveler Zacharias Taurinius (742), when in fact Arnim fabricated the account and ascribed it to a published historical document, the veracity of which itself had been famously questioned.[52] *Caveat lector,* Arnim indicates programmatically: what this narrative presents as "truth" is not true. Witness Golem Bella, the deceptive Jewish simulacrum with the Hebrew word for "truth" hidden on her forehead. By calling attention to its own deception, its own lies, its own *Verstellung,* the narrative hence stages its pervasive hidden "Jewishness" self-reflexively and critiques its effects thematically. Even with Charles's abdication, the narrator reports, Western culture still cannot rid itself of this "Jewish" spirit. The "base lust for money" that enabled Charles to do so much but hindered him from completing his reign has seduced and tortured successive generations, and resulted in the failure to construct a unified Germany (737).

But despite its overt anticapitalist, anti-"Jewish" political agenda, the text also inscribes a contradictory, complementary conclusion. In conjoining Charles and Isabella in life and in death—and including the mandrake root man in this equation—the text underscores the essential unity and the shared destiny of Christian and Gypsy, German and Jew. The text ends with the vision of Isabella enthroned in the heavens above, presiding as the divine leader over a unified people: the text ends with the dream of a unified Christian Germany under Isabella's star, a star that—like Isabella herself—stands under the sign of the Jew.

This chapter has demonstrated how latent anti-Semitism can infuse overtly anti-Semitic literature with surprising subtlety and theoretical sophistication. On the surface, "On the Distinguishing Signs of Jewishness" might seem to be just lame bad humor, an impressive compendium of highly offensive anti-Semitic slurs designed to be funny. This witty endorsement of anti-Semitism is dangerous in and of itself; all the more so, given the stridently serious anti-Jewish sociopolitical agenda of the Christian German Table Society. Yet beneath the pernicious humor, through the pernicious humor, Arnim develops a powerful semiotic theory of "Jewishness." The essay unabashedly embraces an overt, Jew-specific anti-Semitism. At the same time, it constructs a more general rhetorical conception of "Jewishness" as a catchall, a scapegoat, a *pharmakos* for everything foreign, feared, abjected from the German. "Jewishness" becomes a shifting, seductive, pervasive signifier, an often hidden, but always obliquely legible sign of everything that remains antithetical to—and indispensible for—the formation of an Enlightened German identity. This semiotic theory likewise informs *Isabella of Egypt*. As we have seen, "Jewishness" figures only peripherally in the surface storyline, but is in fact a core feature of this complex, intentionally confusing novella. In true Romantic fashion, Arnim's texts present theory as praxis: both are *about* the discursive construction of the figure of "the Jew," and both stage this theory self-reflexively. Significantly, in both texts, the semiotic articulation of "Jewishness" is fundamentally political in nature. Arnim constructs anti-Semitism as a paradoxical discourse both grounded in and freed from any specific historical referent, and integral to the very notion of German culture.

CHAPTER FOUR

∽

Reading Blood

Annette von Droste-Hülshoff's *The Jews' Beech Tree*

The preceding chapters have traced the development of an increasingly sophisticated theory of literary anti-Semitism from Lessing's pro-Jewish writings, which undercut themselves in a self-reflexive, self-critical Enlightenment gesture, through Schiller's poetic and political rewriting of history, which questions the origins of the Judeo-Christian tradition and squarely locates the source of anti-Semitism in the Jews themselves, to Arnim's racially grounded semiotic theory, which aims to identify hidden "Jewishness" in Christian German society in order to exclude hidden "Jewishness" from Christian German society: paradoxically, "Jewishness" becomes the foundational sign against which Christian German society defines itself. In his construction of the semiotic "Jew" Arnim invokes anti-Semitism as an Enlightenment ethos instrumental in defining the "German," and consciously plays with language to advance his Romantic political agenda, to make anti-Semitism seductively, aesthetically attractive. Many of the themes and critical gestures operative in the texts examined thus far are crystallized in Annette von Droste-Hülshoff's *The Jews' Beech Tree* (*Die Judenbuche,* 1842). This beautifully written, unassuming narrative inscribes a programmatic theory of latent literary anti-Semitism, a self-reflexive theory of the structure and function of latent anti-Semitism in literature. Thematically and structurally, the text is about the subconscious effects of the power of the word to create—and transmit—prejudice. Ironically, the novella itself has performed precisely this function in German culture.

The Jews' Beech Tree is one of the most popular and critically acclaimed German novellas of the nineteenth century, yet there has been little agreement about how to interpret this enigmatic text. Set in rural Westphalia at the end of the eighteenth century, the narrative revolves around a central figure, Friedrich Mergel, and his presumed complicity

with a band of wood pilferers. In the course of the novella four characters die under questionable circumstances in the vicinity of a beech
tree, into which a cryptic Hebrew inscription is carved following the
death of the third victim, the Jew Aaron. Although it is suggested Mergel may have murdered Aaron, no conclusive evidence substantiates this
claim. Indeed, when the final victim is found hanged in the Jews' beech
tree, presumably in retribution for Aaron's death, the corpse is identified as Mergel and buried in the knacker's yard like carrion, yet there
is reason to believe this identification may be incorrect. Mergel apparently has been masquerading as his doppelgänger Johannes, a bastard
presumably fathered by Friedrich's uncle Simon, who so resembles Friedrich that even his own mother cannot tell the two apart. Moreover, it is
unclear whether the death of Friedrich/Johannes is a murder or a suicide.
This information would seem essential to understanding why the narrative action ends with the unceremonious interment of the corpse in the
knacker's yard, a singular detail that has received little attention in the
secondary literature.

I believe that Friedrich/Johannes is denied a Christian burial because
he is a Jew, traveling incognito, as it were, as a Christian in Christian
society, and that *The Jews' Beech Tree* is a profoundly anti-Semitic text.
In addition to its blatantly anti-Semitic depiction of those people identified as Jews in the narrative, the novella displays a covert anti-Semitism
in its treatment of the protagonist Friedrich Mergel, whose name belies
his putative Christian identity: "Mergel," or marl, a mixture of clay and
calcium carbonate used as fertilizer, points to the "mixed blood" coursing
through the Mergel family's veins, imbuing it with a pariah status derived
from the anti-Semitic association of Jews with dung. The name "Mergel"
is one of many clues interwoven into the novella linking the family to
the overtly anti-Semitic register that runs throughout the text. This interplay between overt and latent anti-Semitism is related thematically to the
indeterminacy structuring the narrative. The text's programmatic refusal
to confirm conclusively the identity of key characters reflects its author's
fear of the Jews' legal emancipation and subsequent assimilation into
mainstream Christian society in the course of the nineteenth century: this
is a text about Christian society's inability to recognize "the Jew" in its
midst.

My interpretation departs significantly from previous scholarship
on *The Jews' Beech Tree*.[1] Most analyses to date have concentrated on
problems of genre (is the text a novella or a detective story?), illuminated
various aspects of the novella by providing sociohistorical background
material and tracing the text's genealogy, or attempted to resolve the

ambiguities inherent in the plot (who killed the Jew and who is hanged in the beech tree?). Several astute critics have realized the text offers no resolution to these questions, and have focused instead on the indeterminacy structuring the narrative.[2] However, no one has attempted to link this narrative indeterminacy to the text's treatment of anti-Semitism. Indeed, the issue of anti-Semitism remains unmentioned in most analyses. Many of those commentators who do remark on the text's treatment of Jews have not regarded this as a major theme, and have excused Droste's documented anti-Semitism as understandable in its historical context. A few critics even have argued the novella is philo-Semitic simply because its author chose to write about Jews.[3]

Remarkably, prior to the present analysis, first published in 1998, there had been only one study providing any substantive evaluation of anti-Semitism in the narrative, yet this groundbreaking article is somewhat limited in scope. In an excellent and informative discussion, Karin Doerr underscores what she calls the "specter" of anti-Semitism in and around the text, arguing that commentators routinely have glossed over the novella's blatantly anti-Semitic descriptions of the Jews as rogues, liars, cheaters, dogs, and pigs, and that the history of the novella's critical reception is itself anti-Semitic.[4] Doerr, however, does not recognize the latent anti-Semitism embedded in the narrative, and hence does not consider how crucial this anti-Semitic register is to an understanding of the novella as a whole.

The very fact that Droste constructs her Jewish characters from an extensive and deeply ingrained tradition of stock anti-Semitic stereotypes—and makes no attempt to present a balanced or realistic picture of Jewish cultural and religious identity—hints at the presence of a narrative subtext in the novella, a subtext that demands to be contextualized and interpreted sociohistorically. As Sander Gilman has proposed, stereotypes "carry entire realms of associations with them, associations that form a subtext within the realm of fiction. In the case of works claiming to create a world out of whole cloth, such a subtext provides basic insight into the presuppositions of the culture in which the work arises and for which it is created."[5] Droste, I will argue, was acutely aware of these stereotypical associations, and crafted them into a subtextual narrative about the danger of unexposed Jewish identity in nineteenth-century Germany.

In the following analysis I will focus on the narrative function of anti-Semitism in the text, demonstrating *The Jews' Beech Tree* is both a detective story and a novella according to Goethe's famous definition of the genre.[6] The "unheard of event that really occurred" around which the novella revolves documents the influx of "Jewish" blood into the Mergel family, an event encoded on the lexical level of the narrative. Theodor Fontane, representative of a series of distinguished critics who have viewed *The Jews' Beech Tree* as a flawed masterpiece, errs in his assessment that the novella tells two stories—Simon's and the Jews'—and that Droste should have picked one or the other in developing her plot.[7] These two storylines are in fact one and the same, and the novella displays a remarkable narrative cohesion once its anti-Semitic subtext is elucidated. The first part of my analysis situates the text historically as a document in the debate about the Jews' legal emancipation and assimilation into mainstream Christian society in nineteenth-century Germany.[8] The second discusses the methodology I use in my textual analysis. The following three sections identify and interpret the extensive anti-Semitic discourse that informs the novella. After tracing the Jewish genealogy of Friedrich Mergel and his family, I examine a series of narrative circumstances linking this unsavory clan to those people identified as Jews in the novella. Finally, I turn to the conclusion of the text, where Mergel is condemned because of his Jewishness, and then briefly consider the implications of this reading in light of the emergence of modern anti-Semitism at the end of the nineteenth century.

There were four main phases in the development of Jewish emancipation in nineteenth-century Germany.[9] The first, we recall, extended from 1781 to 1815, and began with a public debate in various print media fueled in large part by the French Revolution and the Napoleonic era. As a direct result of the Revolution Jews in France were granted full civic equality in 1791–1792, a right extended to Jews in the French-occupied territories of Germany under Napoleon's reign. Among these regions was Droste's native Westphalia, which forms the setting for *The Jews' Beech Tree*. In this area Jews received full legal rights in 1808, earlier than in most other parts of Germany, and Westphalia hence might be seen as a harbinger of the emancipation process in Germany at large. To be sure, this era of emancipation did not last long. In Westphalia some restrictions were imposed on Jews' rights in 1813;[10] two years later at the Congress of Vienna the civil rights of most Jews in Germany were rescinded. The second phase of the emancipation process, the period from 1815 to 1847, was characterized by an intense public debate about the "Jewish Question." Some two thousand five hundred books, pamphlets and essays devoted to this topic were published between 1815 and 1850;[11] *The Jews' Beech Tree*, in my estimation, counts among these documents. The third phase of emancipation was marked by the 1848 revolutions, during which the "Jewish Question" was hotly contested; the fourth extended from 1850 to 1871, when Jews throughout Germany finally were granted full civic equality.

The issue of assimilation went hand in hand with the emancipation debate. As a prerequisite for emancipation Jews were expected to abandon all characteristics that made them recognizable as Jews outside the religious sphere. In clothing, speech, and comportment Jews henceforth would be indistinguishable from Christians.[12] This call for social integration inspired both ire and angst among those who openly opposed the Jews' legal emancipation and those who harbored anti-Semitic sentiments. If Jews were no longer marked as such, how would Christians be able to recognize them in the general population? Precisely this question forms the crux of *The Jews' Beech Tree*.

There can be no doubt that Droste was anti-Semitic. A significant number of gratuitous negative comments addressing topics like Jewish physiognomy, Jews and money, and the identification of Jews in mainstream Christian society are strewn throughout her personal correspondence.[13] Moreover, the "Jewish Question" was of great concern to her as a Catholic Biedermeier author. Overtly hostile toward the increasing influence of Jews on the German cultural scene,[14] she vehemently condemned "Young Germany" as a "Jewish" movement that threatened Christian bourgeois society, saying derisively of the Young German leader Heinrich Laube: "Isn't Laube a Jew? At least he has everything that distinguishes this people's authors—spirit, wit, antipathy against all existing forms, especially the Christian and bourgeois ones,—grandstanding,—pomposity, and a stentorian manner of grabbing the word in the literary world for himself,—one-sidedness that doesn't come from reason, but from pure darkness,—in short—if he's not a Jew, he certainly deserves to be one [. . .]."[15] (Ironically, Laube, who was not Jewish, later attacked the "foreign Jewish element" that had "penetrated everywhere" into the midst of German society and literature, at the same time claiming he did not oppose the Jews' emancipation.)[16] It is no accident, I would propose, that the genealogy of *The Jews' Beech Tree* coincides with the second phase of Jewish emancipation in Germany (1815–1847). Droste possibly began taking notes for the story as early as 1818, then completed most of the work on the text in two stages: the first in the 1820s; the second between 1837 and 1840. Some twenty years after its inception the novella was published in 1842, in the wake of the Young German movement.[17]

The contextualization of the novella within the Jewish emancipation debate provides a plausible explanation for Droste's enduring interest in her subject matter, though biographical circumstance certainly contributed to her initial choice of topic. *The Jews' Beech Tree* is loosely based on a somewhat fictionalized report of a Westphalian Jew's murder in 1782 published in 1818 by Droste's uncle, August von Haxthausen, and then further fictionalized by Droste in her novella. In Haxthausen's *History of an Algerian Slave,* Hermann Winkelhannes murders the Jew Pinnes in 1782, runs away and becomes a slave for twenty-five years, and in 1807 returns to the crime site and hangs himself out of remorse.[18] *The Jews' Beech Tree* departs significantly from its literary-historical prototype, which, as Droste put it, "is entirely unsuited to MY Mergel."[19] One striking difference between the two stories is the highly stylized Christian rhetoric of Droste's version, largely absent in Haxthausen's. The introduction of this emphatically religious dimension may have been a calculated move to situate the text within the Jewish emancipation debate,[20] a hypothesis substantiated in part by two other major modifications Droste made to the narrative. In addition to changing the name of the protagonist to the semantically charged "Mergel," Droste altered the time of the novella's setting so the action concludes on the eve of the French Revolution, the event that ultimately led to the Jews' legal emancipation.[21]

The novella's title was coined by Droste's publisher Hermann Hauff but approved by Droste, who noted with no small irony that Hauff had "baptized" her story "The Jews' Beech Tree."[22] The choice of title likely was not fortuitous. A popular "Jews' Beech Tree" tale circulating widely at the time related the account of Maria Buchen, "Mary's beech," a tree in Franconia into which a statue of the Virgin Mary had been placed. Over time the tree trunk had grown over the hollow where the statue stood, obscuring the image. According to legend no Jew was able to pass by the tree without drawing his knife and unknowingly stabbing the icon, a transgression for which he was then put to death.[23] The significance of this tale to Droste's novella is profound: in both accounts "The Jews' Beech Tree" serves as a means for identifying and condemning Jews.

Droste's text was published in the *Morning Paper for Educated Readers* in the spring of 1842. In the same issue the journal ran a lengthy exposé on "The Jewish City in Prague," an article that ostensibly argues for the Jews' emancipation but whose rhetoric is demonstrably anti-Semitic.[24] Droste, who interpreted the piece as being about "the position of the Jews everywhere," at first felt threatened by the essay because she feared it might detract from her readership, but later concluded it might actually increase interest in her novella.[25] Read in this context, it is entirely plausible *The Jews' Beech Tree* instantiates a political agenda. Composed as a warning against the influx of Jews into German society, this "portrait of customs from the mountainous region of Westphalia"[26] is, in its author's words, "purely NATIONAL, and very worthy of note."[27]

Throughout the novella Droste uses subtle and subconscious rhetorical persuasion to advance this political agenda, wittingly obscuring a narrative subtext beneath the surface storyline. In this she shared the proclivity of many Biedermeier authors for encoding messages in their writings. In a succinct statement that might be taken as a programmatic description of the narrative principle structuring the novella, Droste announced: "Brevis esse volo, obscuro fio" ("I want to be brief, I'm making obscure").[28] Concealed in the language of the narrative itself, the anti-Semitic subtext of this carefully crafted tale is developed with lyrical precision, a linguistic feat hardly surprising for an author whose primary output was poetry.

In the following analysis I will focus on the semantic network of etymologies, ellipses, and allusions coalescing around the figure of Friedrich Mergel, arguing that Mergel is a Jew according to a racial or "blood" definition, and that the text depicts the fate of the "Jew" masquerading as a Christian in Christian society. Much of my analysis hinges on lexical and etymological evidence. This methodology is justified—indeed sanctioned—by the text itself. Droste challenges her reader to read accordingly in the novella's prologue, an opaque poem that forms the programmatic core of the narrative:

> Where is the hand so delicate, that without erring
> It can sort out the confusion of a narrow mind,
> So steady, that without quaking, the stone it
> Can throw at a poor atrophied being?
> Who dares to measure the force of boastful blood,
> To weigh each word, that unforgotten
> Into a young breast the tenacious roots drove,
> The secret soul-thief of prejudice?
> You lucky one, born and protected
> In the world of light, raised by a pious hand,
> Put aside the scale, never allowed you!
> Let the stone lie—it will strike your own head!
>
> Wo ist die Hand so zart, daß ohne Irren
> Sie sondern mag beschränkten Hirnes Wirren,
> So fest, daß ohne Zittern sie den Stein

Mag schleudern auf ein arm verkümmert Seyn?
Wer wagt es, eitlen Blutes Drang zu messen,
Zu wägen jedes Wort, das unvergessen
In junge Brust die zähen Wurzeln trieb,
Des Vorurtheils geheimen Seelendieb?
Du Glücklicher, geboren und gehegt
Im lichten Raum, von frommer Hand gepflegt,
Leg hin die Wagschal', nimmer dir erlaubt!
Laß ruhn den Stein—er trifft dein eignes Haupt!— (3)[29]

The themes of error, confusion, decidability, blood, prejudice, and retribution are underscored in the verse in an overt hermeneutic challenge.
The poem consists of three complex sentences, each four lines long. The
first and second sentences take the form of queries, while the third is an
exhortation, presumably an answer of sorts to the questions posed in
the previous lines. The first sentence asks: Where is the hand so delicate
it can sort out the confusion of a narrow mind, so steady it can unerr-
ingly stone a poor atrophied being without itself quaking? The second
sentence repeats the question, this time as a challenge: Who dares measure the force of boastful blood, to weigh each word that, unforgotten,
drives its tenacious roots into a young breast, to weigh each word that
is the secret soul-thief of prejudice? This text dares us to read blood,
dares us to read on the lexical level, to weigh each word and its roots,
to remember each unforgotten word in its various contexts, to consider
the word the secret soul-thief of prejudice.[30] The final sentence elucidates
this puzzling image with a caveat for the lucky one born and protected,
raised by a pious hand, in the world of light: Put away the balance,
don't try to measure yourself using this scale, don't throw the stone or
it will strike your own head. It is entirely possible to interpret this as
a simple exhortation against prejudice ("judge not lest ye be judged"),
but I would suggest quite the opposite is the case here. Read in view of
Friedrich Mergel's fate in the ensuing narrative, the final line of the poem
warns: you, too, may have "Jewish" blood coursing through your veins,
and you, too, shall be judged accordingly.

I want to be very clear about the nature of the claims I make here
and throughout my textual analysis. I am not arguing my reading is the
only possible one. Such an assertion would be foolhardy in light of the
fact that the text derives its narrative force from indeterminacy, from the
programmatic avoidance of proof.[31] Many of the passages I discuss can
be interpreted using explanations other than the ones I offer. The crucial
point is not that my reading *is* correct, but that it *can be* correct, given

the textual evidence. Precisely this interpretative ambiguity is at stake in the novella. In a central passage Droste thematizes this irresolvable tension between verity and verisimilitude, proof and plausibility, by offering a Kleistian rendition of Boileau: "the truth does not always appear to be true" ("le vrai n'est pas toujours vraisemblable" [34]), and then steadfastly refusing to verify the "truth" of any of the matter at hand.[32] This refusal to confirm basic information like character identity is significant in a narrative where the polarization between Christian and Jew is stark. Contextualized historically, Droste's narrative voices an anxiety, the fear Christian society will be unable to recognize the assimilated Jew. Droste responds to this fear by arguing that in the face of uncertainty "Jewish" blood will manifest itself. Many readers will find my analysis disturbing, and may take issue with the lexical evidence I offer in support of my thesis.[33] To these critics I respond: Droste explicitly invites this type of interpretation, and my reading is every bit as valid as any other explication of the given evidence. My analysis has the additional advantage of interpreting many significant textual details glossed over or inadequately understood in the scholarship to date. Moreover, it explains the narrative function of anti-Semitism in the text, rather than merely commenting on its presence.

Before turning to the text a few prefatory comments about Droste's narrative technique are in order. First, the narrator distorts facts and dissembles in her presentation. Twice she purports to render an objective account of a historical event: "In a poeticized history ["erdichtete Geschichte": also, made-up story] it would be wrong to thus disappoint ["täuschen": also, deceive] the reader's curiosity. But this all really happened; I can add or take away nothing"; "This really happened according to all main details in September of the year 1789." ("Es würde in einer erdichteten Geschichte unrecht sein, die Neugier des Lesers so zu täuschen. Aber dieß Alles hat sich wirklich zugetragen; ich kann nichts davon oder dazu thun" [25]; "Dieß hat sich nach allen Hauptumständen wirklich so begeben im September des Jahrs 1789" [42].) The narrator's comments could be taken at face value, yet Droste did change a number of crucial details in the historical account, including the years of action. This *is* "erdichtete Geschichte," a made-up story or poeticized history, and a disjunction exists between the historical record and narrative "fact." Even if we were to accept the narrative "facts" as true (a somewhat problematic step, since Droste wrote for an audience who may well have been familiar with both the historical record and Haxthausen's fictionalized version of the event), the narrator's assertion that her account is accurate "according to all main details" implies her report may be inaccurate with regard to minor details. In short, we are dealing with a manipulative narrator whose voice cannot be trusted. Second, despite the narrator's claim she cannot add to or detract from the truth, a number of embellishments and ellipses are evident in the novella. Finally, as we will see, the text constantly quotes and rewrites itself, creating a narrative palimpsest that must be read on many levels.

The following analysis traces the narrative sequence of the novella, highlighting those aspects of the text that detail Friedrich's Jewish provenance. Roughly speaking, the first part of the narrative (pp. 3–26) documents Friedrich's genealogy as "Jew," while the second (pp. 27–42) exposes his true identity and condemns him because of his Jewishness.

In the opening paragraph we are told Friedrich Mergel was born in 1738 into a historically noteworthy milieu that is isolated and protected from modernization, where a foreign face still attracts attention. The population of the region is distinguished by all the vices and virtues, originality and narrow-mindedness that flourish under such conditions. The inhabitants' notions of right and wrong have become somewhat confused. Or rather, in addition to the official legal code a second form of law was in force: the law of public opinion (3). The text does not clarify the contents of the legal code in question, and the ensuing narrative introduces two major legal issues current at the time of the novella's writing. The first is the matter of timber rights on public grounds,[34] a topic hinted at in the next sentence and developed in the following paragraph's description of the area's thriving wood-pilfering industry. The second is the debate about the "Jewish Question," a question the text never overtly raises but perhaps obliquely alludes to in the narrator's remark that a foreign face still attracts attention in the region. The narrator then broaches the issues of interpretation and evaluation, suggesting that these themes have political ramifications of central importance to the novella: "It is difficult to view that time impartially ["unparteiisch": impartial in a political sense]; since its disappearance it has either been arrogantly censured or ridiculously praised [. . .]" ("Es ist schwer, jene Zeit *unparteiisch* in's Auge zu fassen; sie ist seit ihrem Verschwinden entweder hochmüthig getadelt oder albern gelobt worden [. . .]" [3, emphasis mine]). Having framed her "portrait of customs" ("Sittengemälde") as a politically charged, historically specific hermeneutic exercise, the narrator concludes the paragraph by subtly introducing a religious dimension into her discussion of the problematic legal code: "For he who acts according to his conviction, as lacking as it may be, will never completely fail, whereas nothing has a more *soul-killing* effect than to invoke the external law against one's inner sense of justice" ("Denn wer nach seiner Ueberzeugung handelt, und sey sie noch so mangelhaft, kann nie ganz zu Grunde gehen, wogegen nichts *seelentödtender* wirkt, als gegen das innere Rechtsgefühl das äußere Recht in Anspruch nehmen" [4, emphasis mine]).

The Mergel family history is then set into this sociohistorical context. Town B. has just been presented as a peasant town whose inhabitants are distinguished by narrow-mindedness, questionable morality, and a penchant for wood pilfering. But there is something different and decidedly worse about the Mergel family. Significantly, the rhetoric the narrator uses to describe this alterity recalls the foreignness of the "foreign face" ("fremdes Gesicht") that still attracts attention in the area (3). The Mergels have moved into a homestead and destroyed its modest prosperity through "much disorder and bad economy" ("viel Unordnung und böse Wirthschaft"): the house is dilapidated and the fields overrun with "foreign cattle [. . .], foreign corn, [. . .] more weeds than cabbage" ("fremdes Vieh [. . .], fremdes Korn, [. . .] mehr Unkraut als Kraut" [5]). From the beginning, then, the Mergel family is depicted as a destructive force that threatens the local economy and introduces the "foreign" into the old order.[35]

We then are presented with Friedrich's father, Hermann Mergel, who drinks, batters his first wife, and consorts with "foreign girls" ("fremde Mägde" [5]). In light of this illustrious behavior it is unclear why the former town beauty Margreth Semmler, known for her wit and economic expertise, chooses to marry the town drunk: "thus what had *driven* her to this step was incomprehensible to everyone. We *believe* we have found the cause precisely in her self-conscious perfection" ("so mußte es Jedem unbegreiflich seyn, was sie zu diesem Schritte *getrieben*. Wir *glauben* den Grund eben in dieser ihrer selbstbewußten Vollkommenheit zu finden" [5, emphasis mine]). But the tentative nature of the narrator's assertion and the compulsion expressed in the verb "driven" suggest there may well be another explanation. Indeed, as we will see, Margreth's professed probity proves to be a sham,[36] and her brother Simon later intimates the forty-year-old Margreth marries because of her sexual drives (9–10). Soon after the marriage Margreth is seen running from the house with her clothes disheveled and her hair hanging wildly around her head, hastily digging herbs from the garden and disappearing into the barn. The narrator provides one possible reason for this bizarre behavior: it was rumored Hermann beat Margreth for the first time, though she herself never reports this (6). Margreth's silence again calls the narrator's explanation into question. Another possible interpretation of her puzzling behavior is related to her sexual drive: some herbs are known to induce abortion, a suggestion I will return to shortly. At this point I would merely draw attention to the fact that there is a one-year gap in the narrative. The next event we are told of, which by virtue of its narrative position would seem to elucidate Margreth's mysterious behavior in the garden, is the birth of Friedrich Mergel in the second year of the marriage. (In an early draft of the manuscript Friedrich is born in the first year of the marriage,[37] indicating this one-year gap is significant.) Margreth is said to have cried bitterly when handed the child. Her grief is perhaps due to her unhappy relationship with her husband, but the text later suggests another possible explanation: Hermann may not be the father of the child.

Margreth's rectitude is drawn into question in the elliptical description of her husband's death, an event that occurs when Friedrich is nine years old. The reader never receives a precise account of the circumstances surrounding the death. We are told only that Hermann, who had gone to a wedding one stormy winter evening, was found dead in the woods (8). Simon later intimates Hermann fell down drunk and froze to death (12), but a surfeit in narrative information renders this explanation somewhat suspect. Although the narrator reports Hermann had left home early because of the storm, the distance between the site of the wedding and the Mergel house is only three-quarters of a mile. Perhaps this is a considerable stretch for a drunken man to navigate in a storm, but the narrator also recounts that Hermann, who apparently has reformed his untoward behavior and become a devoted father, had promised Friedrich he would return home that night (6). The death itself is glossed over in a remarkable narrative ellipsis, and the text delicately suggests Margreth may have played a significant role in Hermann's demise. Friedrich anxiously awaits his father's return, but Margreth sends the boy to bed, ignoring his assertion that someone is knocking on the door. It is only the wind, she claims, adding that the Devil, who is standing outside the door, will hold Hermann tight (thereby intimating that someone is in fact at the door). After several hours Friedrich wakes up and hears his mother praying. She tells Friedrich to join in, remarking he already knows half the Lord's Prayer. (That a nine-year-old boy knows only half the Lord's Prayer indicates that the seemingly devout Margreth has been seriously remiss in her son's education.)[38] Friedrich again hears knocking; again Margreth dismisses his claim. This time the boy insists he hears voices. The wind abates, and Margreth, hearing the hubbub outside, replies: "They're bringing me the pig again" (7). There is no clear way to interpret this statement. Perhaps the scenario of the drunken Hermann being brought home has been repeated many times before; perhaps this is the second time Hermann returns home that night. When Margreth does get up, she unpiously flings her rosary onto a stool and goes to the hearth before stomping obstinately through the house to open the door. She does not return, and the narrator reports: "Twice a foreign man came into the room and appeared to look for something anxiously" (7). Margreth's trip to the fireplace before opening the door suggests she may have burned the sought-after object, and her willfully ignoring the knocking Friedrich hears hints she may have had a hand in Hermann's death.

Margreth's behavior after the corpse is brought home is even more damning, and again raises the question of her motivation for marrying Hermann in the first place. The narrator insinuates that the seemingly distraught Margreth engages in an incestuous affair with her brother Franz on the very night of her husband's death:

> Her brother stayed with her and the whole night long Friedrich, who had been ordered to stay in bed under the threat of severe punishment, heard the fire crackling in the kitchen and a sound like sliding back and forth and brushing. Little was spoken, and quietly, but now and then sighs penetrated through that, as young as the boy was, went through his very being.

> Der Bruder blieb bei ihr und Friedrich, dem bei strenger Strafe im Bett zu bleiben geboten war, hörte die ganze Nacht hindurch das Feuer in der Küche knistern und ein Geräusch wie von Hin- und Herrutschen und Bürsten. Gesprochen ward wenig und leise, aber zuweilen drangen Seufzer herüber, die dem Knaben, so jung er war, durch Mark und Bein gingen. (8)

While this might be interpreted as a description of Margreth and her brother readying Hermann's corpse for burial, it is by no means clear what actually happens here, and textual evidence points strongly to sexual activity. Friedrich is ordered to stay in bed, suggesting he should not see the adults' activities; he hears rhythmic rustling noises and the fire crackling (fire is a common metaphor for sexual "burning" or desire, and Droste uses this image elsewhere in the text [9–10]); and the penetrating sighs the young boy does not understand cut him to the quick. Moreover, Franz's suggestion to Margreth that they both have three masses read and make a pilgrimage to Werl (8) is ambiguous: perhaps these actions are to be taken in memory of the unshriven Hermann, yet the siblings' contrition also indicates that they may be guilty of some sin.

The first characterization of Jews in the text follows this incestuous interlude, a narrative link that will prove significant later in the novella. Hermann's corpse is carried off; curiously, there is no mention of it being buried. Margreth, faced with the prospect of raising her son alone, asks Friedrich whether he plans to be pious or to lie, drink, and steal. Friedrich hedges the question and replies that Hülsmeyer steals: he recently thrashed Aaron and took six groschen from him. Margreth retorts: "If he took money from Aaron, then the cursed Jew certainly cheated him in the first place. Hülsmeyer is an upright, established resident, and the Jews are all scoundrels ["Schelme"]" ("Hat er dem Aaron Geld genommen, so hat ihn der verfluchte Jude gewiß zuvor darum betrogen. Hülsmeyer ist ein ordentlicher, angesessener Mann, und die Juden sind alle Schelme" [8]). In one short utterance Margreth characterizes the Jews as damned, moneygrubbing, deceiving, and, in implicit opposition to the "established resident" Hülsmeyer, foreign.

Margreth's concluding remark that the Jews are all "scoundrels," *Schelme,* is profoundly important to the ensuing narrative. Commentators routinely have interpreted this derogatory term in its watered-down meaning of "rogue" or "rascal." In this context this attribution is certainly justified, but in keeping with the prologue's challenge to read the roots of words, I would suggest the text also brings into play the literal meaning of the term. *Schelm* in its original meaning refers to "flayed livestock" or a "fallen animal," a usage still current in nineteenth-century dialect, and the term also can be applied to human corpses. From this its other meanings are derived: *Schelm* in its secondary sense refers to "a contagious disease" or "pestilence"; its tertiary meaning is "base person, deceiver, thief, misleader, traitor."[39] Strikingly, the dead Hermann becomes a *Schelm* in at least the first and third senses of the word, tacitly linking him to the anti-Semitic register Margreth summarily invoked. Local lore has it that his blue corpse becomes the phantom rogue of the forest who engages in antics like frightening a slumbering timber thief by showing off his swollen blue face through the leaves (9), a caper that anticipates the scene at the end of the novella when young Brandis lies down for a nap and peers through the leaves to find the dead—and no doubt blue—Friedrich/Johannes hanging in the beech tree (42). Hermann's postmortem metamorphosis into a *Schelm* is the first hint there might be something "Jewish" about the Mergel family. Significantly, this identification will be mirrored at the novella's conclusion in the parallel—and even more damning—transformation of Friedrich/Johannes, whose scarred corpse is hastily buried in the knacker's yard, thereby becoming a *Schelm* in the original sense of the word ("flayed livestock, fallen animal").

Hermann's transformation into a *Schelm* has a profound effect on Friedrich's development. Friedrich is so disturbed by the sight of his father's blue corpse that he refuses to speak about it, and when the other boys tease him about his phantom father, he howls, hits, and stabs out "with his little knife" (9), arguably a threatening phallic gesture that will take on significance in light of the circumcision motif soon to be introduced in the text (a hypothesis I will return to).[40] Friedrich's strong reaction to the children's taunting is perhaps brought on by the subconscious realization that Hermann is a "phantom" father in another sense of the word: he may not be Friedrich's true father. As if to substantiate this conclusion, Friedrich often is seen at his shepherd's post pulling thyme from the earth (9), pathological behavior recalling the strange occurrence in the year before his own birth when Margreth pulled herbs from the garden and disappeared into the barn (6). My suggestion that Margreth's foray into the herb garden was connected to an unwanted pregnancy now gains credence: the herbal link between mother and son serves to introduce Friedrich's genealogy, detailed in the next scene of the text.

The mysterious circumstances surrounding Margreth's marriage and Friedrich's birth are amplified when Margreth's brother Simon comes to visit following the demise of Hermann Mergel. Simon's visit is noteworthy because he has not come to his sister's house since her "foolish marriage" to Hermann twelve years before (9). Since Simon himself is hardly an upright character, we are left to speculate about the reasons for his strange reaction to his sister's marriage. (I would suggest at this point that the reason is sexual.) The motivation for his current visit apparently is professional: the text implies he has come to enlist Friedrich as a lookout for his wood-pilfering band. He therefore arranges a "deal" with Margreth, "a sort of adoption" of the "sister's son" (a "Handel" with Margreth, "eine Art Adoption" of the "Schwestersohn" [11, 10, 16]). This terminology is significant, since the narrative focus of the scene is on familial resemblances, and not on Simon's wood-pilfering activities. Though very little factual information is conveyed here, a series of ellipses in the narrative points to a subtext detailing Friedrich's genealogy.

The scene begins with a characterization of Simon, a portrayal all the more remarkable in that he is the only figure to be described in any detail in the narrative:

> Simon Semmler was a small, restless, scrawny man with fish eyes
> bulging from his head and a face altogether like a pike's, an uncanny

companion ["ein unheimlicher Geselle"] whose boastful reserve
often alternated with an equally affected trueheartedness, who
would gladly have presented himself as an enlightened mind but
was instead regarded as a disagreeable, quarrel-seeking ["Händel
suchend": literally, deal-seeking] fellow, a guy everyone preferred
to avoid [. . .].

Simon Semmler war ein kleiner, unruhiger, magerer Mann mit vor
dem Kopf liegenden Fischaugen und überhaupt einem Gesicht wie
ein Hecht, ein unheimlicher Geselle, bei dem dickthuende Verschlossenheit oft mit ebenso gesuchter Treuherzigkeit wechselte, der gern
einen aufgeklärten Kopf vorgestellt hätte und statt dessen für einen
fatalen, Händel suchenden Kerl galt, dem Jeder um so lieber aus
dem Wege ging [. . .]. (9)

On the etymological level the text suggests that this "uncanny fellow"
("unheimlicher Geselle") is not at home in this society: "unheimlich,"
"uncanny, strange, weird" is derived from *un-home-ly;* and "Geselle,"
"fellow, companion," is the root of "Gesellschaft," society.[41] The ensuing
characterization indicates what is so strange, so "un-home-ly," so unso-
cial, about Simon: this is a stereotypical anti-Semitic description of a
Jew, and I would propose that Simon, the conniving, deal-seeking "fiery
man" with the bulging fish eyes and the Semitic name whose red coat-
tails trail after him like fiery flames (11), is in fact a Jew.[42] In anti-Semitic
literature Jews frequently appear as the Devil,[43] and Simon's "pike face,"
which glosses the folktale in which the Devil appears in the form of a
pike,[44] underscores this demonic association. To be sure, not all demons
are Jews, but Simon's biblical name provides the key to the significance
of this particular Devil figure to Droste's narrative. Of the many Simons
in the Old and New Testaments, the most well known is Simon Magus.
Acts 8: 9–24 relates the account of Peter contending with the magician
Simon and eventually converting him to Christianity. No later document mentions Simon's conversion, and in popular anti-Semitic literature
he often is cited as the prototype of the Jewish sorcerer.[45] (Droste, who
asserted in an early draft of the manuscript that "the Jews are practicing
magic,"[46] tacitly invokes this stereotype by linking Simon to the timber
thieves who mysteriously spirit away wood.) Perhaps in part because of
linguistic circumstance, the historical Simon became a foe of the early
Church. Simon's claim to be "somebody great" resonates with the title
"Great Power," a phrase applied to God or God's representatives, and
later accounts detail Simon parading as Christ. Hence, for centuries

heresiologists have cited Simon as an example of how demonic forces can mimic Christianity, arguing that Simon is a false Christ or an Antichrist.[47] In view of the anti-Semitic stereotype of the Jew as Antichrist,[48] this ecclesiastical history suggests the relevance of the eponym to Droste's narrative: the demonic Simon, masquerading as a Christian, is a Jew.

Moreover, Simon, the "character who is the key" to the entire novella,[49] represents the anti-Semitic stereotype of the licentious Jew incarnate, and this identification provides the key to Friedrich's genealogy. The text raises the distinct possibility that an incestuous relationship existed twelve years before between Simon and his sister (a possibility rendered even more probable by the strong suggestion of sexual activity between Margreth and her brother Franz on the occasion of Hermann's death). Margreth quakes violently when she sees Simon, who "since his sister's foolish marriage *had not crossed her threshold*" ("seit der thörichten Heirath seiner Schwester *ihre Schwelle nicht betreten hatte*" [9, emphasis mine]). Perhaps this mundane turn of phrase metonymically masks a sexual transgression,[50] since Margreth then asks: "Do you want to see how things are going with me and my dirty son?" ("Willst du sehen, wie es mir geht und meinem schmutzigen Jungen?" [9]). Her query raises the obvious question: what makes Friedrich "dirty"? Her brother answers with a slew of homilies ending with an innuendo about the forty-year-old Margreth's sexual drives: "'But when an old house burns, there's no extinguishing the fire.'—A flame as red as blood flew over Margreth's careworn face" ("'Aber wenn ein altes Haus brennt, dann hilft kein Löschen.'—Über Margreths vergrämtes Gesicht flog eine Flamme so roth wie Blut" [9–10]). Margreth's flame-red blush reiterates the image of inextinguishable sexual desire, and the description of Simon not stepping over Margreth's "threshold" resonates synecdochically with the burning house metaphor. Moreover, the ensuing exchange suggests on both lexical and narrative levels that Friedrich may be the product of an incestuous relationship between Margreth and Simon. Like the conniving Simon, who is characterized by "reserve" ("Verschlossenheit" [9]), Friedrich is "perfidious and reserved," "sly and cunning" ("tückisch und verschlossen," "schlau und gewichst" [10]). Margreth then broaches the issue of Friedrich's paternity, remarking: "He has a lot from you, Simon, a lot" ("Er hat viel von dir, Simon, viel" [10]). Simon replies Friedrich is truly his "father's son," and his response indicates that it is unclear who Friedrich's father really is:

> "Hey, here comes the companion! Father's son! He swings his arms just like your blessed husband. And look at that! Truly, the boy has my blond hair!"

A secret proud smile ["ein heimliches, stolzes Lächeln"] crept over the mother's features; her Friedrich's blond curls and Simon's reddish brush!

"Ei, da kommt der Gesell! Vaterssohn! er schlenkert gerade so mit den Armen wie dein seliger Mann. Und schau mal an! wahrhaftig, der Junge hat meine blonden Haare!"
       In der Mutter Züge kam ein heimliches, stolzes Lächeln; ihres Friedrichs blonde Locken und Simons röthliche Bürsten! (10)

Margreth's "secret proud smile" suggests there is not merely a familial resemblance between Friedrich and Simon, but a filial relationship.[51] This suggestion is underscored on the lexical level: Margreth's "secret" ("heimlich": literally, home-ly) smile resonates with the description of Simon as an "uncanny" ("unheimlich": literally, un-homely) fellow, indicating that the root of what is uncanny and secret here, the root of the familial resemblance between Friedrich and Simon, is to be found in the "home." Remember the "burning house" metaphor documenting Margreth's sexual drive and the sexually charged description of Simon not entering Margreth's home, his not crossing her "threshold" after her marriage: on the lexical level a subtextual story of incest is narrated here, a subtextual story accentuated by the fact that Simon's "reddish brush" ("röthliche Bürsten") recalls, in close textual proximity, the sexually charged "sliding back and forth and brushing" ("Hin- und Herrutschen und Bürsten" [8]) punctuating the night Margreth and her brother Franz spent together in front of the crackling fire.
       The likelihood that Simon may be Friedrich's father is further strengthened by Margreth's extremely troubled reaction to the appearance of Johannes Niemand, a bastard child apparently sired by Simon whose maternal lineage remains unexplained. Johannes so resembles Friedrich that Margreth at first cannot tell the two boys apart. Moreover, her face turns pale as a sheet when she sees Johannes (15)—a detail that will prove significant to my analysis—and the narrator's description of her reaction to the boy hints at a narrative ellipsis that might explain his true parentage: "no, that was not her child! And yet—Friedrich, Friedrich! she called" ("nein, das war ihr Kind nicht! und dennoch—Friedrich, Friedrich!' rief sie" [13]). One logical explanation for Margreth's emotional and linguistic reactions to this strong fraternal resemblance is that the two boys are in fact brothers and Margreth and Simon are the boys' parents.[52] Recall the unexplained circumstances surrounding Margreth's marriage to the town drunk

Hermann, her mysterious foray into the herb garden soon after the marriage, and the one-year gap in the narrative preceding Friedrich's birth.
These ellipses suggest that Margreth may have been pregnant when
she married Hermann, that she perhaps had used the herbs to try to
induce an abortion, and that the ungainly Johannes, who perhaps bears
the scars of a failed abortion attempt, may have been born during the
first year of the marriage. Moreover, the coupling of Margreth and
Simon is enciphered onomastically in the unexplained "old story" about
Gretchen Siemers (21), whose first name is a diminutive form of Margreth, and whose last name elliptically combines the names Simon and
Semmler.[53]

Perhaps this is merely idle speculation. After all, the narrator reports
Margreth is extremely upset that Simon has been so "ungodly" as to
sire a child out of wedlock (15), suggesting he is the only culprit here.
Remember, though, that the narrator cannot be trusted, and Margreth's
behavior on the occasion of her husband's death clearly indicated she
is not as pious as she pretends to be. Indeed, when Margreth tries to
explain away the strange similarity between Friedrich and Johannes, the
text indicates her own family history may be tainted by "foreign" (read
"Jewish") blood:

> Similarities prove nothing. Why, forty years ago she herself had lost
> a little sister who looked just like the foreign peddler. What one
> doesn't like to believe when one has so little and by not believing
> would lose the little one does have!

> Aehnlichkeiten wollen nichts beweisen. Hatte sie doch selbst vor
> vierzig Jahren ein Schwesterchen verloren, das genau dem fremden
> Hechelkrämer glich. Was glaubt man nicht gern, wenn man so wenig
> hat und durch Unglauben dieß wenige verlieren soll! (15–16).[54]

The narrator's wry comment indicates that Margreth may well be holding onto false beliefs in dismissing these physiognomic similarities.
While there is no direct evidence the foreign peddler or "Hechelkrämer"
either fathered the child or was a Jew, lexical evidence points strongly
to this conclusion. A "Hechel" is a comb for dressing flax or hemp. This
etymology is significant, since the textile trade—especially the linen
industry—was a major source of employment for Jews in eighteenth-
century Germany.[55] Moreover, tales in which business and sexual
transactions are intermixed are common in anecdotes concerning Jews.[56]
Perhaps most indicative of the genealogical connection between the

peddler and the Semmler family are the lexical links Friedrich shares with both the "Hechelkrämer" and Simon:

> A foot above the others his blond head bobbed up and down like a pike somersaulting in the water; on all sides girls screamed as he flung his long flax hair in their faces [. . .].

> Fußhoch über die Andern tauchte sein blonder Kopf auf und nieder, wie ein Hecht, der sich im Wasser überschlägt; an allen Enden schrien Mädchen auf, denen er [. . .] sein langes Flachshaar in's Gesicht schleuderte. (27)

The flaxen-haired Friedrich, who jumps up and down like a pike, is at once connected to Simon the pike-faced "Jew" (9) and to the foreign "flax-comb" peddler who may have fathered at least one illegitimate child in the Semmler family.[57] It seems there may in fact be Jewish blood on the maternal side of Friedrich's family, and Friedrich and Simon may in fact be Jews according to a liberal interpretation of the matrilineal definition of Jewish law.[58]

To be sure, Simon and Friedrich likely do not know they are Jews. Their "Jewishness" derives from the "Jewish" blood coursing through their veins, condemning them to egregious behavior. The transgressions they are accused of on the narrative level are wood pilfering and murder, yet the text offers no conclusive evidence they are guilty of either wrongdoing. Moreover, all the members of their society—from the villagers to the aristocracy—are of the same moral ilk as Friedrich and Simon, but only Friedrich and Simon are punished for their corrupt behavior. This suggests that what is of interest here it is not so much whether Friedrich and Simon committed a particular crime, but the etiology of their alterity. A series of strategically placed clues links the two to the overtly anti-Semitic descriptions of those people identified as Jews in the novella, and an examination of this interplay between overt and latent anti-Semitism reveals the significance of Friedrich's and Simon's Jewishness to the narrative at large. Their real crime lies neither in a particular action nor even in the unwitting concealment of their true identity, but in the very fact they are Jews.

Friedrich and Simon are marked as unchristian companions from the start of their relationship. Moreover, their unchristianness is explicitly connected to the beech tree motif soon to be identified with the Jews in the narrative. After the meeting with Margreth in which he arranges to adopt Friedrich, Simon brings the boy home. The fiery Devil figure walks through the woods and the sunburned Friedrich follows his "leader," to whom he bears a strong family resemblance (11). As they walk, Simon questions Friedrich's moral character. After asking whether Friedrich drinks (a question the boy does not answer), Simon alludes to Hermann's death in the part of the Breder Forest they are now approaching, and then asks whether his mother prays as much as she used to:

> "Yes, two rosaries every night."—"So? and you pray with her?"—
> The boy laughed, half embarrassed, with a crafty side-glance.—
> "My mother prays the first rosary in the dusk before dinner, and
> I'm usually not back yet with the cows. She prays the other one in
> bed, and I usually fall asleep." "So, so, comrade!"
>
> These last words were spoken under the canopy of a wide beech
> tree, which arched over the entrance to the ravine.

> "Ja, jeden Abend zwei Rosenkränze."—"So? und du betest
> mit?"—Der Knabe lachte halb verlegen mit einem durchtriebenen
> Seitenblick.—"Die Mutter betet in der Dämmerung vor dem Essen
> den einen Rosenkranz, dann bin ich meist noch nicht wieder da mit
> den Kühen, und den andern im Bette, dann schlaf ich gewöhnlich
> ein."—"So, so, Geselle!"
>
> Diese letzten Worte wurden unter dem Schirme einer weiten Buche
> gesprochen, die den Eingang der Schlucht überwölbte. (11–12)

With a crafty side-glance Friedrich follows his uncle, both literally and figuratively, into the realm of the beech tree, a "very dark," "gloomy," "completely dark [ominous]" ("sehr dunkel" [11], "düster" [11], "ganz finster" [12])—read "Jewish"—abyss marked by foreignness, mystery, and murder.[59]

Under Simon's tutelage Friedrich grows into his definition as "Jew."[60] From the very beginning of his association with his uncle, Friedrich becomes preoccupied with money and outward appearances (14, 16). This is significant, since the Jews are the only (other) characters in the novella repeatedly associated with money, a common anti-Semitic attribute.[61] Moreover, Friedrich leads a double life, a detail increasingly important to the narrative at large. Not only does he have a true double, the bastard Johannes, he also appears alternately as "the town dandy" and a "ragged shepherd's lad" (16). This malleability of character presumably allows Friedrich to join Simon in his clandestine activities, but the text suggests much more is at stake than the simple tale of two timber thieves. His double life is a manifestation of the fact he is a Jew masquerading as a Christian, a charade in which Simon also participates. After sending Brandis to his death by misdirecting him down the path passing by a beech tree (an arboreal signifier again suggestive of Friedrich's "Jewishness"), Friedrich decides to go to confession, and is confronted by the wild-haired, pale, horribly strange-looking Simon, the presumed murderer of Brandis. Perverting the biblical Commandment against bearing false witness, Simon warns Friedrich not to bear any witness whatsoever against him, adding: "Go in God's name, but pray *as/like a good Christian*" ("Geh' in Gottes Namen, aber *beichte wie ein guter Christ*" [25, emphasis mine]), a locution that subtly draws attention to what Friedrich is not. Grammatical flux notwithstanding, Friedrich apparently is unable to pray either as a good Christian or like a good Christian, since the narrator laconically reports, "Friedrich did not go to confession that morning" (26). This incident, which makes little impression on Friedrich (26), serves as a catalyst to complete his transformation into a two-faced, untrustworthy man (read "Jew"):

> Outwardly he was orderly, sober, seemingly truehearted, but cunning, boastful and often crude, a person no one could delight in, least of all his mother, and who still had achieved a certain dominance ["Uebergewicht": excess weight] in town due to his feared boldness and his even more feared cunning, a dominance that was all the more recognized the more people realized they didn't know him and were not able to figure out what he was ultimately capable of.

> Er war äußerlich ordentlich, nüchtern, anscheinend treuherzig, aber listig, prahlerisch und oft roh, ein Mensch, an dem Niemand Freude haben konnte, am wenigsten seine Mutter, und der dennoch durch seine gefürchtete Kühnheit und noch mehr gefürchtete Tücke ein gewisses Uebergewicht im Dorfe erlangt hatte, das um so mehr anerkannt wurde, je mehr man sich bewußt war, ihn nicht zu kennen und nicht berechnen zu können, wessen er am Ende fähig sey. (26)

The duplicitous Friedrich has become so boastful, crafty, and treacherous that his fellow villagers fear and no longer know him. In short, Friedrich has become a dangerous foreigner in their midst.

The first part of the narrative, which documents the genesis of Friedrich's threatening alterity, ends at this juncture. While this alterity is linked only vaguely to Jews in the first part of the novella, every scene in the second part underscores Friedrich's connection to the Jews. This point bears emphasizing: from a narrative structural vantage, Friedrich's subsequent development and demise are inextricably intertwined with a "Jewish" storyline.

Indeed, the first narrative sequence of the second part, the death of the Jew Aaron, strongly suggests that Friedrich is a Jew. The villagers celebrate a wedding, and Friedrich asserts his rights as the town dandy, dancing wildly and commanding attention. The previously analyzed sentence intimating Friedrich's Jewish genealogy occurs at this narrative nexus: "A foot above the others his blond head bobbed up and down like a pike somersaulting in the water; on all sides girls screamed as he flung his long flax hair in their faces [. . .]" (27). Recall that this sentence links the flaxen-haired, pike-like Friedrich lexically to Simon the pike-faced "Jew" and to the foreign "flax-comb" peddler who may have fathered at least one illegitimate child in the Semmler family. This interpretation is further substantiated when the sentence is considered in its narrative context. At the wedding Friedrich basks in his role as town dandy until his double Johannes makes a fool of himself by stealing butter. This behavior reflects badly on Friedrich, who angrily calls his sidekick a "ragged dog" ("Lumpenhund" [28]). (This apparently innocuous invective, which obliquely recalls the textile industry of the "flax-comb" peddler or "Hechelkrämer" who may be a Jew, is repeated in the descriptions of Friedrich as "ragged" ("zerlumpt" [11]) and a "ragged shepherd's lad" ("zerlumpte[r] Hirtenbube" [16]), the Mergel family as a "ragged clan" ("Lumpenpack" [19]), and in the name of the Jew "Ragged Moises" ("Lumpenmoises" [34]), who confesses to killing a coreligionist named Aaron.)[62] The semantic network linking the ragged Mergel family to shabby Jews resonates in this narrative context. Friedrich is profoundly embarrassed by the villagers' laughter: "the general laughter cut through his soul" ("das allgemeine Gelächter schnitt ihm durch die Seele" [28]), a phrase that implies he has suffered a religious injury. He attempts to regain his composure by boastfully showing off a fancy watch, but the Jew Aaron shows up at this inopportune moment to demand payment for the timepiece and mocks the delinquent Friedrich for his poverty. The resultant exchange documents the most blatantly anti-Semitic sequence in the entire text:

> The barn roared with laughter; many had crowded into the yard.— "Grab the Jew! Weigh him against a pig!" some shouted; others had become completely serious.—"Friedrich was pale as a sheet," an old woman said [. . .].

> Die Tenne hobte von Gelächter; manche hatten sich auf den Hof
> nachgedrängt. —"Packt den Juden! wiegt ihn gegen ein Schwein!"
> riefen Einige; andere waren ernst geworden. —"Der Friedrich sah
> so blaß aus wie ein Tuch",—sagte eine alte Frau [. . .]. (29)

Doerr has proposed this passage invokes the stereotypical association of Jews with pigs in its most virulent form, that of the *Judensau* (Jews' sow), a motif that refers to the obscene or lascivious behavior of Jewish males.[63] This association is significant, since the narrative again hints at a subtext detailing Friedrich's Jewish genealogy. Lexical evidence suggests Friedrich's reaction to the taunt equating Jew and pig is due to much more than wounded pride. The old woman's observation that Friedrich is "pale as a sheet" reiterates almost verbatim Margreth's reaction to seeing Friedrich's double Johannes for the first time: "Her face was pale as a sheet" ("Ihr Gesicht war bleich wie ein Tuch" [15]). The textile reference again recalls the trade of the "Hechelkrämer" or "flax-comb peddler" who may have fathered at least one child in the Semmler family; and the identification of the Jew Aaron as an "occasional trader in used goods" ("gelegentlicher Althändler" [29]) points to the possible Jewishness of the "Hechelkrämer," the only other peddler mentioned in the text. On the lexical level Margreth's and Friedrich's identical sheet-white faces bear witness to the Jewish blood in the Semmler family. Margreth's ashen expression alludes to the incestuous relationship with Simon that apparently resulted in two children. Friedrich, whose "soul" has just been cut open, pales not only because he has been humiliated in front of his neighbors, but also in direct response to the taunt itself. On a subconscious level Friedrich knows *he* is the Jew who should be weighed against a pig.[64]

As if to substantiate this conclusion, the image of the balance on which Jew and pig serve as counterweights recalls the prologue's challenge to the reader to dare to measure the force of boastful blood and the scale conveniently provided for this purpose. Friedrich, described as "boastful" ("prahlerisch") and having "a certain overweight" ("ein gewisses Uebergewicht" [26]), is one addressee of the final lines of the verse, which admonish the lucky one born and protected in the Christian world of light: "Put aside the scale, never allowed you! / Let the stone lie—it will hit your own head!—" ("Leg hin die Wagschal', nimmer dir erlaubt! / Laß ruhn den Stein—er trifft dein eignes Haupt!—" [3]).[65] Read in view of the ensuing narrative, the prologue warns Friedrich to put aside the scale because it will measure him for what he is: a Jew. Friedrich apparently does not heed this warning, since the text suggests he does indeed throw the stone that strikes his own head. Aaron is killed by a single blow to the head, and Friedrich is implicated as the murderer. He and Johannes leave town, only to return as Friedrich/Johannes, who apparently dies in retribution for Aaron's death.

The narrative circumstances following Aaron's death merit close consideration, since these passages provide most of the overt descriptions of Jews in the text. After Aaron's corpse is found, his nameless wife goes to the squire to beg for justice for his murder. Doerr has discussed the contrasting Old and New Testament images depicted in the scene.[66] On a stormy, frightening night Aaron's wild-haired wife bursts into the safe Christian haven of the squire's home to demand Old Testament revenge for Aaron's murder: "'An eye for an eye, a tooth for a tooth!' these were the only words that she blurted out now and then" ("'Aug um Auge, Zahn um Zahn!' dieß waren die einzigen Worte, die sie zuweilen hervorstieß" [31]). In direct opposition to this witch-like, rain-dripping Old Testament image emerging from the stormy night, the squire's pious wife leads a prayer to ask for protection from the elements. Significantly, she recites the beginning of the Gospel of St. John: "In the beginning was the Word and the Word was with God and God was the Word" ("Im Anfang war das Wort und das Wort war bei Gott und Gott war das Wort" [30]). In a certain sense, this verse forms the crux of the entire novella. Not only does it reiterate the power of the word underscored in the novella's prologue, it also demands to be read literally in its narrative context. The contrasting images of the witch-like vengeful Jew and the pious, virtuous Christian suggest God—the Christian God—is indeed the word here.

But the text is much more subtle than to simply juxtapose Jewish and Christian realms in this passage. The description of Aaron's wife bursting into the pious Christian scene is an intratextual citation of two earlier narrative sequences detailing Friedrich's genealogy and subsequent development into a "Jew," Margreth's mysterious trip to the herb garden and Simon's interference with Friedrich's plans to go to confession following the death of Brandis the forester:

> The door was flung open and the wife of the Jew Aaron rushed in, pale as death, her hair wild around her head, dripping with rain.

> On one such day—no longer a Sunday—she [Margreth] was seen rushing from the house in the evening, without bonnet or neckerchief, her hair hanging wildly around her head, throwing herself down in the garden next to an herb bed, and turning over the earth with her hands [...].

In the bedroom door stood Simon, almost naked, his thin body, his
uncombed, tangled hair and the paleness of his face in the moon-
light gave him a horribly transformed appearance.

Die Thüre ward aufgerissen und herein stürzte die Frau des Juden
Aaron, bleich wie der Tod, das Haar wild um den Kopf, von Regen
triefend. (30)

An einem solchen Tage—keinem Sonntage mehr—sah man sie
[Margreth] Abends aus dem Hause stürzen, ohne Haube und Hals-
tuch, das Haar wild um den Kopf hängend, sich im Garten neben
ein Krautbeet niederwerfen und die Erde mit den Händen aufwüh-
len [. . .]. (6)

[. . .] in der Kammerthür stand Simon, fast unbekleidet, seine dürre
Gestalt, sein ungekämmtes, wirres Haar und die vom Mondschein
verursachte Blässe des Gesichts gaben ihm ein schauerlich verän-
dertes Ansehen. (25)

These passages tacitly document on the lexical level the genealogical
links between Aaron's witch-like wife, "the old witch" Margreth (19),
and Simon (in name the Jewish sorcerer), suggesting they are all necro-
mantic Jews intruding into the pious Christian realm.
    The reaction of the Jewish community to Aaron's murder also docu-
ments the intrusion of Jews into the Christian realm, but this intrusion
is much more blatant than is the case with Margreth, Simon, and Friedrich, since Aaron's coreligionists are overtly identified as Jews. Here, as
in all other passages in the novella in which they are depicted, the Jews
are characterized by numerous anti-Semitic stereotypes.[67] Aaron's wife's
demand for Old Testament justice is carried out by the Jews in the community, who come together in large numbers that seem to threaten the
Christian populace, since the narrator remarks: "From time immemorial
so many Jews had not been seen together in L." ("Seit Menschengeden-
ken waren nicht so viel Juden beisammen in L. gesehen worden" [33]).
True to the anti-Semitic association of Jews with deal-making and
money, they go to the squire "to propose a deal" ("um [. . .] einen Handel anzutragen" [33]). (This image is repeated in the description of
Aaron, "who had fixed his eye on a deal" ("[der] einen Handel [. . .] im
Auge hatte" [31]), in the characterization of Simon as a "deal-seeking
fellow" ("Händel suchende[r] Kerl" [9]), and in the "deal" ("Handel"
[11]) Margreth agrees to when Simon adopts Friedrich).[68] The Jews then

purchase the beech tree marking the site of Aaron's death for a large
sum of money. In a secret ritual instantiating the anti-Semitic stereotype
of the Jew as sorcerer, they hack an enigmatic Hebrew sentence into the
tree that apparently condemns the murderer to the same fate he inflicted
on Aaron. (Droste heightens the sense of mystery surrounding the curse
by withholding the translation of the inscription until the final sentence
of the novella.) As Doerr has argued, the axe they use to hack the sentence into the tree not only recalls the murder instrument that split open
Brandis's skull, but also functions as the Jews' writing instrument.[69] To
expand this, Droste also uses the recurring axe motif to connect Simon,
the probable murderer of Brandis, to the Jews. Indeed, the narrative
strongly suggests Jews are responsible for all three, if not four, murders
in the text: Margreth, who may or may not be a Jew, may have had a
hand in Hermann's suspicious demise; Simon may have murdered Brandis with Friedrich's help; Aaron was killed either by his "coreligionist"
Ragged Moises (34) or by another apparent coreligionist, Friedrich; and
the mysterious curse the Jews hack into the beech tree apparently kills
Friedrich/Johannes. In short, the series of anti-Semitic stereotypes culti-
vated throughout the text culminates in the image of the Jew as murderer.

From here it is but one small step to the ultimate image at the root of
theological anti-Semitism: the Jew as the alleged murderer of Jesus. Precisely this image is at stake at the novella's conclusion, which instantiates
the fate of the racially defined Jew masquerading as a Christian in Christian society. Just as Friedrich lives a double life, he dies a double death.
Friedrich/Johannes apparently either is hanged or hangs himself in retribution for Aaron's death, a murder he may or may not have committed.
Yet at the same time he is identified as a Jew and symbolically crucified
for deicide.

Recall the narrative circumstances leading to the text's conclusion.
Friedrich has fled in the wake of Aaron's murder, taking his doppelgänger Johannes with him. There is some question as to whether he is
guilty of the crime, since the Jew Ragged Moises confessed to killing a
coreligionist named Aaron, but then hanged himself before the details
of the murder could be investigated. It is unclear how to interpret this
event, since, as a magistrate remarks: "le vrai n'est pas toujours vraisemblable" ("the truth does not always appear to be true" [34]). Certainly
the hanged "dog of a Jew" Ragged Moises ("Hund von einem Juden"
"Lumpenmoises" [34]) anticipates the image of the "ragged dog"
("Lumpenhund" [28]) Johannes / "ragged," ("zerlumpt" [16]) "dog-
hole" ("Hundeloch" [19]) destined Friedrich hanged at the novella's

conclusion, suggesting we read the redaction of the Boileau quote in light of the narrative's programmatic confusion of characters and religious identities. The resolution of the novella will reveal the improbable truth of the hanged man's racial identity as Jew.

Twenty-eight years after Aaron's murder a crooked man returns to Town B. on Christmas eve bearing "the marks of long suffering" ("den verzogenen Ausdruck langen Leidens" [36]) and the villagers, "nigh astonished that he still looked like other people" (36), identify this Christ figure as Johannes.[70] He has been a slave in "heathen" Turkey, and has come home seeking return into Christian society and a Catholic burial (39). The text is almost overdetermined in its attempt to establish the Christianness of this wretched character, but several oblique details suggest quite the opposite: he is unable to join in the first stanza of the prayer on Christmas eve celebrating the pure birth of Christ (35–36), a pure birth he does not share; he has a limping gait, an anti-Semitic attribute well established in nineteenth-century discourse;[71] he eluded capture when pursued for Aaron's murder by hiding behind the large cross in the churchyard until frightened away by lightning bolts flashing directly over the church tower (38), an image that concretizes the narrative subtext of the Jew avoiding detection by hiding behind a Christian façade until flushed out by supernatural intervention; and he has escaped slavery by being fished out of the Bosporus under circumstances he is warned not to divulge ([38]; in Droste's source material these circumstances center around a pogrom, a detail the author chose to omit from her narrative).[72] Moreover, the text documents the man's Jewishness on the lexical level. His statement: "They fished me out of the Bosporus" (38) links him to the novella's other fish figures, Simon the pike-faced "Jew" and the pike-like Friedrich. The Baron's reaction to this statement also situates the returned figure within the semantic register of "foreignness" ("Fremdheit") associated with the Mergel family and the Jews throughout the text: "The Baron looked at him in an alienated way ["befremdet": in a "foreign" way, strangely] and raised his finger in warning" ("Der Baron sah ihn befremdet an und hob den Finger warnend auf" [38]). Finally, the squire's deepest sympathy with the poor scoundrel [Schelm] (39) recalls Margreth's pronouncement "the Jews are all scoundrels [Schelme]" (8) and the transformation of the dead Hermann into a Schelm (scoundrel, flayed animal).

Nine months after his return into Christian society, this reborn Christian cripple is revealed for what he is, a Jew, a genealogy first documented in the demise of his family members. Margreth, originally respected as "very smart and economical" (5), dies the object of derision, "in complete mental apathy" (37), and in arrears with "debtors" ("Wucherer":

moneylenders, usurers [33]), a signifier identified as "Jewish" in the next paragraph of the text: vide the Jew Money-Lender Joel ["Wucherjoel," 33]). But her brother's ignominious end indicates the family's indebtedness to Jews is not merely monetary. Simon, who becomes a beggar and expires "in a foreign barn on the straw" ("in einem fremdem Schuppen auf dem Stroh" [37])—an image that inverts the pure birth of Jesus in the manger—dies as an Antichrist, thereby capping off the series of anti-Semitic associations linked to this Devil figure. However, his demonic character lives on in his heir (10).[73] One day Friedrich/Johannes does not return from his errands, and the squire visits the cripple's room, looks around but quickly leaves, since "he felt very oppressed in the stuffy, narrow little chamber" ("ihm ward ganz beengt in den dumpfen, engen Kämmerchen" [41])—an intertextual gloss on *Faust* and Gretchen's uncanny ability to sense the Devil in her stuffy little room. Two weeks later Friedrich/Johannes's body is discovered hanging in the Jews' beech tree emitting an odor described as "disgraceful" or "shameful" ("schändlich" [41]), a term suggestive of moral or religious transgression and perhaps also of the *foeter judaicus*, the "Jewish stench."[74] As Moritz has pointed out, the manner in which the corpse is found mirrors the discovery of the Jew Aaron's body: Aaron's corpse is found in a leaf-covered grave (31) and the squire orders the searchers to look for Johannes's body in the "Graben" in the leaf-covered woods (41); in both cases a dog finds the corpse; and in both cases a shoe identifies the dead man.[75] These parallels suggest that in death Friedrich/Johannes will be revealed to be a Jew, a hypothesis supported by the text's conclusion.

One other seemingly innocuous detail of Friedrich/Johannes's new life also points to his non-Christian provenance. The cripple makes his living carving wooden spoons, a craft that brings to mind the two other instances of woodcarving in the text: the Jews' inscription of the beech tree and young Friedrich's preoccupation with carving before Brandis's death. This latter event merits close attention: in effect, it reiterates the Jews' marking of wood as "Hebrew." The boy sits at the edge of the Breder Forest, apparently serving as a lookout for Simon and his timber thieves. He passes the time carving wood, committing a "wood sin" or "wood sacrilege" ("Holzfrevel" [17]) of his own: "[he] whittled a willow staff whose knotty end he was trying to give the shape of a formless animal ["eines ungeschlachten Thieres"]" ("[er] schnitzelte an einem Weidenstabe, dessen knotigem Ende er die Gestalt eines ungeschlachten Thieres zu geben versuchte" [18]). The "ungeschlachtes Thier" he attempts to carve is not merely a formless animal; on the lexical level the phrase documents the "Jewish" blood flowing through his Christian veins. Most—although not all—of the animal images occurring in the text are applied to Jews, and the adjective "ungeschlacht" is especially important in this context. In addition to its definition of "formless," "ungeschlacht" also means "not of the same family, ignobly born, thus evil in character and custom."[76] Moreover, "ungeschlacht" is etymologically related to "schlachten," "slaughtering," "butchering," suggesting a link to the novella's two "Schlächter," or butchers, Solomon and Aaron, who are both Jews (29, 31). These lexical associations take on even greater significance in light of the fact that Friedrich carves the "ungeschlachtes Thier" from "the knotty end" of the staff: the phallic symbolism is clear. In short, Friedrich attempts to mark himself a Jew by symbolically circumcising himself, a conclusion bolstered both by the threatening phallic gesture he had made with his "little knife" when taunted about his father (9) and by the rewriting of the scene later in the text. The last time he is seen before he is found hanging in the beech tree, Friedrich/Johannes again sits at the edge of the Breder Forest carving a spoon. This time he completes his symbolic circumcision: "but he cut it completely in two" ("er schnitt ihn aber ganz entzwei" [40]). Symbolically marked as a Jew, he enters into the forest whose "criss- and *cross*paths ("*Kreuz*- und Querwege") he studiously had avoided (40, emphasis mine), and there he meets his fate.

Just as Simon's death reenacts the birth of Jesus in a negative mode, the death of Friedrich/Johannes reenacts Jesus's death, also in a negative mode. Tellingly, this "Christian" figure is accused of masquerading as someone innocent and is symbolically crucified for his crime: his rotting, wormy corpse is found hanging in the Jews' beech tree. Doerr has identified the threefold symbolism in this image.[77] First, hangings are referred to as crucifixions in folklore. Even more significant is the fact that this locution was used in blood libel cases where Jews allegedly hanged or killed Christians, a detail I will return to shortly. Finally, the Holy Cross is said to have been fashioned from beechwood, and the inscribed beech tree perforce recalls the inscription on Jesus's cross. The putrid corpse is cut down and the noose removed, revealing a broad scar that the squire regards "with great attention" (42).[78] Not only does the scar on the corpse mirror the beech tree scarred by the Hebrew inscription, it refers metonymically to the one other scar hinted at in the text: the mark of circumcision Friedrich/Johannes symbolically inscribed on himself. The squire then exposes the dead man's transgression, saying:

> "It is not right that the innocent one should suffer for the guilty one; tell all the people: that man"—he pointed to the dead body— "was Friedrich Mergel."

> "Es ist nicht recht, daß der Unschuldige für den Schuldigen leide;
> sagt es nur allen Leuten: der da"—er deutete auf den Toten—"war
> Friedrich Mergel." (42)

One way to interpret the squire's religiously charged words is this:
"Who is the innocent one who suffered for the guilty? Not him: he's
not Christ ("er ist nicht Christ"); he's not Christian." Anathematized,
Mergel's corpse (if the corpse is in fact Mergel) is then unceremoniously
disposed of: "the corpse was quickly buried in the knacker's yard" ("die
Leiche ward auf dem Schindanger verscharrt" [42]), a locus semantically
encoded as "Jewish" by the fact that the only butchers mentioned in the
narrative, Salomon and Aaron (29, 31), are both Jews. (The semantic
coding of the "knacker's yard" or "Schindanger" as "Jewish" is corrob-
orated by Droste's source material: in Haxthausen's account Hermann
calls the Jew Pinnes "you cursed knacker's dog of a Jew" ("du ver-
flogte Schinnerteven von Jauden" ["Schinner" is a Low German form of
"Schinder" and "teve" means "dog"[79]], and the Jew's corpse is found par-
tially flayed).[80] Ashes to ashes, dust to dust, Mergel to Mergel. With this
astounding literalization of metaphor the crucified Mergel is identified
for what he really is: the "King of the Jews" is a *Schelm* in the original
sense of the word ("flayed animal, fallen animal").[81] As if to substantiate this conclusion, the text ends with the deciphering of the Hebrew
inscription carved in the beech tree, suggesting that we, too, decipher the
"Hebrew" (read Mergel) inscribed in Droste's *Jews' Beech Tree.*

Yet the inscription suggests that much more is at stake in this symbolic
crucifixion than the simple identification of a Jew. Remember that hangings were referred to as crucifixions in blood libel cases in which Jews
allegedly had killed Christians. This locution recalls its ultimate derivation,
the allegation that the Jews crucified Jesus. If the Jews are responsible for
Jesus's death, the ultimate punishment according to the Old Testament "an
eye for an eye" mentality underscored in the novella would be to crucify
the Jews in return. In light of the fact that Mergel's hanging in the beech
tree symbolically reenacts Jesus's crucifixion on the beechwood cross, this
is precisely what the Hebrew inscription implies: "If you approach this
spot, what you did to me will happen to you" ("Wenn du dich diesem Ort
nahest, so wird es dir ergehen, wie du mir gethan hast" [42]). Mergel does
not die merely in retribution for Aaron's murder, a crime he may not have
committed; as a Jew, he is symbolically crucified for deicide.

There is a final etymological twist to the beech imagery in the text.
Buche ("beech") is etymologically akin to the words "Buch" ("book")
and "Beuche" ("lye used to remove natural impurities from textiles"),[82]

a derivation that evokes the textile metaphors associated with Jews in the text. This is precisely what the Jews' beech tree accomplishes: the removal of the "natural impurity" (read Jew) that has stained Christian society. *The Jews' Beech Tree* as text shares the same goal. This is why Droste ends her novella with the erroneous statement: "This really happened according to all the major details in September of the year 1789" ("Dieß hat sich nach allen Hauptumständen wirklich so begeben im September des Jahrs 1789" [42]). By situating her text historically at the juncture of the French Revolution, the event that led to the Jews' emancipation in Westphalia, Droste warns her German compatriots of the dangers of allowing "Jewish" blood into Christian society. The Mergel family is Catholic by confession, but this is perforce a specious identification according to the blood definition of the narrative. The message this disquieting text promotes is clear: a Jew by any other name is still a Jew, and should be disposed of accordingly.

A final methodological consideration is in order here. Given the text's programmatic indeterminacy we cannot know for certain that Mergel is in fact a Jew according to a racial or blood definition, but the text offers ample and compelling evidence that repeatedly suggests he is. Throughout my analysis I have chosen the stronger reading that concludes Mergel actually is a Jew, but we also must consider the alternate reading. Even if Mergel is not Jewish, he surely has all the anti-Semitic attributes of a "Jew," and functions, like Arnim's Gypsies, as a semiotic Jew, or as what Lauckner has called a "surrogate Jew" in the text.[83] Whether Mergel is in fact Jewish is ultimately of little consequence to the narrative: the mere suggestion that he *may be* a Jew is what is really at stake here. Singularly worse than those people identified as Jews, singularly worse than the narrow-minded Christians, Mergel, true to his name, represents an aberrant mixture—a deviant "Jewish" element—that has entered into and should be removed from German culture.

To be sure, Droste did not valorize the corrupt Christian society she depicted in her novella, yet she also did not temper the text's systemic anti-Semitism. Instead she crafted a tale of indeterminacy that would resonate subliminally within the context of the debate about the "Jewish Question" for decades to come. Certainly the text admits many different interpretations and refuses to offer proof positive of a single one, but the prologue's challenge to the reader to measure blood and weigh words against the backdrop of prejudice validates the type of analysis I have laid out here. That the text *can* be interpreted in this manner is significant; indeed, Germany's unfortunate history lends urgency to this reading. The insidious discourse of anti-Semitism permeating the novella is so subtle and complex that it has eluded critical attention for over one hundred and fifty years. Problematic as this reception history may be, it accentuates one of the central themes of the text: the subconscious effects of the power of the word, how the word turns into "the secret soul-thief of prejudice" ("des Vorurtheils geheimen Seelendieb" [3]). Disturbingly, the novella first became a popular critical success when it was republished in Heyse and Kurz's *Treasure Trove of German Novellas* (*Deutscher Novellenschatz*) in 1876, at the brink of the era of modern anti-Semitism. The novella immediately attained canonical status and soon became required reading in school curricula.[84] *The Jews' Beech Tree* thus might be seen as a very small but significant factor in fueling the nationalist fervor that exploded in the Third Reich. This fact alone suggests that we must take its anti-Jewish rhetoric very seriously.

This chapter has offered a fundamentally new interpretation of the structure and function of latent anti-Semitism in an enduring classic of nineteenth-century German literature. Following Droste's lead, her exhortation to consider each "unforgotten" word and its roots, I have grounded my reading in lexical evidence and etymologies, and have argued that an extensive network of signifiers narrates a subtextual story about identifying and exposing the hidden "Jewishness" that has permeated the farthest reaches of German society, the rural setting of the isolated village B. We have seen similar themes and rhetorical strategies at work in other texts analyzed thus far: in Lessing's characterization of Christoph as being, very possibly, a crypto-Jew, a hidden Jew; in Schiller's universal historical analysis of the origins of "Jewishness" as a hereditary disease that marks the Jew as the permanently dangerous "other"; and in Arnim's semiotic construction of a hidden "Jewishness" that pervades Christian German society and is both antithetical and integral to its definition. Droste, more explicitly than Lessing, Schiller, or Arnim, programmatically focuses on the function of language in the discursive construction of "Jewishness." By design, *The Jews' Beech Tree* masterfully theorizes the power of the written word to subconsciously create and transmit prejudice.

≈

Natural Anti-Semitism

Adalbert Stifter's *Abdias*

The question of reading, of how to read "the Jew" and "the Jewish"—
so central to Droste-Hülshoff's *The Jews' Beech Tree*—is posed in
a different form in Adalbert Stifter's *Abdias*. The explict focus of this
contemporaneous novella is on interpretation: the text presents a hermeneutic theory of literary anti-Semitism. Ironically, as was the case
for Droste's unassuming narrative, this placid, poetically beautiful text,
steeped in metaphors of nature that mask its revolutionary aesthetic program, originally was not read for "the Jew" at all.

Stifter's *Abdias* was first published in the *Austrian Novella Almanac of
1843* to rave reviews, catapulting its young author to instant fame.[1] "A
lion's claw," trumpeted the *General Newspaper;* "a pearl," proclaimed the
Sunday Paper.[2] The cynosure of a volume highlighting recent advances in
Austrian novella writing, *Abdias,* the critics agreed, forged an exciting,
new, contemporary aesthetic: "unequivocally the most significant, the
best contribution to the volume"; a work of "rare originality"; "thoroughly original"; "darkly original"; "bold and original"; "pregnant";
"exquisite"; "enchanting"; "fresh and powerful"; "sensational"; Stifter
is "a child of our times."[3] Remarkable praise indeed for the singular story
of a pockmarked, swarthy, Job-like Wandering Jew who emigrates from
the timeless ruins of a Roman outpost in Africa to Stifter's present-day
Austria—a plotline that moves, along with its peripatetic protagonist,
from Romantic travelogue to contemporary cultural criticism. Abdias is
the paradigmatic embodiment of the "Jewish Question" that informed
Austro-German political discourse in the 1820s through 1840s: the
intense public debate about Jewish emancipation and assimilation. To
be sure, the novella's earliest reviewers did not recognize the political
import of the text, faulting the narrative's second half, set in Austria, as
distinctly weaker than its exotic African opening, and appreciating only

peripherally the significance of the Jewishness of its title figure. And by 1848, one year after the second version of the novella was published in a revised *Study Edition* (*Studienfassung*), Stifter was accused of "Zeitfremdheit," of writing a piece that was "alien to the times." In stark contrast to the socially engaged authors of Young Germany and the "Vormärz" period, Stifter, the critics charged, ignored contemporary issues. Lauded as a maverick poet not five years before, Stifter now was dismissed as an outmoded "nature poet" whose writing had lost its relevance.[4] Ironically, it is precisely in its nature metaphors that *Abdias* inscribes an incisive cultural critique. Unaware though they were of the ideological significance of nature to Stifter's writing, the novella's earliest reviewers were right to underscore the bold novelty, the fundamental modernity, and the darkness of the text's penetrating aesthetic. Stifter's *Abdias,* I will argue, is a profoundly political text that casts anti-Semitism as a natural phenomenon and constructs a discursive critique of the nature of "the Jew" in contemporary Austrian society and art.

At stake in the following analysis is a broad theoretical issue: how to read for and evaluate discourses of anti-Semitism in a literary text. *Abdias* itself poses this question as its prime narrative motivation. Yet the reception history of the text offers a striking example of the reluctance on the part of *Germanistik* as a discipline even to read the figure of the Jew in a major nineteenth-century narrative, let alone assess the text's programmatic anti-Semitism. Until recently, most criticism has glossed over the title character's Jewishness as largely incidental to the novella, either ignoring the issue completely or according it marginal attention.[5] The novella's earliest reviews are arguably representative of most Stifter scholarship in this regard. Diffuse and contradictory, the scattered comments in these documents indicate a liminal awareness of Abdias's ethnicity, but a lack of critical engagement with its significance to the text as a whole. The reviewers note in passing the persecution the children of Israel must endure in the novella, see Abdias as combining the distinctive character of the Mosaic people with the rigid tenacity of the desert population of Africa, identify Abdias as a modern Job, assert that Abdias has a "fiery flame in place of the usual soul," remark on the glaring contrasts that arise of necessity in his character, and identify the "rigid, peculiar character" of this "son of Israel" as detracting from the poetics of the novella.[6]

Much of the criticism that does recognize the centrality of Abdias's Jewishness to the text dates, disturbingly, from the Third Reich. Perhaps unsurprisingly, given the political context in which the reviews were written, there is little agreement in this scholarship on how to interpret the text's programmatically conflicting pro-Jewish and anti-Semitic gestures. In a chilling analysis written in 1935, Margarete Susman interprets the lack of clarity in the novella's depictions of Jews as reflective of a lack of moral clarity in the Jews themselves: Abdias comes from a Jewish community living at the edge of the world, itself scarcely human, a community that has forgotten its divine origins and focuses instead on amassing riches. Susman reads the trajectory of Abdias's life—the unnecessary killing of his devoted dog, the beloved daughter struck down by lightning, his derangement—not as destiny, but as divine judgment. Susman sees the rise of the Nazis in the same vein, exhorting her fellow Jews to read the text as a warning to a modern European Jewry that has lost its Jewish identity and strayed from its divine calling.[7] Writing in 1938, Urban Roedl launches a spirited attack against the Third Reich's appropriation of Stifter as "the true poet of *Blut und Boden*," arguing that Stifter the man clearly was pro-Jewish, and that Stifter the author intentionally chose a Jew to illustrate his theory of destiny. In Roedl's assessment, *Abdias* is the most profound depiction, the highest celebration of the Jewish spirit that can be found in German letters.[8] In his 1942 analysis of *Abdias* in light of Nazi ethnogeny or *Rassenkunde,* Wolfgang Heybey agrees that Stifter himself may not have been anti-Semitic, but maintains that the healthy racial instincts of the Aryan come to the fore in his writing: Abdias is a Jew "we couldn't depict more drastically today," a Jew motivated by greed, money, and sex, a Wandering Jew whose Jewishness manifests itself everywhere.[9] Writing in *The Menorah Journal* in 1948, John Urzidil lauds Stifter as the greatest pro-Jewish German author, a truly Enlightened spirit to whom Lessing pales in comparison. Urzidil maintains that Stifter portrays the very heart of the Jew, with its strengths and weaknesses, but does not simply wish to promote the fashionable agenda of "toleration" in vogue at the time: "His Abdias was hardly the type to be joyfully welcomed by advanced city Jews; on the contrary, they must have sensed rather an exposure of their assimilationism which Stifter had not intended."[10] *Ex negativo,* Urzidil identifies the crux of the text: Stifter's intentional "exposure of the Jews' assimilationism," which, as Urzidil correctly ascertains, "advanced Jews" would not "joyfully welcome."

More recently, Kurt Gerhard Fischer has taken the entire discipline of *Germanistik* to task for its failure to come to grips with—much less recognize—the centrality of the Jew to *Abdias*. In Fischer's assessment, both Stifter and his text clearly are philo-Semitic: Abdias is representative of the Jews in general, a Nathan figure of sorts, and the irreconcilable extremes in Abdias's character are a product of the circumstances into which he is born. Stifter, Fischer argues, takes anti-Semitic stereotypes as a given, and aims to suppress, if not overcome, them in his novella.[11] Similarly, Ruth Angress maintains that the novella is not anti-Semitic. In her reading, Abdias is portrayed without condescension, indeed, with a certain respect. Yet at the same time Abdias is depicted as the product of a blind, misguided, cursed race, a characterization, Angress concedes, that is on closer evaluation problematic.[12] Finally, in an incisive analysis of the text's rhetorical strategies, Joseph Metz considers the "formidable intersections of the Semitic and the semiotic in Stifter's narrative," and optimistically "hopes to discover in these signs a subversion of the anti-Semitic discourses they at first glance appear to uphold."[13] Metz's far-reaching investigation considers how the text's discourse of Jewishness intersects with its themes of epistemological anxiety and hermeneutic uncertainty and comes to embody the crisis of the concept of nation in Stifter's Austria. In line with a cadre of distinguished critics who correctly discuss the text's oscillation between reason and unreason,[14] the "irreducible ambivalence" of its self-referential metaphorics,[15] and its proffering of countless substitutes for meaning in place of "meaning,"[16] Metz ultimately reads the text as suspended between anti-Semitism and anti-anti-Semitism.[17]

But a text's refusal to construct meaning, its presentation of polyvalence and ambivalence in place of meaning, itself ironically constructs meaning on the metatextual level—i.e., in the broader context of nineteenth-century discourse in general—and this meaning demands closer consideration in a narrative replete with anti-Semitic stereotypes. *Abdias*'s shiftiness, its slipperiness, its moral ambivalence—all quintessentially stereotypical "Jewish" traits—are striking in a text that programmatically takes as one of its central concerns the discursive construction of "Jewishness." At the very least, the narrative conspicuously calls attention to its own deployment of anti-Semitic rhetoric.[18] More controversially, one might hypothesize that the text enacts its own "Jewishness" self-reflexively, and in so doing presents a unified aesthetic theory.

In what follows, I want to explore this hypothesis by analyzing the discursive construction of the Jew in *Abdias* in conjunction with the extensive metaphorical and thematic network of nature that structures the narrative. This approach is indicated by the novella's famously opaque metaphysical introduction, which offers three interpretative paradigms for understanding the cosmos, paradigms that are explicated in part by the life story of the Jew Abdias. On its most basic thematic level, the metaphysical introduction makes patently clear that *Abdias* is a text about interpreting the nature of "nature" and the nature of "the Jew," a project that clearly has ideological implications for Stifter. As Walter Benjamin has noted, Stifter treats "social relations" as "nature relations" and "history" as "nature" in his writing:[19] "historical reality and ideology are almost always presented in Stifter as simple descriptions of the laws of Nature and of human nature," Eric Downing observes in his reading of Benjamin.[20] Downing goes beyond Benjamin in demonstrating that Stifter intentionally maps politics and history onto nature in his writing, presenting subjective and ideological values as immanent natural laws.[21] In its purportedly objective descriptions of nature, I will argue, *Abdias* inscribes an inherently anti-Semitic, anti-assimilationist political agenda.

The very fact that its title figure is a Jew whose Jewishness is emphatically thematized marks *Abdias* sociohistorically as a document in the debate about the "Jewish Question." In the 1820s through 1840s Austria, like Germany, was engaged in a spirited and intense public discussion about the legal and social status of Jews. This dialogue was played out in large part in the print media.[22] With Joseph II's Edict of Toleration of 1782, Austria had been the first European country to grant Jews the right to become naturalized subjects, but the government did not pursue the issue of legal rights for its Jewish subjects further until forced to by the 1848 revolutions.[23] (This political stagnation, we recall, stood in marked contrast to other European countries: in France, Holland, Prussia, and many other German states, Jews made decisive advances toward full legal integration in the wake of the French Revolution and the Napoleonic era.) In Austria in the early 1840s—the setting of Stifter's *Abdias*—the legal status of Jews remained static, dating back to the 1782 Edict of Toleration. Jews were limited by law in their choice of place of residence and their choice of occupation, but these restrictive regulations were largely ignored in actuality. Vienna was legally closed to most Jews, but thousands lived there in flagrant violation of the law. Jews entered into professions technically illegal to them, enjoyed increased economic prosperity and social stature, and freely participated in intellectual and cultural life. These activities were openly tolerated by the authorities. So conspicuous were Jews' contributions to commerce and industry that their presence in the capital became an "unavoidable necessity."[24]

Yet there was no shortage of anti-Jewish sentiment either in the government or in the general population. Opponents of emancipation used Jews' professional achievements as an argument against granting them legal rights or citizenship, maintaining that the Jews would come to dominate and control fields like medicine and commerce. Katz cites

the case of Count Ferdinand Schirnding as an example of a liberal who
subscribed to such reasoning. Schirnding, well known for his *Austria in
the Year 1840* (*Österreich im Jahre 1840*), a cultural survey of the Austrian state in which he had first addressed the "Jewish Question," argued
in 1842 that Jewish industrialists controlled the factories while Christian
workers did the real labor for them, and that these "alien" Jewish industrialists, motivated purely by self-interest, should be granted protection
by the commonwealth, but not the rights of citizens. In 1845 Schirnding
intensified his anti-Jewish rhetoric, again opposing citizenship rights for
Jews because of their economic, social, cultural, and religious isolationism. Throughout his writings Schirnding regarded the Jews as a "state
within the state," alien, aloof, and exclusive. Schirnding's view was typical of foes of emancipation. As Katz argues, the perception of the Jews
as a foreign social entity fueled opposition to emancipation.[25] The liberal
moment in Schirnding's reasoning was his willingness to consider citizenship rights for Jews, provided they give up "Jewish" occupations like
commerce and trade, and "amalgamate with the blood of Christianity"
through intermarriage: "As long as it [the Jewish people] does not engage
in agriculture and handicraft and as long as it separates itself in the close
bond of internal marriage and the unification of blood, so long is the
emancipation of Judaism unthinkable."[26]

Schirnding's call to integrate Jews into Christian society by eradicating
their "Jewishness"—a common theme in the emancipation debate—
is itself anti-Semitic, in that it assumes that Jews are characterized by
inherently negative traits that must be eliminated as a prerequisite for
emancipation. This argument underscores an essential dimension of the
emancipation debate. The real issue for many Germans and Austrians
was not citizenship rights for Jews per se, but concern about the Jews'
"foreign" national character and its relationship to German and Austrian
national character, and, closely related to this perception of the Jews as
"alien," concern about the Jews' moral character. Improving the moral
character of the Jews as a nation was the real prerequisite for emancipation for Schirnding and many fellow thinkers.[27]

The discourse of "Jewishness" Stifter engages in *Abdias* resonates
in its rhetoric and argumentation with Schirnding's contemporaneous
writings on emancipation and assimilation. (This is not to argue for
intertextuality, but to contextualize *Abdias* sociohistorically as a cognate
document in the debate about the "Jewish Question.") Stifter's Abdias,
dark, horrifically plague-scarred, and African—the embodiment of common nineteenth-century anti-Semitic stereotypes that cast "the Jew" as
black, Negroid, African, and syphilitic[28]—settles into a remote corner of

Austria, circumventing the law to acquire his homestead (a clear parallel to real-life Jews openly living in Stifter's Austria in violation of the law). In Austria the Jew Abdias conspicuously maintains his "African spirit,"[29] building a house suited to desert conditions, wearing his turban and caftan, amassing money, and sticking to himself (in Schirnding's terms, Abdias remains "alien," "self-interested," and "exclusive"). But when his blind daughter Ditha is struck by lightning and begins to see, Abdias gradually begins to assimilate, turning from the "Jewish" professions of trade, deal-making, and usury to the "Christian" profession of farming (recall Schirnding's requirement that Jews must give up commerce and engage in agriculture before emancipation would be conceivable). When Ditha reaches sexual maturity, Abdias thinks about finding a husband for his blond, blue-eyed daughter. Abdias's preference would have been his fellow African Uram. But Uram, unable to withstand the Austrian climate, has died, and Abdias does not pursue the matter further. Presumably, prospective suitors would come from the predominantly Christian local population. But before any "unification with Christian blood" (Schirnding) can occur, the Aryanized Ditha is struck down by lightning. Read in its sociohistorical context (see also Schirnding), the storyline itself inscribes an anti-assimilationist political agenda.

But of course the novella is a good deal more complex than this in its treatment of the "Jewish Question" on both the narrative and discursive levels. Certainly the text's metaphysical introduction and its programmatically conflicting pro-Jewish and anti-Semitic gestures demand interpretation in light of the "Jewish Question." Moreover, Stifter's narrator explicitly calls attention to the rhetorical construction of "the Jew" from the start of the text:

> It is the Jew Abdias of whom I wish to tell.

> Es ist der Jude Abdias, von dem ich erzählen will. (239)

This one-sentence paragraph from the novella's metaphysical introduction highlights one of the text's central concerns: the act of narrating the Jew; more precisely, of constructing the image of "the Jew" through the language, content, and structure of the text itself. Despite the volition expressed in the above assertion ("of whom I *wish* to tell"), the narrator purports to have undertaken the project without an overt agenda and assigns the reader the task of following the account impartially, keeping any experiential images of Abdias he or she may have in mind—but holding the "bitter feeling" occasioned by contact with the real-life Jew in check—and then passing judgment on the nature of the Jew *as it is depicted in the narrative:*

> Whoever has perhaps heard of him, or perhaps even seen the ninety-year-old bent figure sitting in front of the little white house, do not regard him with bitter feelings—neither curses nor blessings, he reaped both abundantly in his life—rather, in reading these lines, once again hold his picture ["Bild": also, image] before the eyes. And he who has heard of this man should follow us, if it pleases him, to the end, *since we have simply tried to depict his essence,* and then he should pass judgment on the Jew Abdias, according to the promptings of his heart. (emphasis mine)

> Wer vielleicht von ihm gehört hat, oder wer etwa gar noch die neun-zigjährige gebückte Gestalt einst vor dem weißen Häuschen hat sitzen gesehen, sende ihm kein bitteres Gefühl nach—weder Fluch noch Segen, er hat beides in seinem Leben reichlich geerndtet—sondern er halte sich in diesen Zeilen noch einmal sein Bild vor die Augen. Und auch derjenige, der nie etwas von diesem Manne gehört hat, der folge uns, wenn es ihm gefällt, bis zu Ende, *da wir sein Wesen einfach aufzustellen versucht haben,* und dann urtheile er über den Juden Abdias, wie es ihm sein Herz nur immer eingibt. (239, emphasis mine)

In short, this is a narrative about evaluating the discursive construction of the Jew: about judging the image of the Jew, the essence of the Jew as it is depicted in the text. And this is a judgment of the heart, the narrator reports, with profound metaphysical implications. The life course of the Jew Abdias raises fundamental questions about "Providence, destiny, and the ultimate ground of all things" ("Vorsicht, Schicksal und letzten Grund aller Dinge" [239]).

The following analysis considers why "the ultimate ground of all things" is linked to the aesthetic image or "Bild" of a Jew in a narrative that is so obviously *not* presented in an objective manner.[30] The narrator's purported impartiality is strikingly at odds with the carefully crafted language, structure, and content of the text itself, which contains a pronounced surfeit of stock anti-Semitic themes and stereotypes. Indeed, this anti-Semitic register is so overdetermined in the opening paragraphs of the novella that it perforce draws attention to itself, pointedly emphasizing the prime significance of the title figure's Jewishness. "Hidden" on the surface of this bizarre narrative is a discourse of anti-Semitism.[31] *Abdias* consciously enacts the process of representing the Jew as a discursive construct, and this is why the Jews in this text are repeatedly represented as aesthetic objects, as *Bilder.* In drawing attention to the very constructedness of its subject matter, *Abdias* stages a self-reflexive aesthetic in which both nature and art take on a metaphysical "Jewish" ground.

And this is precisely the point of the novella's metaphysical prologue: to signal the reader to read the nature of nature and the nature of the Jew in the text, to signal that "Jewishness" is the narrative principle of the text. The point is not to determine which of the three paradigms the narrator introduces for interpreting the nature of nature—fate ("Fatum"), destiny ("Schicksal"), or the "bright flower chain" ("heitre Blumenkette") of cause and effect (237–38)—provides the best template for reading the life story of the Jew Abdias. The Job gloss that opens the narrative arguably stands as a warning to the reader *not* to attempt to read the text metaphysically. (As God demonstrates in the Book of Job, human beings cannot fathom the nature of the cosmos, and should not try to fathom the nature of the cosmos.) To attempt to do so here is to be tricked into thinking the text's recondite metaphysical introduction can be understood by reading the text itself, a hermeneutic trap the narrator explicitly cautions the reader to avoid:

> We do not wish to *brood* ["grübeln": literally, to dig deeply] further how it might be in these things, but simply tell of a man, in whom *some of this was presented,* and of whom it is uncertain whether his destiny was more curious, or his heart. In any case, one is inspired by life courses like his to ask: "why this now?" and one is *lured into a gloomy brooding* about Providence, destiny, and the ultimate ground of all things. (emphasis mine)

> Wir wollen nicht weiter *grübeln* wie es sei in diesen Dingen, sondern schlechthin von einem Mann erzählen, *an dem sich manches davon darstellte,* und von dem es ungewiß ist, ob sein Schicksal ein seltsameres Ding sei, oder sein Herz. Auf jeden Fall wird man durch Lebenswege wie der seine zur Frage angeregt: "warum nun dieses?" und man wird in ein *düsteres Grübeln hineingelockt* über Vorsicht, Schicksal und letzten Grund aller Dinge. (239, emphasis mine)

Importantly, Abdias's life story only *partly* represents the metaphysical prologue—it replaces and at the same time displaces—the prologue, luring the reader into a "düsteres Grübeln," a "gloomy digging around" of interpretation, an activity clearly troped as "Jewish" on the semiotic level of the text.[32] The following analysis interprets the disunity in the textual representation of the Jew Abdias as programmatic in nature. The text uses irony, disjuncture, and disbelief to call into question the production of meaning.[33] The narrative is structured by a series of metonymic gestures in which meaning is displaced—like the Wandering Jew Abdias—in a constant chain of deferral.[34] And this is why the Jew's fate is linked to "Providence, destiny, and the ultimate ground of all things" ("Vorsicht, Schicksal und letzten Grund aller Dinge"). Abdias's life course narrates a rupture in the production of meaning, the establishment of a metaphysical "Jewish" ground. In a text that enacts the problem of "Jewishness" self-reflexively, a text about "Vorsicht"—foresight, Providence, and caution—a text about "Schicksal" or fate, a text about the "ultimate ground of all things," the "letzten Grund aller Dinge"—about metaphysics, about the nature of things, about first and last principles— the Jew—perforce the emblem of the originary in the Judeo-Christian tradition—becomes starting point, process, and destiny of all things.

Before turning to a closer examination of the text's discursive construction of "Jewishness," a brief word about the two versions of the novella is in order. The *Journal Edition* of 1842 and the stylistically superior *Study Edition* of 1847 differ subtly but significantly in their rhetorical construction of "Jewishness," irrefutable evidence that Stifter intentionally foregrounded the issue in his text. While some of these textual alterations do not fit neatly into a pattern—Stifter eliminated a few anti-Semitic stereotypes, but introduced many more—there is a qualitative difference between the two versions. Compared to the earlier *Journal Edition,* the Jews of the *Study Edition* are largely affectless; their characterizations are more ambiguous; and the motivations for their behavior are more ambivalent. When Aron sends Abdias out into the world to earn money, for example, in the earlier *Journal Edition* the father's hands shake and he sobs, and Abdias rides away with a broken heart (J110). Abdias then endures fifteen years of money-seeking activities out of respect for his father and his father's might (J114), "and in so doing, contradicted his heart and his head" (J113). These emotional and motivational descriptions are eliminated completely in the *Study Edition.* Similarly, Abdias's feelings of remorse for causing his African neighbors' misfortune, his emotional reaction to Ditha's birth and his joyful reconciliation with his wife Deborah, his sadness on leaving Africa, his tender care of his daughter during the boat journey across the Mediterranean— all are described in much greater detail in the *Journal Edition* than in the *Study Edition*. These changes clearly are programmatic in nature. From the beginning, Stifter had intended to depict Abdias and his fellow Jews "with the iron toughness unique to his people" ("mit der eisernen Zähigkeit, die seinem Volke eigen ist" [J110])—a phrase introduced in the *Journal Edition* but excised in the revision. Emphasizing their "iron toughness" by eliminating descriptions of their emotions and motivations, Stifter in effect dehumanizes the Jews in the *Study Edition*. These textual variations raise an important methodological consideration: precisely what the status of "the" text *Abdias* is, when, in fact, there are two extant texts, both published by the author. It is not my intent here to offer a comprehensive philological comparison of the two versions. In working out my textual analysis, I did construct such a comparison, and found that the earlier *Journal Edition* bolstered—but did not change—my reading of the more polished *Study Edition*. The following discussion is based primarily on the *Study Edition,* the version most commonly read today, but I will refer to the *Journal Edition* on occasion. Unless otherwise noted, page citations are to version "B," the "book" or *Study Edition* of the critical edition (*HKG* I, 5); references to the *Journal Edition* (*HKG* I, 2) are marked by a "J."

The opening description of Abdias the Jew's provenance, replete with anti-Semitic rhetoric presented in what appears to be a straightforward factual summary, stands as a program for reading "Jewishness" throughout the text. The text deliberately foregrounds the issue of Abdias's "Jewishness" in the sheer quantity of anti-Semitic descriptors it employs. Yet at the same time this anti-Semitic rhetoric is embedded in a narrative-descriptive account that neutralizes this language, presenting anti-Semitism as completely natural. Deep in the deserts of the Atlas mountains, the narrator begins, is an old Roman city lost from history (239)—in the *Journal Edition*, "an old, mysterious Roman city," "an old Roman city full of secrets" ("eine alte, geheimnißvolle Römerstadt" [J107])—which for centuries has had no name and no inhabitants. The territory now lies uncharted in the European consciousness, and it inspires feelings of "uncanniness" ("Unheimlichkeit") and superstition in the local Berber population (239). To the outside world the only residents of this eerie, forlorn region are jackals, which, in actuality, share their living space with an invisible—and in the *Journal Edition* "enchanted" ("verzaubert" [J113])—Jewish community. The description of this jackal-Jewish community differs markedly in the two versions of the text. First, in the implication in the *Journal Edition* that the Jews and the jackals are not only cohabitants, but also co-species. Second, and more significantly, in their descriptions of how the Jews came to be living in this remote region of Africa. The passage in the *Journal Edition* reads:

> Only one species shared with the jackals. Children of that species ["Geschlecht": also, family, race] that for four thousand years had had to disperse, that had had to wander since its first father had wandered, and in this wandering stayed more the same in itself than all others who are firmly established on every point of this earth. Dismal, black, dirty Jews went like shadows through the ruins from time to time, went out and in, and lived within with the jackals, which they sometimes fed.

> Nur ein Geschlecht theilte mit dem Jackal. Kinder jenes Geschlechtes waren es, das seit viertausend Jahren theilen mußte, das, seit sein erster Vater wanderte, wandern mußte, und auf dieser Wanderung sich gleicher blieb, als alle andern, die da fest und seßhaft sind auf jedem Punkte dieser Erde. Düst're schwarze, schmutzige Juden gingen wie Schatten zuweilen in dem Trümmerwerke herum, gingen drinnen aus und ein, und wohnten drinnen mit dem Schakal, den sie manchmal fütterten. (J107)

Compare this with the version in the *Study Edition:*

> Yet in addition to the jackals there lived, unknown to the entire rest of the world, other inhabitants in the ruins. They were children of that race ["Geschlecht"] which was the most exclusionist in the world, petrified yet pointing to a single point [of origin], but scattered in all countries known to man, and a few drops of them were spattered, as it were, by the ocean into this remote region. Dismal, black, dirty Jews went like shadows through the ruins from time to time, went out and in, and lived within with the jackals, which they sometimes fed.

> Dennoch lebten außer den Schakalen, der ganzen übrigen Welt unbekannt, auch noch andere Bewohner in den Ruinen. Es waren Kinder jenes Geschlechtes, welches das ausschließendste der Welt, starr blos auf einen einzigsten Punkt derselben hinweisend, doch in alle Länder der Menschen zerstreut ist, und von dem großen Meere gleichsam auch einige Tropfen in diese Abgelegenheit hinein verspritzt hatte. Düstre, schwarze, schmutzige Juden gingen wie Schatten in den Trümmern herum, gingen drinnen aus und

ein, und wohnten drinnen mit dem Schakal, den sie manchmal
fütterten. (240)

In the *Journal Edition* the Jews have been wandering for four thousand years—have *had* to wander for four thousand years—yet have not
changed at all in their peregrinations. The nature of the Jew remains
constant over time; all Jews are "der ewige Jude," the Eternal Jew, the
Wandering Jew, the same everywhere. In the *Study Edition* the trope of
the Wandering Jew has been replaced, importantly, by a metaphor of
nature. The Jews, "the most exclusionist" of all peoples, are petrified
("starr") to their point of origin and hence the same everywhere and
the same over time, yet they are dispersed over all regions of the world.
The Jews have been "spattered" ("*ver*spritzt"), as it were, by the ocean
(in a perverse natural act, as the prefix *ver* in "verspritzt" indicates) into
this remote region of northern Africa, suggesting that the Jews' very
presence in Africa—and, by extension, in Austria—although naturally
occasioned, is unnatural.[35] The ensuing description of these unnatural
Jews is introduced in a phonologically remarkable sentence—employed
in both versions of the text—that is structured by the repetition of
sounds and poetic cadences: "Düstre, schwarze, schmutzige Juden gingen
wie Schatten in den Trümmern herum, gingen drinnen aus und ein, und
wohnten drinnen mit dem Schakal, den sie manchmal fütterten." ("Dismal, black, dirty Jews went like shadows through the ruins from time
to time, went out and in, and lived within with the jackals, which they
sometimes fed.") Built up around the vowels *u, ü,* and *a,* in combina-
tion with the consonants *m* and *n* in particular, the sentence uses a series
of words beginning with *sch* to fuse the "*sch*warze, *sch*mutzige Juden"
("the black, dirty Jews") qua "*Sch*atten" ("shadows") with "*Sch*akale"
("jackals"), creating a phonological emblem that will resonate throughout the text. Moreover, the mellifluous poetic language of the sentence
is jarringly at odds with its anti-Semitic content. The Jews are dismal,
black, dirty, shadowy figures who live with "Raubthiere" (literally: "robbing animals," i.e., scavengers [242])—like "Raubthiere" and as fodder
for "Raubthiere"[36]—in the rubble of a "dead" Roman city (242), "an old
Roman city lost from history" (239), in an atemporal setting that calls the
Jews' status as the originary people into question. The Jews make their
living dealing in gold, silver, and pestilence-infested textiles, occasionally
infecting themselves with the plague and perishing. (In the *Journal Edition* the Jews deal only in plague-ridden rags and woolen goods [J107];
the stereotypical association of Jews with money—gold and silver—is a
notable addition to the *Study Edition*.) And now and then a Jew is killed

by a Berber, causing the entire tribe to howl (240), hyena-like (257), and to exact Old Testament justice by murdering a Berber in turn. "This is how this people was," the narrator summarizes matter-of-factly in what is clearly not a matter-of-fact report, "and Abdias came from them" ("So war dies Volk, und von ihm stammte Abdias her" [240]).

The narrative descriptions of Abdias and his family likewise read like a veritable dictionary of stock anti-Semitic themes and stereotypes. Abdias's father Aron is the richest man in the community, and this "dark secret" ("düstere Geheimniß") hangs silently over the dead city (242). The family living quarters, marked by a triumphal arch (240), are decrepit, the outer chambers bare, but inside are hidden rooms in which jewels are piled high. (In the *Journal Edition* the secret inner chambers are piled high not merely with jewels, but with "everything that pleases the senses" [J108].) Aron's wife Esther spends her days sumptuously surrounded by and ensconced in the richest finery, finery as good as (if not better than [J108]) the Sultana's (242). Apart from his wife, the narrator reports, Aron's most valuable "jewel" (242) is his son, the epitome of Oriental beauty (242). Yet so intent is Aron on bodily pleasures that the licentious Jew "forgets" to educate Abdias (243).[37] His mother Esther, the "Jewish mother," babies him, dressing him up, frequently in girl's clothing, covering him with jewels, and putting makeup on him (243). Hardly a poor, hardworking family struggling to eke out a meager existence in the harsh desert climate, as some critics would have it,[38] Abdias, Aron, and Esther are not what they would seem to be. In the words of the narrator in the *Journal Edition:* "Even if it also seemed as if the black flag of poverty and need waved over the pile of rubble, inside it was very different" ("ob es auch schien, als wehe die schwarze Fahne der Armuth und Noth über dem Trümmerhaufen, so war es doch innen anders" [J108]).

The anti-Semitic descriptors intensify in the narrative characterization of the adult Abdias. Among his fellow Jews Abdias is an object of Jewish self-hatred.[39] He is despised for his excessive wealth, secretiveness, avarice, and cunning. He engages in money-hoarding, deal-making, and usury, seeking riches by any means possible: "He sought wealth in all his travels and defiantly amassed it in glowing greed" ("Den Reichthum suchte er auf allen Wegen, er trotzte ihn bald in glühendem Geize zusammen" [250]), the narrator reports, introducing one of the token traits that will come to define Abdias, his "glowing greed" or "Geiz." Abdias repeatedly unearths hidden coins from stones and sand, an action that suggests the Jew's connection to money is natural (285–86). Importantly, Abdias is, by nature, a figure of speculation, an economic figure, for both

Muslims and Jews alike, and the text underscores his essential economic nature using nature metaphors. Melek spares Abdias's life so that he can "swell up and bear fruit"—money—again ("Jetzt gebt ihn frei, daß er wieder anschwelle und Früchte trage" [256]). Likewise, the greedy Jews of the *Journal Edition*—not content with receiving simple reparations, but intent on becoming richer than ever—invest in Abdias: "Even if he brought losses to us, he's the man who can think up the ways and means of lifting us up again and making us richer than ever. Let's keep him" ("Wenn er uns auch zu Schaden gebracht, so ist er wieder der Mann, der Mittel und Wege ersinnen kann, uns neuerdings emporzubringen, und reicher zu machen, denn je. Lasset uns ihn aufbewahren" [J120]).[40] With his "glowing greed" and fundamental economic nature—traits that mirror and magnify defining features of his fellow money-centered Jews—Abdias is troped as the quintessential stereotypical Jew from the start of the text.

An extensive array of stock anti-Semitic stereotypes complements Abdias's essential economic characterization. Like his father before him, Abdias indulges in sensual pleasures (250). He is reviled as a traitor for revealing the community's very existence. He is a man of unusual beauty who "inherits" the plague in Odessa: "he inherited the evil pestilence of pox" ("[er hatte] die böse Seuche der Pocken geerbt" [249]) and his face becomes pockmarked with scar lines that are "unspeakably ugly" ("die Narbenlinien seines Angesichts, die so unsäglich häßlich waren" [251]). Yet these inherited, "unspeakably ugly" natural scar lines in fact speak volumes in the text. In the *Journal Edition* his fellow Jews interpret his pockmarks as divine judgment, as "God's writing" ("Gottes Schrift" [J116]). And indeed, the "crossed scars" ("gekreutzte Narben" [327]) that disfigure his blackened face mark the Wandering Jew Abdias with both the sign of Cain and the very sign of anti-Semitism, the sign of the cross, branding the Jew as the crucifier of Jesus.[41] Abdias is malicious to Christians and Muslims (245). He is driven by vengeance and dreams of murdering his nemesis Melek, conquering the world, and subjugating its inhabitants (253)—an act of vengeance, the narrator of the *Journal Edition* reports, that would have been carried out with his harassed, jackal-like African nature (J128). By nature and in intent, the Jew represents a threat to Christianity and to Islam, to the very world order.

The Jew's perverse nature is further underscored in the descriptions of Abdias's familial relations. His improbably blond, blue-eyed daughter is born under highly questionable circumstances. Before his illness his wife Deborah remains infertile, and after he recovers from the plague Abdias apparently has no physical contact with his wife, who loathes him and turns away "forever" from his hideous visage (249). But "the ugly head of a neighbor, who perhaps could least restrain his lust ["Gierde": also, greed]" (258) that appears in the doorway when Ditha is born clearly draws Abdias's paternity into question and suggests that the Jews as a whole are a licentious, ugly people. (In the *Journal Edition* the neighbor's ugly head merely appears in the doorway [J121]; the ensuing description of the Jews' "Gierde" was added to the *Study Edition*.) With his questionable fatherhood, Abdias also stands as a figure of illegitimacy, a figure of transgression who challenges the traditional paternal order. Already present in the fatherly neglect and maternal spoiling that characterize his childhood, this divergence from the paternal order comes to be a defining feature of the adult Jew Abdias: "But he no longer acted in the manner of the patriarchs" ("Dieser aber that nicht mehr nach Art der Väter" [J113]), the narrator of the *Journal Edition* reports.

The text clearly indicates that the transgressive, perverse nature of the Jew is not restricted to social relations, but also inheres in the Jew's very body, indeed, is the essence of the Jew's very nature. Abdias literally turns from white to black to white; this fluctuation in the Jew's skin color is notable not only because of the obvious stereotypical association of "white" with "good" and "black" with "bad," but also because the image of the "dark" Jew always is related to the image of the "diseased" Jew.[42] Abdias goes mad, evoking the stereotypical characterization of Jews as mentally diseased. Abdias is a "fiery" Jew with an unnatural glow about his person (257, 328–29, 335), and hence is associated with the Devil. He takes on many different guises. He is troped as the Wandering Jew who migrates from northern Africa to Austria, implicitly threatening the populace. His relationship with his beautiful daughter, whose naked limbs he bathes in a marble basin while the water glows "like diamonds" in her blond hair (310), has marked—albeit muted—incestuous overtones. Tellingly, in the *Journal Edition* Abdias even conflates Ditha with his wife Deborah in his dreams (J153). Similarly underscoring his perverse nature, Abdias is cast as the effeminate Jew on both the thematic and structural levels of the text: as a child his mother frequently dresses him up as a girl (243); he and Ditha, his "identical image" ("Ebenbild"), who ironically looks nothing like him (307), are repeatedly identified as flowers (242, 327, 341); in the *Journal Edition* he cares for Ditha "like a mother and a maid" ("wie eine Mutter und Magd" [J134]); and the section headings of Abdias's "life course" are named after the three women in his life.[43]

Finally, capping off this list of anti-Semitic attributes, Abdias the Jew is characterized as a murderer. Abdias is twice accused of killing his wife, a charge the narrator tacitly, but repeatedly, endorses. The narrator situates the first accusation in a position of structural prominence as the final sentence of the second section: "Abdias was said to be the one who had killed her" ("Abdias sei es eigentlich gewesen, der sie um das Leben gebracht habe" [272]).[44] The narrator uses the indicative mood, rather than the subjunctive, in reporting the second accusation: "Mirtha said nothing, since she hated the man Abdias because he had killed his wife" ("Mirtha redete nichts, da sie den Mann Abdias haßte, weil er sein Weib umgebracht hatte" [289]).[45] The narrator draws a clear parallel between the death of Abdias's beloved dog Asu, whom Abdias intentionally but mistakenly shoots and then leaves to bleed to death, and the death of his wife, whom Abdias forgets to care for properly after she gives birth, likewise leaving her to bleed to death "like a helpless animal" (267). Indeed, following the tragic death of his dog, Abdias returns home wearing the bloodstained clothes of a murderer: "his clothes all stained with the blood of the murdered animal" ("alle Kleider mit dem Blut des ermordeten Thieres besudelt" [318]). The narrator draws a second clear parallel between Abdias raising his blind daughter after her mother's death and his raising the young dog Asu, "whose mother was murdered and whom he had taken in and raised when the puppy was still blind" ("Er hatte ihn einstens, weil man seine Mutter erschlagen hatte, und er noch blind war, aufgelesen und erzogen" [315]), a statement that again raises the specter of murder associatively. Finally, the narrator reports that Abdias's long shadow fell over the corpse of his dead wife (270), likewise indirectly indicating his culpability. Similarly, the text suggests that Abdias is responsible for his daughter's death. Ditha, "a venerable enigma who had emerged from his being" ("ein ehrwürdiges Räthsel, aus seinem Wesen hervorgegangen" [306]), inherits her propensity for attracting lightning strikes from her father: from childhood onward Abdias repeatedly is seen with an electric glow about his person (257, 328–29, 335). And when Abdias crosses the Mediterranean en route to Austria with his daughter, he fears they will be harmed by storms. But these storms do not—yet—materialize: "since his time had not come, or rather, Abdias carried his misfortune with himself, without realizing it" ("denn seine Zeit war nicht gekommen, oder vielmehr, Abdias trug sein Unglück mit sich, ohne es zu ahnen" [J134–35]), the narrator of the *Journal Edition* reports, drawing a clear connection to the storm that will later kill Ditha, a "misfortune" that Abdias "carries with himself" from Africa. The intimation that the Jew, whose face is scarred by the sign of the cross, is responsible for his daughter's death is all the more damning in that Ditha—whose body appears to be marked by "an expression of sweet suffering" ("ein Ausdruck süßen Leidens" [336])—clearly is a Christ figure.

Yet this impressive concatenation of stock anti-Semitic themes and stereotypes in Abdias's characterization is countered by a sustained narrative tenor that implicitly suggests that the Jew Abdias is a good man. Named after the Old Testament prophet Obadiah, Abdias—whose Germanized appellation stands in paradigmatic opposition to *ab deus*—is a man guided by angels: sad, dark angels and glowing angels (253, 296); a man who is good to animals, slaves, and neighbors (249); who honors his parents, respects his wife, loves his dog, and cares for his blind daughter to the best of his abilities; who is successful in his business dealings; who garners the respect of others when he is abroad (and even is savvy enough to understand that this respect is occasioned by his money); a Job figure who endures a series of misfortunes that culminates in the death of his beloved daughter Ditha; and dies an effete old man sitting in front of his white house with a white—i.e., good—face, dreaming futilely of revenge.

However, the narrative construction of the Jew Abdias is not as ambivalent as this summary might indicate. The disjunction in the Jew's characterization surely functions as a metacritique on the nature of "Jewishness," but the text programmatically reinscribes its anti-Semitism at the same time as it critiques it. As a case in point, the text makes some attempt to establish Abdias's stereotypical "Jewish" behavior as completely understandable within its narrative context, but these pro-Jewish gestures are immediately effaced by the text's pronounced anti-Semitic rhetoric.[46] When he realizes Ditha is blind, for example, Abdias decides to amass great sums of money to secure his daughter's welfare after his death. He resolves to economize by dismissing most of his servants and giving up good clothing and good food for himself, and, with the best of intentions, turns his full energy to accumulating money for his daughter. Reverting to his African (read "Jewish") ways, however, Abdias engages in excessive avarice and usury. Strikingly, the narrator's explanation of this "Jewish" behavior recalls and ironically reinforces the extensive network of anti-Semitic descriptors introduced in the opening section of the text, the characterization of the Jews as black, shadowy, dark figures who live like "robbing animals" ("Raubthiere," scavengers), who create feelings of unease in the local population, and who are at best subhuman beings:

> As a result of this decision Abdias now became greedy. [. . .] Just as he had done during his fifteen-year apprenticeship, the gray-haired

Abdias again began to learn how to acquire money and goods, he began to hunt and run, and to gather profit and interest, he began to practice usury, namely with time, and this all the more so, with the fear of a robbing animal, as it were, since he was haunted by the thought of his age and his approaching death. He never allowed himself to rest—the business that he knew, and that had brought him riches in Africa, he took up again, namely trade, he practiced it now, as he had practiced it in Africa—and when on many a night the weather stormed and raged so that the dog crept into his kennel and the polecat into his den, and no people were on the streets, the bent, black shadow of the Jew went across the fields. [. . .] Now that he frequently went among people, they came to know him, and he became an object of hatred and loathing.

In Folge dieses Entschlusses wurde nun Abdias geizig. [. . .] [W]ie einst in seiner fünfzehnjährigen Lehrzeit fing er jetzt bei grauen Haaren an zu lernen, wie man wieder Geld und Gut erringen könne, er fing an zu jagen und zu rennen, und Gewinn und Zinsen zu sammeln, er fing an zu wuchern, namentlich mit der Zeit, und dies alles um so mehr, gleichsam mit der Angst eines Raubthieres, da ihn der Gedanke an sein Alter und seinen nahen Tod verfolgte. Er ließ sich daher keine Ruhe—das Geschäft, welches er kannte, und welches ihm in Afrika Reichthümer eingetragen hatte, nahm er wieder vor, nemlich den Handel, er trieb ihn so, wie er ihn in Afrika getrieben hatte—und wenn es in mancher Nacht stürmte und tosete, daß der Hund in seine Hütte kroch und der Iltis in seinen Bau, und kein Mensch auf der Straße, ging der gebeugte schwarze Schatten des Juden über die Felder. [. . .] [D]a er jetzt viel unter die Menschen kam, lernte man ihn kennen, und er ist ein Gegenstand des Hasses und des Abscheues geworden. (313–14)

Rather than providing an explanation for why Abdias's behavior ought to be understood as something other than "Jewish"—i.e., the caring father merely trying to provide for his blind daughter—the passage establishes through its extensive network of anti-Semitic descriptors that the Jew by nature *is* "Jewish": incessantly greedy, money-driven, usurious, crooked, shadowy, black, subhuman, a fear-ridden "Raubthier," or "robbing animal," compared here not to jackals and hyenas, but to dogs and polecats, the latter carnivorous mammals of the weasel family associated in folklore with superstition and death ("the polecat is the animal of souls and death").[47] Wilder than the wild animals that take shelter in stormy weather, the Jew—or more precisely, "the bent, black shadow of the Jew"—makes his way over fields when no human would venture forth ("no people were on the streets"). As the comparison to the polecat—"the animal of souls and death"—suggests, the Jew is not just a shadow here, but a shade, eerily spooking around like the invisible Jews in his hometown in Africa, who live "like shadows" (240), "with the jackal" (240), inspiring feelings of "uncanniness" ("Unheimlichkeit") in the local population (239). As the purportedly impartial narrator explains in the opening paragraphs of the novella, the nature of the Jew stays constant over time and the world over: "This is how this people was, and Abdias came from them" ("So war dies Volk, und von ihm stammte Abdias her" [240]). No wonder, then, the text implies, that Christians abhor Jews: once his neighbors get to know Abdias, the narrator reports, they hate and despise him. In short, the text does not construct a self-reflexive discourse on the nature of anti-Semitism;[48] it constructs a self-reflexive discourse in which anti-Semitism is eminently natural.

Nowhere is this natural anti-Semitism more acute than in the narrative description of Ditha's death, a death cast as both natural and supernatural. Ditha's demise is all the more significant in that she clearly is the text's icon of Christianizing assimilationism and—as the bolt of lightning that strikes her down suggests—its inherent impossibility. The Aryanized Ditha, the "identical image" ("Ebenbild") of Abdias (307), who ironically looks nothing like Abdias, is of the same natural essence as Abdias: "a venerable enigma who had emerged from his being" ("ein ehrwürdiges Räthsel, aus seinem Wesen hervorgegangen" [306]). And in this her genealogy parallels the genealogy of Christianity from Judaism. Indeed, as Metz has argued, Ditha's seemingly "immaculate" conception, her journey over the desert on an ass, her figuring as the bride called home by the heavenly groom, and her sacrificial death all inscribe her in a "relentlessly Christianizing tropology."[49] Noting that her name is a diminutive form of the biblical Judith, the editors of the critical edition likewise interpret Ditha in the same Christianizing vein: "Judith is considered to be the representative of the true people of God, and as such is a predecessor of Mary, whose color [blue] and whose flower [the lily] are also ascribed to Ditha here."[50] But to read Ditha solely in this Christianizing mode is to overlook an essential element of her cultural genealogy. The biblical Judith is—first and foremost—not a Christ figure or a predecessor of the Virgin Mary, but a savior of the Jews. The Jews had been besieged by the Assyrian general Holofernes and were almost at the point of unconditional surrender. In a daringly subversive act, Judith used her stunning beauty to seduce Holofernes and then famously beheaded him in his sleep, thereby saving her fellow Jews and throwing the Assyrian troops into disarray.[51] That Assyria and Austria are like cases, that Judith's exquisitely beautiful, blond-haired, blue-eyed namesake incorporates a similar subversive threat to Christian society, is clearly what is at stake in the narrative description of Ditha's (super)natural death.

The narrative chain of events leading to Ditha's demise begins with the death of the dog Asu, the beloved creature Abdias had taken in as a blind puppy and raised—like Ditha—because his mother had been murdered. Returning home one day, Abdias stops to rest in a forest and then resumes his travel, but the dog, foaming at the mouth, repeatedly races ahead of Abdias and then turns back in the direction from which they had just come. The "smart Jew" Abdias misreads Asu's bizarre behavior and shoots him, believing the dog is rabid, when, in fact, the dog has been trying to alert Abdias to the money belt he had unwittingly left in the woods. In effect, Abdias kills Asu because of the dog's "Jewish" behavior, which parallels his own: the excessive and incessant focus on money. In the *Journal Edition* the narrator explicitly foregrounds Abdias's "Jewish" nature here. So distraught is Abdias over his own actions that he almost kills himself in the heat of his "African" (read "Jewish") blood: "if it hadn't been for Ditha, he would have without doubt bashed his brains in in the heat of his African blood" ("wäre Ditha nicht gewesen, ohne Zweifel hätte er sich in der Hitze seines afrikanischen Blutes das Gehirn zerschmettert" [J143]). Following Asu's death, Abdias falls ill for some time, and then recovers. At this juncture, the first "wonderful event" ("wundervolle Begebenheit" [318])—in the *Journal Edition* the first "natural wonder" ("Naturwunder" [J143])—of the narrative occurs: "an event that will remain wonderful until we have fathomed those great widespread forces of nature" ("eine Begebenheit, die so lange wundervoll bleiben wird, bis man nicht jene großen verbreiteten Kräfte der Natur wird ergründet haben" [318]). In other words, this is a natural event that is to be read metaphysically: in the terms laid out in the text's opaque metaphysical introduction, as a gloss on the nature of nature and the nature of the Jew. One night Abdias sits in his room calculating how to recoup the financial losses he had sustained during his long illness (319)—a scene that scripts the healthy Jew as a Jew focusing on money—when a storm comes over his house. (In the *Journal Edition* the storm explicitly erupts "over the house of the Jew" [J143].) Suddenly, "a crashing blow" ("ein schmetternder Schlag") shakes the house, sending a bolt of lighting into Ditha's room, miraculously bringing sight to her blind eyes (319). (As the traditional natural signifiers of divinity—thunder and lightning—suggest, Ditha's miraculously cured blindness is to be read in a theological vein. The notion that the Jews are a "blind" people, unable to see the truth of Jesus, dates to Paul; by the Middle Ages Church leaders argued that the only way to cure the Jews of their blindness was through the sudden flash of divine inspiration.)[52]

As a result of this "wonderful event"—this "natural wonder"—the Jew becomes human. Ditha, previously characterized as soulless (308–9), motionless, and dumb, becomes more beautiful and begins to see, to live, to have a heart, to develop into a thinking, speaking human being (327). And, in a parallel development described in the next sentences of the text, Abdias—likewise a "blind" figure who misreads his wife's postpartum distress, his dog's "mad" behavior, and his daughter's blindness, improbably failing to recognize for four years that she cannot see until the thought shoots through his head like a glimmering bolt of lightning ("[ein Gedanke], der sich wie ein Blitz, wie eine leuchtende Lufterscheinung durch sein Haupt jagte" [311]),—also becomes human. Abdias, repeatedly characterized as a shadowy, subhuman "robbing animal," gives up his relentless pursuit of money (326)—the defining feature of his "Jewish" nature—and spends all his time with his daughter. Consequently, his neighbors—who had previously interpreted Ditha's blindness as divine retribution for Abdias's limitless avarice or "Geiz" (314)—no longer know what to make of the Jew:

> As Abdias had suddenly begun to be avaricious several years before, one no longer knew, is he still, or not. He always walked with the girl. All who hated the Jew looked with visible pleasure upon the innocent face of his daughter.

> Wie Abdias vor mehreren Jahren angefangen hatte, plötzlich geizig zu werden, so wußte man nicht mehr, ist er es noch, oder nicht. Er ging immer neben dem Mädchen. Alle, die den Juden haßten, sahen mit sichtbarlichem Wohlgefallen in das unschuldige Angesicht seiner Tochter. (327)

In effect, the lightning bolt that brings sight to Ditha's eyes precipitates a hermeneutic crisis. Christian society no longer knows how to read the Jew, to judge the Jew's true essence, to judge whether the Jew is still "Jewish": "is he still, or not" ("ist er es noch, oder nicht"). Abdias and Ditha become inseparable: the dark, ugly, effeminate Jew and his beautiful, innocent, blond-haired, blue-eyed daughter begin to merge into one, to become acceptable to Christian society, to themselves become—almost—Christian.

Precisely this Christianizing impulse—this move toward assimilating the Jew into Christian society by removing the Jew's "Jewishness"—forms the crux of the text. (And the crux of the nineteenth-century debate about the "Jewish Question"; recall the case of Count Schirnding discussed above.) Yet at the same time, the text inscribes the impossibility of any "natural" assimilation, not because Christian society refuses to welcome the Jew, but because the Jew remains—by nature and by choice—"African" and "foreign." In Austria Abdias wears his turban and caftan and builds a house suited to desert conditions, cultivating his "African spirit" and his isolationism: "he had brought his African spirit and the nature of aloneness to Europe" ("er hatte den afrikanischen Geist und die Natur der Einsamkeit nach Europa gebracht" [334]). Rather than raising his daughter to be a functional member of Austrian society, Abdias speaks Arabic, not German, with Ditha, and infects her with his vulture-like "African" ways: "he threw his Beduin thoughts like vultures of the Atlas Mountains, as it were, at her heart" ("er warf seine Beduinengedanken gleichsam wie Geier des Atlasses an ihr Herz" [335]). Remarkably, Abdias's own "desert nature" ("Wüstennatur" [J152]) even seems to permeate Austrian nature itself: "over the valley there lay a desolate African sun, as it were" ("auf dem Tale lag gleichsam eine öde afrikanische Sonne" [334]). (Elsewhere the narrator clearly marks this "African" nature as "Jewish," reporting that "the desert sun" shines "like a big, round diamond" [247].)[53] Tellingly, the *Journal Edition* uses nature metaphors to cast Abdias—and not the Austrians—as xenophobic, again suggesting that it is the Jews, not the Austrians, who by nature resist assimilation. Abdias regards Austria and its inhabitants to be "unnatural" ("unnatürlich" [J150]). In his estimation the Austrians are not people, but "trained beings" ("abgerichtete Wesen"), and he vows that his daughter will not become one of them (J150). Emphasizing the Jew's own sense of foreignness on Austrian soil, the narrator reports Abdias's bitter disappointment with his life in Europe: "he was a foreign tree in this land and his daughter a foreign apple on this tree" ("er war ein fremder Baum in diesem Lande und seine Tochter ein fremder Apfel auf diesem Baume" [J150]). According to the text's extensive register of nature metaphors, Abdias and Ditha are—by nature and by choice—incompatible with Austrian nature.

Moreover, as the lightning bolt that strikes Ditha down suggests, nature itself—or, more precisely, the higher principle that orders nature—opposes the Jews' assimilation. (In the programmatic preface to

Many-Colored Stones [*Bunte Steine*], Stifter will later argue that spectac-
ular natural phenomena like lightning bolts are not in and of themselves
grand events that should be accorded great significance: "because they
are only effects of much higher laws. They appear in single instances and
are the result of one-sided originary causes ["Ursachen"]" ("weil sie nur
Wirkungen viel höherer Geseze sind. Sie kommen auf einzelnen Stellen
vor, und sind die Ergebnisse einseitiger Ursachen" [*HKG* 2, 2: 10]). In
the case of *Abdias,* the higher principle ordering nature, the one-sided
originary force guiding nature, is, unapologetically, God.[54] When Ditha
reaches sexual maturity, Abdias despairs in finding a husband for her.
In the *Journal Edition* he even looks to divine intervention for help in
marrying off his angel of a daughter, frequently believing in his arrogance that it must be so that an angel would come to her and announce a
groom, as had happened with the patriarchs Isaac and Jacob (J151–52).
To which the narrator laconically rejoins: "All that remains for us is to
relate how this groom came" (J154), indicating that the lightning bolt
that kills Ditha is divinely ordained, that Abdias in fact gets precisely
what he had hoped for.

But the lightning strike that kills Ditha does much more than simply punish Abdias's hubris; it also eliminates the subversive threat Ditha
poses to Christian society. In the words of the narrator, the sexually
mature Ditha is, by nature, a stunningly beautiful—and specifically Jewish—woman: her body is characterized by "a slenderness completely
unique to their climate and their tribe" ("[eine Schlankheit], die ihrem
Klima und Stamme aber ganz besonders eigen ist" [J154]); in the revised
Study Edition this remark is truncated to a simple reference to "Ditha's
tribe" ("Ditha's Stamme" [336]). Yet at the same time, her sexually tense
adolescent body also seems to bear "an expression of sweet suffering"
("ein Ausdruck süßen Leidens" [336]), marking the Jewess as a Christ
figure. And it is precisely this dual marking as both Christian and Jew
that constitutes Ditha's subversive potential. The sixteen-year-old Ditha,
who eschews the traditional black clothing of her fellow Jews (334),
is the epitome of ideal Austrian beauty: her blond hair and blue eyes
implicitly make Jew and Christian indistinguishable, clearly posing a
natural threat to the local Austrian populace. The same storm that brings
sight to Ditha's eyes with a lightning bolt—removing the distinguishing
feature that differentiates her from her Austrian neighbors—destroys the
neighbors' harvest (322). As if to underscore the fundamentally destructive nature of this seemingly positive natural event—the Jew cured of
blindness becoming "Christian"—the storm ends with a shimmering
rainbow stretched over "the entire dark ground":

> The region was very still, the sun had just sunk in the deep evening,
> in the east, the direction the entire storm moved, a broad, shimmer-
> ing rainbow stretched over the entire dark ground.

> Die Gegend war sehr stille, die Sonne ging eben im tiefen Abend
> unter, und spannte im Morgen, wohin eben das ganze Gewitter
> hinauszog, einen weiten schimmernden Regenbogen über dem gan-
> zen dunklen Grund desselben. (322)

In contrast, the storm that lovingly "kisses" Ditha to death with a lightning bolt that emerges from the parted curtain-like clouds of heaven
(340) when she is on the cusp of sexual maturity pours "abundant blessings on all beings" and ends, as did the storm that brought her sight,
with a rainbow, a rainbow stretched this time not over "dark ground,"
but over brightness:

> The storm, which had kissed the child's life from her head with its
> soft flame, poured abundant blessings on all beings on the same
> day, and ended, like the one that had given her sight, with a beauti-
> ful rainbow in the wide morning [eastern] sky.

> Das Gewitter, welches dem Kind mit seiner weichen Flamme das
> Leben von dem Haupte geküßt hatte, schüttete an dem Tage noch
> auf alle Wesen reichlichen Segen herab, und hatte, wie jenes, das ihr
> das Augenlicht gegeben, mit einem schönen Regenbogen im weiten
> Morgen geschlossen. (341)[55]

The rainbow, of course, is the sign of the postdiluvian covenant, in which
God promises "Noah, his offspring, and every living creature with him"
that they will not be flooded out again and commands them to go forth
and multiply (Genesis 9). Reading the biblical gloss, presented here in
the form of a natural sign, together with the other nature metaphors
in the passage reveals a subtextual—and perhaps subliminal—anti-
assimilationist message couched in completely natural terms: the
sexually mature Jewess Ditha, visually indistinguishable from the Austrians, would give birth to Jewish children visually indistinguishable from
Austrians were she to go forth and multiply, and this is why her death
brings "abundant blessings" to the local population.

To be sure, the text itself warns against attaching fixed meaning to
nature: we are dealing with a text in which natural laws apparently can
be inverted, where nature enacts "the incomprehensible" with impunity

(237). But we also are dealing with a text in which nature glosses over the disaster of a boy's drowning with a silver mirror, lovingly curling itself around his hair and then hiding this disastrous history beneath its placid surface (237). And we are dealing with a text that demands to be read on the metaphysical level, suggesting we read its nature metaphors programmatically. *Abdias* narrates a subtextual story about the naturalization of Jews in Austria, about what happens when an illegal Jewish homestead becomes as natural as the stones that surround it (303). Ditha and Abdias, who arrive in Europe with the "foreign, weathered color" ("fremde verwitterte Farbe") of wild animals (300), become "natural people" ("Naturmenschen") spending all their time in nature (333), until nature metes out their fate in the form of a lightning bolt, a "foreign weathering" or natural decomposition (a "fremde Witterung" or "*Ver*witterung"). In the semantic register of nature running throughout the narrative, the text suggests that the naturalized Jews Abdias and Ditha—like their African coreligionists who trade themselves to death by dealing in plague-infested textiles—are responsible for their own fate. Ditha, who wanders repeatedly on the "seams" ("Säume") of fields and hills (332, 334, 336, 337), draws attention to the textual status of nature, and ends up speaking herself to death in her strange natural language.[56] Similarly, when Abdias turns from the quintessentially "Jewish" professions of deal-making and usury to the (for Jews) forbidden professions of land acquisition and farming, he reaps a natural crop: Ditha's death comes at "harvesttime" ("die Zeit der Ernte" [336]).[57] Nature in this narrative is neither innocent nor impartial; in this narrative the text of anti-Semitism is written in nature as natural.

In a stunning inversion of natural law—a stunning extension of natural law, perhaps—the naturalized Jew becomes the metaphysical ground of a prosperous Austrian nature. Following her death, the "lily" Ditha is planted in the ground (341), and nature—flowers and grass—literally sprout "from her limbs" ("aus Ditha's Gliedern sproßten Blumen und Gras" [341]). (The nature that sprouts from Ditha's body clearly is to be read metaphysically. The flower imagery recalls the most enduring image of the novella's metaphysical prologue, the "bright flower chain" ("heitre Blumenkette") that perhaps structures the cosmos, and the narrator's ensuing proleptic comment about "flower people" is explicitly cast in metaphysical terms: "whether the human being himself is a flower in that chain? who can fathom that? [who can ground that?]" ("ob er [der Mensch] selber eine Blume in jener Kette ist? Wer kann das ergründen?" [238]). Abdias likewise returns to nature, comes too to ground

Austrian nature. The Jew goes mad, then emerges from insanity, and sits in front of his house and dreams of returning to his original "nature," to Africa, to vengeance, and to murder: "All of a sudden he awakened again and wanted to travel to Africa to stab a knife into Melek's heart; but he no longer was able to" (341). (In the *Journal Edition* the narrator overtly draws attention to Abdias's "African" nature here, reporting, "the people regarded him as an African robbing animal [*Raubthier*]" [J157].) Although the old man no longer can make the trip back to Africa, the Eternal Jew has not lost his vitality. Abdias sits in front of his house for more than thirty years after Ditha's death—"How long afterward, no one knows" (342)—saying nothing, but looking silently at the sun (341). Eventually he loses his black color (342), blends in with, and becomes part of, the Austrian landscape, part of Austrian collective memory, part of Austrian history: "Many people saw him sitting on the bench in front of his house" (342), the narrator reports. And in death the Wandering Jew ends his "life course" and becomes rooted in Austrian soil, becomes part of Austrian nature, still looking silently at the sun:

> One day he no longer sat there, the sun shone on the empty place, and on his fresh grave, from which tips of grass already *peered out*.
>
> How old he was, no one knew. Some said, well over one hundred years.
>
> Since then the desolate valley has been fertile, the white house still stands, indeed since then it has been made more beautiful and has been expanded, and all is the property of the sons of Abdias's trade partner.
>
> Thus ended the life and the career [*Laufbahn*, also "trajectory"] of the Jew Abdias. (emphasis mine)

> Eines Tages saß er nicht mehr dort, die Sonne schien auf den leeren Platz, und auf seinen frischen Grabhügel, aus dem bereits Spitzen von Gräsern *hervor sahen*.[58]
>
> Wie alt er geworden war, wußte man nicht. Manche sagten, es seien weit über hundert Jahre gewesen.
>
> Das öde Thal ist seitdem ein fruchtbares, das weiße Haus steht noch, ja es ist nach der Zeit noch verschönert und vergrößert worden, und das Ganze ist das Eigenthum der Söhne des Handelsfreundes des Abdias.
>
> So endete das Leben und die Laufbahn des Juden Abdias. (342, emphasis mine)

Abdias, the transgressive figure who breaks Jewish communal law and Austrian state law, who effortlessly crosses the physical boundaries of desert and sea, and the metaphysical boundaries of time and death, looks forth from the grave, grounding a prosperous Austrian nature: his desolate valley becomes fertile; his house, larger and more beautiful. And all this comes to benefit the sons of the trade partner who had arranged Abdias's illegal homestead, his entrance into Austrian economy and culture. In life and in death, Abdias remains an economic figure, a figure of speculation. The Austrian society that welcomes the Jew—invests in the Jew—profits from the Jew: the Jew becomes the metaphysical condition of possibility of a prosperous Austrian culture.

At the same time, the text inscribes a complementary, contrary conclusion: the Austrian society that welcomes the Jew, that does business with a Jew whose family deals primarily in clothing and tattered rags (241)—the plague-infested fabrics of Jewish trade (240)—itself becomes Judaized: the Jew becomes part of Austrian nature. (The notion that modern civilization is "Judaized" has a long history in anti-Semitic polemics. In his contemporaneous essay "On the Jewish Question" ("Zur Judenfrage," 1843) Karl Marx famously argues precisely this point, maintaining that bourgeois society, with its focus on capitalism, has become completely Judaized, and that the social emancipation of the Jews implies the emancipation of society from Judaism.)[59] Like Abdias himself—who breaks down the border between black and white and arrives in Europe severely plague-scarred but apparently disease-free (299)—this Judaization of Austrian culture is, according to the logic of Stifter's text, not all good, not all bad, but it is, irradicably, "Jewish."

And it is precisely this "Jewish" essence, we recall, that the reader has been assigned to evaluate after following the narrator's depiction of the Jew to the text's conclusion. The reader is to judge the essence of the Jew "according to the promptings of his heart" (239), the narrator states, seemingly rendering every judgment of the Jew subjective, every assessment of the text's discursive construction of "Jewishness" defensible. Yet the attentive reader who *has* followed the purportedly impartial narrator to the text's end will see that the novella clearly articulates a political agenda in its descriptions of the nature of nature and the nature of the Jew, an agenda that resonates in light of one of the core issues in the debate about the "Jewish Question": the notion that improving the Jews' national character and moral character is a prerequisite for emancipation. The narrator's programmatic assertion that the nature of the Jew remains constant over time, the same everywhere, belies the notion that such improvement of the Jew's character is possible. Indeed, the text's opening description of the Jews living like "robbing animals" in the rubble of a dead Roman city lost from history arguably stands as a cautionary message from one Roman empire to another (Holy) Roman empire. On the metatextual level, *Abdias* narrates the story of the introduction of "the Jew"—that unstable disrupter of meaning—into Austrian society: into its economy, its nature, and its art.

This chapter has argued that *Abdias* presents a hermeneutic theory of literary anti-Semitism couched in metaphors of nature. This is a text *about* interpreting discursive constructions of "Jewishness," a project that has political, aesthetic, economic, and metaphysical implications for Stifter. Stifter casts the figuration of anti-Semitism as integral not only to the sense of the nation (here Austria), but also to nature itself. Anti-Semitism becomes not merely part of culture, as it was for Arnim and Droste, but an essential component of the very world. As was the case for Arnim and Droste, the novella's representation of "Jewishness" informs its own mode of narration. Many of the values and features these texts discursively assign to "Jewishness" function, programmatically, as their own organizing structure, their own narrative principle: slipperiness, craftiness, hidden motives, duplicity, moral ambivalence, inscrutability. These texts systematically embody, even embrace, their own "Jewishness" self-reflexively. In some ways, these texts reverse the original paradox of Lessing's works, where the overt philo-Semitism was subtly countered by unexpected anti-Jewish tensions and rhetorical gestures. Here, the texts' more exposed anti-Semitism is paired with an implicit valorizing of many "Jewish" qualities at the level of narration itself. How to understand and interpret the nature of, and reasons for, this paradox is precisely Stifter's theoretical innovation.

~

CHAPTER SIX

Framing the Jew

Franz Grillparzer's *The Jewess of Toledo*

Franz Grillparzer's grand "historical tragedy" *The Jewess of Toledo* (*Die Jüdin von Toledo*, 1851/1872) takes as its premise a lie: the fabrication that Alfonso VIII's humiliating defeat at the Battle of Alarcos in 1195 was divine retribution for his amorous involvement with a Jewish woman, an allegation with no historical basis. No evidence indicates unequivocally that such an affair ever took place, let alone led to Alfonso's defeat, yet this anti-Semitic myth has served as a theme for a long tradition of literary compositions that inspired Grillparzer's "historical" tragedy. Grillparzer certainly was aware his subject matter was grounded in an anti-Semitic legend, and the scapegoating of the Jew is central to his play. At the same time, the text very obviously pits philo-Semitism against anti-Semitism repeatedly and programmatically, thereby foregrounding one of its central themes: the representation of the Jew. Like Stifter's *Abdias*, *The Jewess of Toledo* revolves around the question of interpretation, reprising many of the rhetorical strategies analyzed in previous chapters, and, like *Abdias*, the hermeneutic challenge this text poses is overtly political, as suggested by the play's very plotline. In this "historical tragedy" a Jewish woman seduces a king and causes the downfall of his realm: this is a play about the consequences of the state's love affair with "the Jew." Thematically, structurally, and discursively, *The Jewess of Toledo* effects a trenchant critique of the dangers of philo-Semitism.

Historically, the disciplines of *Germanistik* and German Studies have largely ignored "the Jew" in this text.[1] Most scholars have glossed over the play's conflicting representations of Jews completely or dispensed with the topic in very short order, arguing that while the text exhibits a smattering of anti-Semitic prejudice at odds with its pro-Jewish stance, the play is about erotics, power, politics, and the state, and it is largely irrelevant that three of the main characters—not to mention the title figure—are Jews. Taking their cue from an early entry in Grillparzer's diary that identifies sensuality ("die Wollust") as a prime motivation for the king's actions, these readings focus on what happens when Alfonso, a man with little sexual experience, is confronted for the first time with "woman herself, nothing but her sex" (III, 859: 481).[2] Yet the very same diary entry begins by suggesting the king's attraction to the Jewess is not merely sexual in nature: "The Jewess of Toledo. Tragedy. The story of Alfonso the Good of Castile and of Rahel, who ensnares him for so long, *not without suspicion of sorcery,* that she is finally murdered by the king's grandees with the support of the queen" (*HKA* 358, emphasis in the original, underlined three times in Grillparzer's handwritten text).[3] Judging from Grillparzer's own notes, *The Jewess of Toledo* is indeed a play about a king incapacitated by sexual infatuation, but it is of prime importance that Alfonso is infatuated with a Jewish woman suspected of sorcery.

The few critics who have analyzed the play's Jewish figures in any detail have noted the contradictory depictions of Jews evident throughout the text, yet for the most part have failed to offer an adequate explanation for this blatant incongruity. According to nearly all of these readings, the play presents ambivalent statements about the Jews, rather than a unified aesthetic theory. Three lines of analysis—all concentrating primarily on the thematic level—have been proposed.

The first examines Grillparzer's documented statements about Jews and the Jewish emancipation debate in great detail, and then concludes *The Jewess of Toledo* has nothing to do with the "Jewish Question." Regrettably, none of these analyses submits the play to close textual analysis. In *Grillparzer's Attitude Toward the Jews,* for example, Dorothy Lasker-Schlitt explains the conflicting statements about Jews recorded in the playwright's journal and letters by arguing that Grillparzer was a patriotic Austrian whose "racial heritage" was steeped in anti-Semitism and hence was subconsciously conditioned to hate Jews, but was himself tolerant of the Jews and hence a great humanist. Lasker-Schlitt does not include a comprehensive analysis of *The Jewess of Toledo* in her study, claiming that Grillparzer did not write the play to express his views on the Jews, but as a treatise on the state.[4] Harold Lenz (*Grillparzer's Political Ideas and "The Jewess of Toledo"*) and Charlene Lea (*Emancipation, Assimilation and Stereotype: The Image of the Jew in German and Austrian Drama 1800–1850*) likewise assert that the play is about politics and the state, but not the "Jewish Question." Sigurd Scheichl supports these conclusions by citing the play's reception history: since most scholars bracket the text's depictions of Jews from their analyses and still find ample material to interpret, Scheichl maintains, the "Jewish Question" cannot be of central importance to the play.[5] Scheichl's argument raises an important methodological consideration. Many insightful interpretations have not addressed the play's Jewish characters, and many critics who have taken the Jewish characters into consideration have not come to grips with their conflicting representations. But to conclude from this that the "Jewish Question" is of no import to the drama amounts to circular reasoning. Texts by their very nature are multidimensional, and an essential layer of meaning emerges when the play's portrayal of Jews is analyzed in a thoroughgoing manner.

The second line of scholarship asserts that the text wavers irreconcilably between a liberal Josephinist tolerance toward Jews and an ingrained anti-Semitism.[6] In an astute observation representative of this strand of reasoning, Ruth Angress recognizes that the text's pro-Jewish gestures affirm negative anti-Semitic stereotypes, but does not pursue the implications of this remarkable observation.[7] She then concludes that the play is oddly ambivalent in that it both reinforces and retracts these stock characterizations, without considering why this might be the case.

Finally, Dagmar Lorenz stands alone among the critics in providing a plausible explanation for the text's contradictory depictions of Jews. Situating the play against the backdrop of the 1848 revolutions and within the context of the social criticism and concern for oppressed peoples that runs throughout Grillparzer's oeuvre, Lorenz suggests that Grillparzer, while capitalizing on Jewish stereotypes (the Shylock figure, the Jewish seductress, and the Enlightened Nathan figure of reason),[8] counteracts these stock motifs with true-to-life characters whose actions derive from a completely understandable survival instinct. Moreover, Lorenz maintains that the unscrupulous Christian characters are the true villains in the text, and *The Jewess of Toledo* promotes a relatively positive picture of the Jews as "the villains who were not villains."[9]

None of these readings accounts for the textual complexity that informs Grillparzer's drama, and I propose a different methodological approach: one that moves beyond the thematic level of the text to examine its rhetorical structure. At the same time, I suggest a reevaluation of the standard historical contextualization of the play, challenging those scholars who readily discuss Grillparzer's attitudes toward Jews, Jewish emancipation, and Austrian politics, but then inexplicably disregard, downplay, or dismiss the significance of the "Jewish Question" to an understanding of the text.[10]

This chapter argues that *The Jewess of Toledo* is about the formation and concomitant politicization of "the Jew" as a discursive construct. More specifically, to borrow a metaphor from the play, the text *frames* the Jew, in both senses of the word. On the one hand, the text gives shape to the Jew, forms the Jew, sets the Jew in a frame. But at the same time, the text also concocts a false charge or accusation against the Jew, devises a scheme or plot with regard to the Jew, makes the Jew the victim of a frame-up.[11] It is hardly coincidental that the bulk of the text was penned in the years surrounding the 1848 revolutions, formative years in the debate about the Jews' legal emancipation in Germany and Austria. *The Jewess of Toledo* constitutes Grillparzer's contribution to and metacritique of the emerging discourse of anti-Semitism in the Austro-German context.

The following analysis focuses on the construction of the Jew as a discursive figure in *The Jewess of Toledo*. Grillparzer frames the Jew on two levels: on the thematic level, in his manipulation of the historical subject matter; and on the rhetorical and structural levels of the text. The first two sections situate the play historically and thematically within the context of the debate about Jewish emancipation around 1848, and show how Grillparzer draws on a contemporaneous political event, the Lola Montez affair, to cast the "Jewish Question" as a discursive issue. The third and fourth sections demonstrate how the framing mechanism operates both in the play as a whole and in the infatuated king's eloquent defense of the Jews. The analysis concludes with an evaluation of Grillparzer's complex treatment of anti-Semitism.

The Jewess of Toledo is based on a historical fiction.[12] All historical accounts of Alfonso VIII's alleged affair with a Jewish woman can be traced to one source: the *General Chronicle of the Kings of Spain* (*Cronica general de los reyes de España*), written by Alfonso X in 1284, which recounts Alfonso VIII's love for a Jewess named Fermosa ("the beautiful"). During their seven-year relationship the infatuated king is said to have completely forgotten his realm, his reign, and his wife, and lived in seclusion with Fermosa until his grandees, enraged by the situation, murdered the Jewess. While there may be some truth to the account, the conclusion that Alfonso's military defeats were divine retribution for his relationship with the Jewess clearly is fabricated. From the beginning the affair was linked erroneously to a failed crusade Alfonso purportedly undertook with Richard the Lion-Hearted in 1189–1192; in fact, Alfonso did not participate in the Third Crusade. The affair likewise later was blamed for Alfonso's defeat at the Battle of Alarcos in 1195. Yet other early chronicles by Roderich of Toledo and Lucas of Tuy make no mention of the affair, a circumstance that draws both its historical authenticity and historical significance into question. In his 1783 biography of Alfonso, the Marquis of Mondexar provides evidence of the king's state activities during the reputed seven-year affair and concludes: "the relationship with the Jewess is a notorious fable" (*HKA* 320).

Grillparzer conducted extensive research into the historical and literary traditions detailing Alfonso's reputed relationship with the Jewess, and surely knew his subject matter was grounded in an anti-Semitic myth. Grillparzer was familiar with Mondexar's study refuting the account. Moreover, Cazotte's popular novella *Rachel, or the Beautiful Jewess* (*Rachel, ou la belle juive*), which provided Grillparzer's introduction to the theme and which he read repeatedly while he worked on the play, also questions the historical veracity of the story (*HKA* 316–17). That Grillparzer recognized the significance of the Jewish component of the legend is clear from his notes on two sources. Excerpting from Mariana's history of Spain, which charges the king with both criminal and religious transgressions for his affair with the Jewess,[13] Grillparzer writes that Alfonso's defeat at the Battle of Alarcos was said to be God's punishment for the king's "unnatural" relationship with the Jewess of Toledo (*HKA* 369). Of even greater import is Grillparzer's evaluation of Lope de Vega's *The Peace of the Kings, and the Jewess of Toledo* (*Las pazes de los reyes, y la Judía de Toledo*), the other major literary source for his own *Jewess of Toledo*: "Remarkably, Lope de Vega pretty much sides with the Jewess. She is treated nobly throughout, and he even takes away the stain of her Judaism [. . .] by having her want to convert to Christianity before her violent death. Another proof of his lack of prejudice" (*HKA* 372). Grillparzer's rhetoric celebrating de Vega's "lack of prejudice" anticipates his own agenda in *The Jewess of Toledo*. Grillparzer chose not to remove the "stain" of her religion from his title figure, yet at the same time whitewashed the text with a philo-Semitic veneer.[14]

The Jewess of Toledo frames the Jew historically and thematically. The play's title indicates the importance of the Jewish dimension of its subject matter; its historical setting and its designation as "historical tragedy" underscore its historicity.[15] Certainly the historical significance of the subject matter for Grillparzer's nineteenth-century Austrian audience does not lie in an analysis of a relatively minor twelfth-century Castilian king: the play deals with an aspect of Alfonso VIII's reign that has no verifiable historical basis. Poetic license notwithstanding, Grillparzer's choice of source material indicates it is not just that the king allegedly had an affair that is of interest here, but that the affair was with a Jewish woman. Similar accounts of Dutch and Danish kings' indiscretions with Christian women were available to the playwright, but Grillparzer opted instead for the Spanish version of the romance. In the Spanish courtly context a king philandering with a Christian woman likely would have raised few eyebrows, but an affair with a Jewess would have been scandalous.[16] Grillparzer, perhaps capitalizing anachronistically on the Habsburg dynasty's rule in both Spain and Austria, dramatizes the anti-Semitic legend of the Castilian king's ill-fated fling with a Jewess as a thinly veiled contribution to the Jewish emancipation debate in nineteenth-century Austria.

The emancipation debate in Austria, we recall, differed somewhat from its German counterpart.[17] With Joseph II's Edict of Toleration of 1782 Austria had been the first European country to grant Jews limited legal rights, but in the nineteenth century lagged considerably behind France, Holland, Prussia, and the other German states in moving toward full civic and legal equality for its Jewish population. Only with the revolution of 1848–1849 was the conservative Austrian government forced to loosen its restrictions on Jews: among other constitutional articles the revolutionaries wrested from the imperial government was a provision granting equal rights to all citizens, regardless of their religious affiliation. The government retreated from this legal position once the uprisings were quelled, but in practice the revolution resulted in many civic advances for Jews. These advances were not welcomed by some conservative segments of the population, who regarded the revolution, which had had a proportionately large number of Jewish participants, as a "Jewish" plot to force the emancipation issue.[18] In anti-Semitic circles the 1848 revolutions throughout Europe were considered "Jewish" machinations, a view that persists even today. In the years following the revolution full emancipation for Jews became an issue passionately debated on a large scale in newspapers and pamphlets; the anti-Jewish propaganda produced in Austria during this time surpassed that of other European countries both in quantity and virulence.[19]

Grillparzer, astute social critic that he was, participated in this highly charged debate sotto voce, taking detailed notes for *The Jewess of Toledo* in the 1820s and 1830s and finishing the bulk of the manuscript in the years surrounding the 1848 revolutions, but keeping the manuscript tightly under wraps until after his death.[20] Grillparzer had been an ardent supporter of the Vienna uprising in its early stages, but had backed away from this liberal position because he feared that the revolutionaries were going too far, that the proposed reforms would threaten the integrity of the Austrian state. Grillparzer's decision to withdraw his support from the revolution may have had little to do with the emancipation issue, which was only one of many proposed reforms, but the very fact that he worked intensively on *The Jewess of Toledo* at a time when the "Jewish Question" was being widely and forcefully debated indicates his strong interest in the matter.

Grillparzer's reluctance to release the play—or even to discuss its existence—may have been due in part to a shift in the discourse surrounding the emancipation issue. The debate about the "Jewish Question," which had been central to the print media in the 1830s and 1840s, was virtually nonexistent during the 1850s and 1860s. During this time anti-Jewish propaganda with a definite political objective was published almost exclusively by the extreme right,[21] from which Grillparzer surely would have distanced himself. Read in this context, *The Jewess of Toledo* functions as a critique of the crass anti-Semitic rhetoric put forth by opponents of emancipation. But at the same time the play also challenges the pro-Jewish rhetoric of the debate with a subtle anti-Jewish bias.

Grillparzer's attitude toward the Jews and Jewish emancipation has been a topic of some contention in the scholarship. Critics intent on defending Grillparzer against charges of anti-Semitism have been quick to point to the numerous friendly contacts he had with Jews throughout his long career, to the philo-Semitic passages in *The Jewess of Toledo,* and to the fact that he was carried from his sickbed to cast his vote in support of the 1868 referendum that, among numerous other liberal reforms, finally granted Jews in Austria full legal rights. Seen in light of the pervasive anti-Semitism of the era, these actions surely are pro-Jewish, yet they comprise only one aspect of Grillparzer's documented statements and writings about Jews. A more comprehensive account suggests instead a complex ambivalence.[22] Grillparzer also made a number of negative comments about individual Jews throughout his life. His characterizations of the Jews in *The Jewess of Toledo* programmatically draw on stock anti-Semitic stereotypes. His plans for the continuation of his fragmentary play *Esther,* a text that likewise centers on religious tolerance, call for the title figure, an upstanding, good-hearted person, to be revealed to be a doglike scoundrel ("Kanaille") at the end of the play for committing the "crime" of failing to admit that she is a Jew.[23] And his purportedly pro-Jewish political stance is profoundly drawn into question by a quatrain he published in 1865 ostensibly praising emancipation legislation, but at the same time damning the Jews for being Jews:

> *Emancipation*
> Late did one become equitable to your race,
> Burdened with hate, revenge, and disgrace,
> You have all your civil rights now,
> But to be sure, you always still will be Jews.

Emanzipation
Spät ward man billig eurem Geschlechte,
Das Haß und Rachsucht mit Schmach beluden,
Ihr habt nun alle Bürgerrechte,
Nur freilich bleibt ihr immer Juden.[24]

While it is perhaps methodologically unsound to accord this short verse too much interpretative significance,[25] *The Jewess of Toledo* frames the Jews—and the "Jewish Question"—in much the same way the quatrain does.

Even a brief plot synopsis indicates the significance of the "Jewish Question" to *The Jewess of Toledo.* The play opens with the capricious young woman Rahel—together with her father Isaak and half sister Esther— entering into an Edenic English garden off-limits to the Jews when the court is in residence, because the Eve-like Rahel is intent on seeing, and subsequently seducing, the sexy young king, Alfonso. (The English garden that forms the meeting ground between Christian and Jew is an eighteenth-century invention, and critics have long interpreted the anachronism allegorically: Grillparzer mirrors nineteenth-century Austrian society in this twelfth-century Spanish setting.) Rahel and her family are granted legal protection by the magnanimous Alfonso, who states that he has no love of the Jews as a people, but will guarantee the safety of all subjects in his realm. Alfonso, who is married to the cold fish of a queen, Eleanore, becomes infatuated with the voluptuous Jewess Rahel and has an affair with her. This illicit relationship seems to threaten the kingdom from within and without. As Alfonso dallies with his lover in a garden at his "pleasure palace" or *Lustschloß,* a setting reminiscent of the "garden of pleasures," the *Lustgarten* he had built for his wife to no avail, Rahel's father Isaak farcically takes over some of Alfonso's state affairs. Meanwhile, the Moors—who are virtually interchangeable with the Jews as signifiers in the text—arm themselves at the kingdom's borders. (This merging of Jew and Moor subtly suggests that the Jews are non-European, heathen outsiders who threaten the integrity of the Christian state.[26]) Alfonso insists he is aware of the political situation and will end the affair. He resists Rahel's pleas to stay with her and takes decisive steps to address his military and marital problems. But the king's grandees, spurred on by the jealous queen Eleanore, kill Rahel on charges that she embodies a dangerous morality and a threat to the security of the Christian state. Alfonso abdicates and vows to cleanse himself in a Crusade, but there is to be no absolution for this transgression: the play ends with his marching off to crushing defeat at the Battle of Alarcos, apparently divine retribution for his affair with the Jewess of Toledo.

In essence, the play suggests that allowing Jews into Christian society and granting them legal protection threatens the moral and political integrity of the Christian state.[27] This theme clearly resonates with a key sociopolitical issue current at the time of the play's writing: the debate about the Jews' legal and social standing in Austria, an issue that had come to the fore in the 1848 revolutions. Grillparzer's dramatization of the "Jewish Question" was recognized at the play's Vienna premiere in 1873, shortly after the 1868 referendum that finally granted Jews in Austria full legal rights. A review in a leading Viennese newspaper described the Jewish "nation" as breaking into the European populace with volcanic force (likely an allusion to the 1848 revolutions), and accused the playwright of "poetic perfidy" for his treatment of this subject matter.[28] Elisabeth Frenzel voiced a similar sentiment during the Nazi era in her 1941 assessment of the play: "behind Rahel's clan lurks a whole people waiting to break into the body politic."[29]

Stripped of its Jewish dimension, the text mirrors a second key political issue of 1848, the Lola Montez affair, a parallel also duly noted at the play's Vienna premiere by Ludwig Speidel, who surmised that Grillparzer likely had thought of "that dancing piece of world history" in scripting Rahel, and that *The Jewess of Toledo* hence functions as a "pseudonymous fragment" of that era (*HKA* 339). This conjecture is substantiated by the play's subject matter and by the history of the text's genesis. The Montez affair rekindled Grillparzer's interest in working on the drama, which he had begun years before, and he finished the bulk of the manuscript during its aftermath (*HKA* 323). Moreover, Grillparzer's poem "Lola Montez," written in 1847, provides an intertextual gloss on *The Jewess of Toledo*.[30]

That the text functions as an oblique commentary on both the Jewish emancipation debate and the Lola Montez affair has thus been clear since the play's premiere, but to my knowledge no one has considered there might be a connection between the two issues, that they might in fact be one and the same. At stake in both, at least from the standpoint of certain xenophobic segments of society, is the question of citizenship rights for foreigners of questionable morality and shady backgrounds. Whether fortuitously or on purpose, Grillparzer infused the Lola Montez affair with a Jewish component, and *The Jewess of Toledo* constitutes his discursive contribution to and critique of the emancipation debate.

The Lola Montez story was well suited to such manipulation.[31] Lola Montez, one of the more illustrious femmes fatales of the nineteenth century, was born in 1821 in Ireland as Elizabeth Rosanna Gilbert. After eloping with one of her mother's suitors at the age of sixteen, she unceremoniously abandoned her husband and took on a new name and a new identity. As the Spanish dancer Lola Montez, she wandered from country to country and bed to bed, engaging in numerous affairs with men of high standing, most notably with Ludwig I of Bavaria. When the king attempted to grant her Bavarian citizenship and a title of nobility, his entire government resigned in protest. At issue were both Montez's notorious impropriety and the well-founded fear that she was trying to take control of the government. The sixteen-month affair ended only after Montez was forced out of Germany by an angry mob. Politically crippled by these events, Ludwig abdicated in 1848.

On the surface the Lola Montez debacle—outrageous enough in and of itself to a staid public who had followed her sensational career with shocked fascination—would seem to have little to do with the "Jewish Question." But on reflection the two issues bear remarkable similarities: both Montez and the Jews were accused of precipitating the 1848 revolutions, and the discourse surrounding the Montez affair contains pronounced parallels to the contemporaneous discourse on anti-Semitism. Montez was regarded not only as an exotic "other," but also as a sorceress and a foreign spy who had been led by a demon into Bavaria and threatened the purity of the "unmixed" Bavarian people.[32] Her religion also had come under scrutiny when the king petitioned to grant her citizenship.[33] Moreover, in her various exploits Montez displayed a malleability of character consistent with the prototype of the Wandering Jew. With her jet-black hair and striking good looks, Montez was a persona of unknown or questionable origins, a scheming, shifty seductress who took on many identities and left a trail of destruction in her wake. Her assumed Spanish background also fits the profile of a Sephardic—and perhaps even a Marrano—Jew. Montez, of course, was not Jewish, and does not appear to have been perceived to be a Jew at the time. However, the rhetoric surrounding the Montez affair contains significant parallels to the rhetoric of anti-Semitism, and an audience inured to a deeply ingrained anti-Semitism might well have recognized Montez's "Jewish" traits on a subconscious level. Whether Grillparzer wittingly took advantage of these anti-Semitic associations is a matter of pure speculation, but one conclusion is clear: by mirroring her story in *The Jewess of Toledo* Grillparzer implicitly recast the Montez affair as a "Jewish" matter.

In his subtle textualization of the Montez affair Grillparzer attached a seductive and widely despised face to the anti-Semitic fear at the center of the emancipation debate: that admitting Jews (or "Jew"-like characters like Lola Montez) into Christian society would threaten the political and moral integrity of the Christian state. Yet at the same time Grillparzer liberally showcased philo-Semitic sentiments in his play. This textual incongruity suggests that the core of the "Jewish Question" raised in *The Jewess of Toledo* does not lie solely in the thematic parallels between a medieval anti-Semitic legend, the Montez affair, and the nineteenth-century emancipation debate. This thematic allegorical reading does not begin to do justice to the complexity of the subject matter, to the play's conflicting representations of Jews: the programmatic confusion of anti-Semitic and philo-Semitic sentiments perforce draws attention to the rhetorical structure of the text. The real "Jewish Question" in *The Jewess of Toledo* is formulated on the rhetorical level, and this is what makes Grillparzer's infusion of the Montez material into a Jewish context so interesting. Grillparzer's transformation of the Montez affair into a "Jewish" matter reflects on the thematic level what the text accomplishes qua text: the formation of "the Jew" as a discursive construct.

The Jewess of Toledo is a text that stresses its own textuality: relatively little action occurs onstage, and the play is replete with semantic networks that draw attention to its language and structure. Analyzed on the structural and discursive levels, the text's apparently contradictory depictions of the Jews, its seemingly irreconcilable philo-Semitic and anti-Semitic stances, are not as contradictory and irreconcilable as they might seem: the text is inherently, but subtly, anti-Semitic. Thematically, structurally, and discursively, *The Jewess of Toledo* is a text about the transgression of borders, about the dangers of allowing Jews into Christian society. The Jews in this play represent a threat to Christian society from within and without, a threat to the legal, moral, religious, and social foundations of the Christian state, to representation itself. The capricious Rahel, who slips into different roles at will, acts as a shifting signifier, representing truth, contradiction, *Verstellung* (dissimulation; literally, dis-placement that is also mis-placement). In this sense, Rahel is even more of a caricature of the stereotypical shifty Jew than her scheming father, Isaak. Strikingly, her sister Esther, the voice of reason in the play, also proves to be a slippery signifier. At the same time, the king—the only Christian character to express philo-Semitic sentiments—is condemned for his actions and textually transformed into a "Jew."

Structurally, the action of the play is framed by—and frames—its Jewish characters: the Jews have the first and last words in the text, words that explicitly condemn their own actions; and each act subtly censures the Jews as it evaluates the "Jewish Question." The first words of the play, spoken by the Jewish patriarch Isaak, warn Rahel that Jews transgressing into the Eden-like Christian realm face divine retribution. Rahel does not heed this admonition, and act 1 unfolds with the king—God's earthly representative—granting legal protection to the Jews, an executive decision that will bring about the demise of both the Jewess and his own authority. The impropriety of this legislative largess is suggested on the lexical level from the start: the king, a stranger in his own country (I, 108: 454) and hence in some sense equated with the Jews, is repeatedly surrounded by a semantic network of "faults," "flaws," "spots," and "stains" ("Fehl," "Fehler," "Flecken," and "Makel") that tacitly condemns his actions.[34] In act 2 the Jews, under the king's protection, settle into their new home at the heart of the Christian realm.[35] Rahel, exploiting the situation, costumes herself in regal finery and replaces a painting of the king with her own portrait. In this exchange of images (*Bildertausch*) the king—and all he represents—literally is unframed by a Jew and supplanted by a Jewish image (and a feminine one, at that). This metaphor is concretized in act 3, obliquely labeled by the text as "topsy-turvy: the new order" ("Verkehrung"; "die neue Ordnung" [III, 787–88: 479; III, 835: 480]), when the Jews take control of the realm in a parodic show that pushes stock anti-Semitic stereotypes *ad absurdum*. But rather than undermining these stereotypes, the parodic show underscores the danger the Jews pose to the Christian state. Act 3—the structural core of the text—opens with the Shylock-like Isaak farcically overseeing the king's economic affairs. Meanwhile, Rahel facetiously plays with the king's weapons and remarks that his "lance" is well suited to her purposes,[36] indicating she has sexual and military control over Alfonso, a statement the king adamantly denies but the queen and the grandees readily accept. Act 4 presents the mock trial and condemnation of the Jewess, a move that simultaneously condemns the king for his actions and strips him of his power. The execution of the Jewess, which occurs between the fourth and fifth acts, functions as the ultimate reprimand for the game Rahel had played to attract the king's attention in the first place: her exaggerated fear she would be killed and was in need of the king's protection (I, 304–31: 460–61). Ironically, the Jewish seductress is killed precisely because Alfonso grants her this protection. Act 5 culminates in the damning of both the king (a "Jew") and the Jews. The king abdicates and marches off to defeat at the Battle of Alarcos dogged by Esther's trenchant curse. Esther then abruptly retracts her curse when her father, true to his typecasting as the unscrupulous, avaricious Jew, insists on fetching his buried money before tending to his daughter's

burial, leading Esther, in the final speech of the drama, to blame the Jews
for being just as guilty of Rahel's death as the Christians, and to ask for
forgiveness and self-forgiveness for their actions.

But the text goes far beyond a simple condemnation and self-
condemnation of its Jewish characters. The text implies that what is
really at stake in admitting Jews into Christian society is nothing less
than the rewriting of Christian salvation history (*Heilsgeschichte*). The
first words of the play are a theological imperative placed, ironically, in
the mouth of the Jewish patriarch Isaak, warning the Jews in a lightly
accented German to "stay back," that entering into the Eden-like royal
garden will bring about a Fall, a Fall that could be avoided:

> Stay back, don't go into the garden!
> Don't you know it's forbidden?
> When the King takes his pleasure walks here,
> No Jew is allowed—God will condemn them!—
> No Jew is allowed to set foot in this place.
>
> Bleib zurück, geh nicht in' Garten!
> Weißt du nicht, es ist verboten?
> Wenn der König hier lustwandelt,
> Darf kein Jüd—Gott wird se richten!—
> Darf kein Jüd den Ort betreten. (I, 1–5: 451)

The ensuing play dramatizes the Jews' trespass into the Edenic garden
as a transgression against the natural order that will result in divine retribution, not only for the Jews, but also for the Christian society that
admits them.[37] Structurally, the play takes the form of a framed narrative.[38] Before the start of the action the harmonious Christian society is
comparable to an Edenic state and the Adam-like Alfonso is characterized as "immaculate" ("fleckenlos," I, 159: 455). To be sure, this Edenic
state is depicted as ripe for trouble: Alfonso came to power following
a bloody civil war; the Moors are massing at the borders of the realm;
and Alfonso obviously is unhappy with his sexually unresponsive wife.
The play—a "historical tragedy"—begins with the Jews infiltrating into
this precarious Christian Paradise. The body of the text presents Paradise
lost. The Eve-like Jewish seductress Rahel brings about the Fall of the
harmonious Christian state and dies for this sin. Alfonso recognizes the
biblical dimensions of her actions when he likens Rahel to a second Paradise, complete with serpent (V, 1691–1704: 510). The play ends with a
promise of Paradise regained. Alfonso marches off to battle to cleanse

himself of his sins, "God willing: to victory" (V, 1920: 517). But there will be no absolution for his transgression. Alfonso's disgraceful defeat at Alarcos—which occurs after the close of the play—stands as a tacit and divine condemnation of his actions. In short, the text's rewriting of Christian salvation history implies that letting Jews (back) into Paradise brings about the Fall of the Christian state (be it Toledo or Vienna), and for Alfonso and his realm this Fall is everlasting: there will be no Paradise regained, no eternal salvation.[39]

The play's philo-Semitic sentiments are integrated into this basic anti-Semitic structure. Grillparzer incorporates a number of short statements preaching tolerance toward the Jews, and one lengthy and impassioned defense of the Jews, into the play, attacking Christian prejudice and sanctimonious Christian mores, and making the most Enlightened figure, Esther, a Jew. Yet at the same time he fashions his Jewish characters using an extensive array of stock anti-Semitic stereotypes: the Jewish seductress, the Jewish princess, the smart Jew, the shifty Jew, the money-grubbing Jew, the unscrupulous Jew, the Jewish spy, the Jew seizing control of the economy, the Jewish sorcerer, the filthy Jew, the cowardly Jew, the thieving Jew, the crafty Jew, the Jew as the Devil, the Jew as the murderer of Jesus, the Jew as the drinker of Christian blood.

Although the play makes some attempt to counteract a few of these stereotypes, none of the charges against the Jews is dismissed out of hand. Isaak's scheming attempt to seize control of the state economy is depicted as laughable; but it is significant that Grillparzer casts a Jew in this role in the first place, and at the end of the play Isaak remains the unprincipled, moneygrubbing Jew. At the beginning of the play Isaak asserts that his second wife, whom he married for her money, engaged in lascivious behavior, as does her daughter, and he suggests Rahel's foolishness may be the "heritage of disgraceful Christians" (I, 29: 451). Rahel, who will bring about the fall of the Christian state through her affair with Alfonso, thus raises the specter of the dangers of miscegenation throughout the play. Moreover, the text repeatedly suggests Rahel's "mixed" nature masks a demonic core. From the beginning the Jewish seductress is characterized as naive, curious, capricious—almost childlike in her innocence and insolence—but at the end of the play, after seeing the destruction she has wreaked on his kingdom and his family, the king recognizes the Devil in the dead *juive fatale*. In life, Alfonso notes: "She was not beautiful. [. . .] / An evil feature around her cheek, her chin, her mouth, / Something lurking in her fire-gaze / Poisoned, disfigured her beauty" (V, 1848–51: 515). In death her face appears to distort before his very eyes and her corpse seems to stretch out her arms to grab the king (V, 1858–59: 515).[40] These passages can be read literally (i.e., Rahel *is* the Devil), or as a psychological characterization of a king who has come to the sober realization that his affair with the Jewess has been devastating. Either way, the demonic metaphors with which Alfonso describes Rahel are damning.

Similarly, the Jews never are exonerated of the most serious charge raised against them: that Rahel seduces the king using sorcery. When Rahel commandeers Alfonso's portrait, threatens to stick a needle through the painted king's heart, and claims she wants to drink his blood while celebrating the "unholiness" ("Unheil") she has created (II, 590–92: 471), she is dismissed by her sister Esther as a spoiled, wild child who knows nothing of black magic (II, 634–35: 473). But at the same time, the king actually feels a stab in his breast when Rahel threatens to stick a pin through the heart of his painted likeness. His blood races uncontrollably and he becomes disoriented as a result of Rahel's picture games: "And I see things as if in a confused light"; "And how that waves and surges and glows and shines" (II, 627–41: 472–73). The king's response might be interpreted as a normal sexual reaction, rather than his succumbing to sorcery, yet he himself questions whether Rahel practices black magic when he feels the stab in his chest (II, 631: 472). Moreover, when Rahel insists on exchanging the king's portrait with her own, the characters' ensuing fixation on this exchange of pictures (*Bildertausch*)—reinforced by Grillparzer in the stage directions—never lays to rest the accusations of necromancy.[41] To be sure, the king dismisses his wife's assertion that the Jews (or more precisely, "the Moorish people, and all like them" [IV, 1424: 499]) practice black magic: according to Alfonso, Christians are the magicians who create the enchantments they perceive in the world around them (IV, 1429–30: 500), and he says the queen's belief that Rahel is a sorceress is grounded in superstition (V, 1841–43: 515–16). But at the same time, the king remains preternaturally entranced by Rahel's portrait. In a draft of the play dating from 1827 Grillparzer describes this quasi-enchantment: "Rahel's relationship to the king to some extent enchantment. In act 4 when he's prepared to send the Jewess off and the queen demands that he remove a portrait of Rahel he wears around his neck, he's willing to do so. But when he sees the picture he sinks into contemplation and his old passion returns" (*HKA* 369). In the final draft of the manuscript the soupçon of sorcery surrounding the portrait is retained right through to the close of the drama. In act 5 the king flings away the portrait in disgust when he sees Rahel's corpse (V, 1860: 515), apparently freeing himself from its pull, albeit with great difficulty: even after the physical attraction to Rahel has been broken, the king struggles to resist the strong temptation to retrieve the portrait, taking a few steps toward the door before halting in his tracks (V, 1820–21: 514). But in the play's final speech Esther steps into the middle of the theater—emphasizing the high drama of the moment— and pointedly invokes the power of the portrait the king had thrown from himself: "You think you're free of my sister's power, / Because the sting of her impression has been deadened / And you cast away what once lured you" (V, 1928–30: 517). Esther, the play's most Enlightened character, the Jew without reproach, then arguably slips into the role of Jewish sorceress with her ominous threat that the king, troubled by his bad conscience, will be haunted in battle by a heaven-sent, gruesome apparition of her dead sister. Esther's curse is uttered after the Christian characters have left the scene, a staging that indirectly suggests that the Jews are a secretive, powerful people who plot against the Christians and who may be in cahoots with the Moors.[42] Although Esther retracts this curse, her imprecation seems to hold sway: against all expectations, Alfonso will be trounced by the Moors at the Battle of Alarcos, leaving a vague suspicion of sorcery surrounding the other Jewess of Toledo.

That Esther is cast in this ambivalent role at the close of the drama is disconcerting, to say the least, since she is the voice of reason and moderation throughout the play: Esther tries to curb Rahel's capricious antics; she counters anti-Semitic stereotypes (asserting that she and her family are not spies and that Rahel does not practice black magic, and criticizing her father for his fixation on money); she condemns the grandees' "Christian" behavior when they kill her sister; she urges the king to reconcile with his people following Rahel's death; and she utters the last lines of the drama, a plea for forgiveness and self-forgiveness. On the surface, Esther is presented as both human and a humanist; for this reason, many critics have regarded her as Grillparzer's mouthpiece. However, Esther's characterization at the end of the play is much more complex and problematic than this summary might indicate.

Esther's final speech both promotes and problematizes this Enlightenment figure, thereby accentuating the framing mechanism with which the play's Jewish characters are depicted. The speech begins with Esther deploring the Christians for slaughtering her sister in a sacrificial act for their "festival of reconciliation" and being too willing to shake bloody hands with each other after the deed is done (V, 1923–25: 517). Esther is justified in condemning the Christians for their murderous actions, but she comes across as hypocritical when she denounces their reconciliation, since she herself had counseled the king not to kill the grandees as punishment for their insurrection, stating he should leave the grieving to the Jews and work to unify his people (V, 1711–12: 510). But at the close of the play Esther pronounces her ominous curse on the king, threatening that he will be haunted in battle by a vision of her dead sister. Esther then abruptly retracts her curse when her father, true to his typecasting as the unscrupulous, money-centered Jew, insists on fetching his hidden treasure before tending to his daughter's burial (thereby highlighting the exchange the Jewish patriarch was all too willing to make: buried money for a buried daughter), leading the smart Jew Esther to conclude (somewhat illogically) that the Jews, apparently by their very nature, are just as guilty of Rahel's death as the Christians.[43] (Earlier Esther had asserted that she and her father alone—and not Alfonso—were guilty because they had sacrificed Rahel to gain monetary and social favors by being in the king's good graces [V, 1751–54: 511].) Esther is right to assert that she and her father bear some responsibility for their actions, but at the same time she reinforces the stereotype of the Jews as scheming deal-makers who would even give up a family member's life for remuneration. This stereotype is further reinforced by the fact that the Jews obviously are not in need of money when they commence their deal-making with the king: at the start of the play the Jewish princess Rahel flaunts her jewels, pretends to throw them away, and then offers them as ransom in exchange for her life (I, 315–30: 460–61). Similarly, Rahel's death serves to both discredit and promote the stereotype of the cowardly Jew: Isaak cowers under a carpet and Esther faints when the grandees come to kill Rahel. On the one hand, the Jews' behavior is understandable, given the mortal danger they faced, but Esther finds her own actions contemptible: "Pure cowardice. Women's way" (V, 1611: 507). In the final lines of the play Esther, the eminent voice of reason, lays blame on the Jews, as well as the Christians, for Rahel's death, and asks for forgiveness and self-forgiveness for their actions.

Esther's final speech both strengthens and relativizes this philo-Semitic figure. On the surface, the drama ends on a strong humanistic note, and it is significant that a Jew delivers these lines. But at the same time, her condemnation of the Jews blurs an important ethical distinction: the Jews may have speculated with Rahel's person with Rahel's willing consent, but they did not commit murder; the Christians did. Esther is acutely aware of this ethical distinction. When Manrique proudly promotes Christian mercy following Rahel's murder ("Woman, we're Christians"), Esther retorts: "You've certainly shown it. / I praise the Jewess, by God!" [V, 1796–97: 513]. Esther's subsequent condemnation of the Jews, by virtue of both its speaker's Enlightenment authority and its structural position at the close of the drama, stands as a summation of the play's treatment of the Jews in general: the text repeatedly problematizes its pro-Jewish gestures to the point where they lose virtually all argumentative force.

Nowhere is this more apparent than in the speeches of the play's most pro-Jewish proponent, Alfonso, whose eloquent defenses of the Jews are undermined on the thematic, rhetorical, and structural levels of the text, and, most remarkably, are constantly contradicted by the king himself. As a case in point, in his first comment about the Jews—which lays the groundwork for his later remarks—the king decries Christian society's mistreatment of the Jews, vows to protect all subjects in his realm, and admonishes his grandees not to harm the Jews. But in the same breath Alfonso declares that he despises the Jews' idolization of money and therefore has never asked them for advice (I, 288–94: 459). At this point the king might be characterized as promoting an Enlightenment toleration policy that is somewhat wanting, but his subsequent contradictory comments about the Jews point to a much more problematic facet of the text's philo-Semitism that has escaped critical attention.

The king is the only Christian in the text to utter pro-Jewish sentiments, and, with the exception of the passage just discussed, he does so only as a justification for his sexual attraction to Rahel. (The passage above also can be understood in this light: the king vows to protect the Jews in his realm before he even sets eyes on Rahel, and hence establishes himself as a tolerant ruler. But the audience already has been introduced to the Jewish seductress and will interpret the king's words in this sexually charged context.) In fact, the king makes very few pro-Jewish statements, and only one lengthy speech about the Jews. This singular speech—almost always cited out of context in the secondary literature as proof of the play's philo-Semitism—reveals that the king is indeed philo-Semitic, but in the true sense of the word.

The speech—which contains a remarkable exposition of the structure and sources of Christian anti-Semitism—is introduced by the admission the king makes to his confidant Garceran that he is burning with desire for the Jewess, is interrupted by a distracted query the king makes asking Rahel's name, and concludes with a remark intimating that he expects to receive sexual favors from the Jewess in return for his kindness. The speech is situated at the beginning of act 2, when the king, smitten with Rahel, turns to Garceran for advice on how to woo women, and imagines a seduction scenario that begins at an opportune moment when the men of his lover's house are absent and his lover's chambermaid comes to fetch him:

KING: Then you enter and a warm hand
    Grabs yours, leads you through the corridors
    Which, black as the grave and endlessly gliding,
    Increase desire, until finally ambrosial fragrance
    And a pale shimmering coming through the cracks   470
    Show that you've reached the lovely goal.
    The door opens and brightly in the candle glow
    The limbs draped on dark velvet,
    The white arm encased in strings of pearls,
    Leans the desired one with gently lowered head,   475
    The golden locks—no, make that black locks!—
    The raven-black hair of her head—and so on!
    As you can see, I learn quickly, Garceran,
    And the same goes for Christian woman, Mooress—Jewess.
GARCERAN: Since we're fighting for the border   480
    We rightly turn to Muslim women, but the Jewess, Sire—
KING: Don't pretend you're not interested.
    I bet if that girl even glanced at you, you'd be burning up.
    I have no love of this people, but I know that
    What discredits them is our own work;   485
    We lame them, and then despise them when they limp.
    Moreover, there's something great
    In this wandering, transient shepherd race:
    We others are from today, but they reach
    Back to the cradle of Creation, when the Godhead   490
    Still walked in Paradise in human form,
    When the cherubs were the Patriarchs' guests
    And the One God was the judge and the law.
    With the whole fairy tale world is also the truth
    Of Cain and Abel, of Rebecca's cleverness,   495
    Of Jacob, who, in service, wooed Rachel—
    What's the girl's name?
GARCERAN: Sire, I don't know.
KING: Oh!
    From Ahashuerus, who reached out his scepter   500
    Over Esther, who was his wife
    And also a Jewess, a divine protector of her people.
    Both Christian and Muslim trace their family trees
    Back to this people as the oldest, the first,
    So that they doubt us, we don't doubt them.   505

And though, like Esau they frivolously gave up
   their birthright,
We crucify the Lord ten times daily
With our sins, our misdeeds,
And they crucified Him only once.

But let's go! Wait, you stay!   510
Accompany her, and mark well her house.
Perhaps sometime when weary worries press,
I'll visit her and take pleasure in her thanks.
(II, 466–512: 467–68)

Read in its entirety, Alfonso's speech clearly indicates that his philo-Semitism derives largely from his infatuation with Rahel. Alfonso himself admits as much later in the text: motivated by a jealous drive to be her sole possessor, the king confesses that he does not like Jewish men because he cannot stand the thought of these unsavory figures touching Jewish women, especially Rahel: "The women of this race / Are tolerable, even good.—But the men / Filthy-handed narrow-minded usurers, / Such a man should not touch this girl" (IV, 1447–50: 500). Significantly, it is Rahel—characterized by the king as "Truth itself, if distorted" (V, 1685: 509)—who sums up the king's attraction to her with the following words: "He's rough even in tender encounters / He immediately rues every mild word / *And his inclination a hidden hatred*" ("*Und dessen Neigung ein verstecktes Hassen,*" III, 925–27: 483, emphasis mine). Rahel makes this statement while flirting with Garceran in an obvious attempt to regain the king's favor, but her criticism rings true in light of Alfonso's sexually charged comment praising Jewish women and denouncing Jewish men. Rahel's statement, strategically situated at the structural center of the play, is programmatic for the text's philo-Semitism in general. Grillparzer casts Alfonso's philo-Semitism as an infatuation that clouds the mind, masking its true core—a hidden hatred of the Jews—and the text, with its pro-Jewish gestures that are in essence anti-Semitic, enacts Alfonso's philo-Semitic infatuation discursively.

    To wit, consider the content of Alfonso's remarkable speech in context. The king's trenchant critique of Christian anti-Semitism—undercut from the start by the fact that its speaker is an obviously infatuated man—is repeatedly contradicted by the text in a series of subtle reversals of Alfonso's pro-Jewish gestures. The king's speech begins with the recognition of the lethal consequences of a tryst between Christian and Jew. Alfonso imagines himself making his way to the woman through corridors that are dark as the grave, and this deadly threat heightens his desire (l. 467–69). The king then indulges in this sexual fantasy: first replacing blond locks with raven-black hair in his seduction scenario (l. 476-77), then equating Christian and Moor, and finally equating Christian and Jew (l. 479). Garceran, however, criticizes the king for trying to break down the border between Jew and Christian (l. 480–81), and the text, with its repeated insistence on maintaining borders, indicates his reproach must be taken seriously: the Jew—but not the Christian—will die and the king will be defeated at Alarcos trying to defend the borders of his realm, apparently divine retribution for his own border transgression. (That the king's ancestor, Don Sancho, had an affair with a Mooress without suffering the same devastating consequences [II, 771–78: 478] indicates the seriousness of the border transgression between Christian and Jew.) The king then admits his infatuation, denies he loves the Jews as a people, and launches into an extraordinary philo-Semitic analysis of the structure of Christian anti-Semitism.

Significantly, each of the king's assertions in his four-pronged analysis is called into question, subtly undermining his pro-Jewish gestures. First, the king maintains, the Jews' tarnished reputation derives from Christian actions, Christian calumny: "What disfigures them is our work; / We lame them and then despise them when they limp" (l. 486–87). Alfonso elliptically gives voice to a Dohmian line of argument in the emancipation debate: the Jews' perceived focus on money can be explained by the fact that one of the few professions Christian society allows them is moneylending; the Jews are deal-makers because Christians by and large do not allow them to practice skilled trades or to farm; the Jews are wanderers because Christians do not allow them to own land; the Jews live in dark, crowded quarters because Christians dictate they must; and so on. In the emancipation debate the upshot of this argument is clear: give the Jews a fair chance and they will prove to be reputable, upstanding members of society. However, the action of the play refutes this proposal. The Jews largely live up to their stereotypical characterizations when the king gives them free rein in a microcosm of Christian society (the closed environment of the "pleasure palace" or *Lustschloß*), and the result is devastating: Rahel brings about the fall of the Christian state. Rahel's characterization as a *juive fatale* surely undercuts the king's argument, as does the suspicion of sorcery surrounding the Jews throughout the play. Moreover, Isaak's fixation on money suggests the Jews have been so badly lamed by the Christians that their limp, to use Alfonso's metaphor, has become second nature, and the Jews have lost their moral ground: Isaak's insistence on fetching his buried money before tending to his daughter's burial is an extreme characterization. Significantly, a fellow Jew, Esther, condemns his actions, thereby counterbalancing to some extent the skewed ethos Isaak represents, though, as we have seen, her characterization as the voice of reason in the play is problematic.

Second, the king identifies the Jews as the originary people, the guarantors of a divine, prelapsarian truth (l. 488–94). Even after her death the king sees in the capricious Rahel an originary, if somewhat distorted, truth, a truth harking back to Paradise, and he pointedly dismisses Esther's assertion that he overly esteems Rahel (V, 1676–90: 509). However, when the king recognizes the destruction Rahel has wreaked on his family and kingdom, he also sees the Devil in her (V, 1849–50: 515). Moreover, the text's rewriting of Christian salvation history contradicts the king's characterization of the Jews as the guarantors of an originary truth: the king's decision to let the Jews back into Paradise (the "pleasure garden") threatens the core of the Christian state not with a divine Jewish morality or truth, but with the truth of a corrupt "Jewish" morality. As if to underscore this danger, the king interrupts his speech at this point to ask the name of the Jewish seductress (l. 498).

Third, the king continues, the Jews as the originary people have the right to be suspicious of Christians and Muslims, whose religions are historical offshoots of Judaism (l. 502–504), but the Jews foolishly gave up this right like Esau (l. 505), who traded his birthright for a dish of pottage. Ironically, the biblical gloss functions as a critique not only of the Jews, but also of Alfonso, who will give up his birthright (his kingdom) for Rahel. On the semiotic level, Alfonso is equated with a foolish Jew; the Jewess, with a pittance in this comparison.

Finally, the king concludes, the Jews crucified Jesus, but the Christians, with their corrupt behavior, do the same ten times daily (l. 506–508). That the king makes no attempt to examine the veracity of this most serious charge against the Jews is understandable within the historical context of the play, but he nonetheless engages in exaggerated reasoning: from a Christian theological perspective, Christian crimes committed ten times daily would not seem to be of the same magnitude as deicide. This is why Rahel, and not the king, will die for their joint transgression. Both Christian and Jew are warned they face divine retribution for their actions, but their God-sent punishments are strikingly different: the king is stripped of his power; the Jewess, of her life. At this point the king's Enlightened defense of the Jews ends with Alfonso intimating he expects to receive sexual favors from Rahel in return for his kindness (l. 511–12), thereby emphasizing that the king's pro-Jewish rhetoric must be read within the context of his infatuation. This conclusion is substantiated on the structural level of the text: the king's speech is situated at the beginning of act 2, and the bulk of the play works to condemn Alfonso for his pro-Jewish stance and actions.

Moreover, Alfonso's eloquent defense of the Jews is severely compromised, if not nullified, in the very next lines, underscoring once again that the king's pro-Jewish speech must be interpreted within the context of the play's plot and structure: the text's depiction of real-life Jews stands in stark opposition to the image of the great Jewish patriarchs and matriarchs invoked in Alfonso's impassioned speech. Immediately after the king concludes his speech, the cowardly Jewish patriarch Isaak emerges from the garden house where he and his family are sheltered, intending to abandon his misbehaving daughter to save his own skin (II, 517: 468)—hardly a fine representative of the upstanding Jews just depicted in the king's speech. Isaak meets Garceran and the king and apprises them of Rahel's activities in the garden house. Apparently not recognizing the king, Isaak prefaces his account by asking: "Who is the Lord [Ruler]?" ("Wer ist der Herr?" [II, 522: 468]). Does he really not recognize Alfonso? He has seen the king's picture (II, 544–45: 469). Through a subtle wordplay Isaak draws into question the identity and authority of the Christian God and king, mirroring in his rhetoric the threat to the Christian state his daughter concretizes through her actions. Rahel, Isaak reports, entered the garden house distraught, but quickly recovered and began to sing and dance, and displaced a Christian holy object, perhaps a crucifix (II, 531: 469). Rahel then resourcefully used her own keys to open all the cabinets (a description obliquely evoking the stereotypical crafty Jew), and found a collection of costumes left over from the previous year's Carnival play. The costumes, hanging side by side, bring together beggar and king, angel and devil (II, 537: 469), and, the text tacitly suggests, Christian and Jew: Rahel adorned herself in a mantle and crown (not gold, but gilded tin, Isaak shrewdly comments, calculating its monetary value) and declared herself queen (II, 539–43: 469). Note the semiotic associations established in this series: king—angel—Christian, beggar—devil—Jew. Finally, Isaak reports to the infatuated Alfonso, Rahel took a painting of the king from the wall, and is now carrying it around pressed to her bosom and calling it her husband.

This report, it must be emphasized, occurs directly after the king's lengthy defense of the Jews, clearly contradicting his characterizations of the Jews as a harmless people whose bad reputation derives from Christian slander. The capricious Rahel poses a profound threat to both the king and the Christian state: in the ensuing scene the Jewish seductress sticks needles in the king's portrait, threatens to puncture the painted king's heart, and says she wants to drink his blood, raising charges of necromancy and blood libel. She then literally unframes the king's painted image and replaces it with her own.

The twofold threat Rahel poses to the Christian state is played out on the semiotic level in the central topos of the *Bildertausch* (exchange of images). First, the king—and all he represents—is replaced by a female Jewish image, and the text implies this emasculating Judaizing or *Verjudung* will be everlasting.[44] At the end of the play when the king discovers that Rahel is dead, he metaphorically takes over the mothering role Esther has assumed (V, 1621: 507), declaring that he wants to "give birth" to his revenge (V, 1649–50: 508). The feminized Alfonso then abdicates, declares his young son and only heir king, and marches off to battle to cleanse himself of his sins. But Alfonso will suffer humiliating defeat at Alarcos, and the boy, propped up onstage by two women (V, 1901: 516), will be killed by a falling brick (comparable, perhaps, to a thunderbolt from heaven) after the close of the drama.[45] In the *Bildertausch* the image of the Christian king is compromised on two levels: through a chiasmic play the king—God's earthly representative—is textually transformed into an effeminate "Jew"; the Jewess Rahel, into a Christ figure who will die for the sins of all guilty parties—both the Christians and the Jews—in the play.[46]

The second threat Rahel poses to the Christian state in the *Bildertausch* is to its orderly delimitation. The text repeatedly emphasizes that it is not just the fact Rahel takes the king's picture that is at stake here, but that she takes it from its frame, and Alfonso is inordinately concerned that she return his portrait to its proper frame. When Rahel first appropriates the king's painting, the text redundantly reports the action in both stage directions and dialogue: "RAHEL *returns with a picture without a frame:* Here is the king's portrait, freed from its frame" (II, 568: 470). When the king demands that she return his portrait, he insists she return it to its frame (II, 627: 472), and then checks to see if she has carried out his orders: "But did she also put it in its frame?" (II, 742: 477). Finally, the stage directions at the beginning of act 5 specify among the signs of destruction: "a painting [presumably of the king], half ripped from its frame" (V: p. 506).

This framing topos is programmatically linked to the text's insistence on maintaining borders.[47] An extensive semantic network running throughout the text casts political, religious, legal, and moral transgressions as violations of the border: the Jews cross the legal border into the Edenic garden and hence into the heart of the Christian state; the

Moors constantly threaten to attack the borders of the kingdom; Garceran is sent to the border of the realm to atone for slipping into a lady's chamber to spy on her—a moral border violation; the king breaks down the queen's door—a physical border violation—in a metaphorical rape [IV, 1540: 503]; and, most significantly, the king eliminates the border between Christian and Jew, legally, linguistically, and sexually— the ultimate border transgression, for which he is damned. When Rahel unframes the king's portrait, metaphorically freeing him from his proper boundaries and rendering him capricious like herself, Alfonso commits his most serious border infractions: he is overwhelmed by his infatuation and has an affair with the Jewess; and he loses sight of the fact the Moors are massing at the borders of his realm. The action of the play attempts to restore the king to his proper frame, both literally and figuratively, so that he can defend the borders of the realm. Both enterprises fail. In unframing the image of the king, Rahel brings about the downfall of the Christian state and effects the transformation of its highest authority, the king, into a "Jew." She represents an intractable threat to representation, delimitation, order. As Alfonso recognizes at the start of the play, Rahel introduces a profound chaos that must be eradicated from the harmonious Christian state: "These confused images begone!" ("Nun aber fort mit diesen wirren Bildern!" [I, 398: 464]). This optative will not be realized within the borders of this programmatically confusing text.

The Jewess of Toledo presents a complex critique of the Jewish emancipation debate in nineteenth-century Austria. On the one hand, the play showcases pro-Jewish sentiments and makes some attempt to present Jews in a positive light, and Alfonso's extraordinary analysis of the structure and sources of Christian anti-Semitism is remarkable in its depth and precision. Nonetheless, these pro-Jewish gestures are repeatedly undercut on all levels of the text, most strikingly in Grillparzer's casting of Alfonso's philo-Semitism as an infatuation that clouds the mind, an infatuation that is irreparably destructive: the play's action ends with "The whole castle completely destroyed, ravaged, devastated" ("Das ganze Schloß, zerstört, verheert, verwüstet" [V, 1627: 508]). In short, *The Jewess of Toledo* narrates a subtextual story about the cataclysmic dangers of allowing Jews into Christian society.

Importantly, the text also criticizes the villainous Christian society it depicts: there are no heroes in this historical tragedy. As Dagmar Lorenz has argued, the play's revolutionary potential lies precisely in this negativity. Alfonso's society is sick. In his portrayal of twelfth-century Toledo, Grillparzer mirrors an ailing Austria around 1848, a country in need of a fundamental restructuring of its political, social, and ethical foundations.[48]

Seen from this vantage, *The Jewess of Toledo* arguably might be interpreted as a pro-Jewish text *ex negativo*. Such a reading might consider the possibility that the play works to expose the structure of anti-Semitism, enacting a critique akin to Horkheimer and Adorno's *Dialectic of Enlightenment*. The challenge to this kind of analysis is that the text not only reinscribes itself in the very discourse it critiques (as one might perhaps expect, following Horkheimer and Adorno's schema), but also rewrites the rhetoric of anti-Semitism on a more sophisticated level.

Given the play's casting of the Lola Montez affair as a "Jewish" matter, its characterization of Rahel as an openly sensual woman, and its merging of Jew and Moor as almost interchangeable signifiers throughout the text, a case also might be made for interpreting *The Jewess of Toledo* as a discourse on the "other" in nineteenth-century Austro-German society, rather than as a discourse on anti-Semitism per se. However, the text's conspicuous foregrounding of the figure of the Jew and the centrality of the "Jewish Question" to the politics and discourse of the era both speak against such a generalizing reading. The play's casting of the Montez affair as a "Jewish" matter, its characterization of the sensual Rahel as the Jewish sorceress, its merging of Jew and Moor, its semiotic transformation of Alfonso into an effeminate "Jew," and its programmatically conflicting characterizations of the Jews as shifty, shifting signifiers all attest that this text does not reduce "the Jew" to one signifier among many; it stages the formation of "the Jew" as a discursive construct.

This chapter has analyzed a text written around the time of the 1848 revolutions, and published posthumously in 1872, at the historical juncture when the Jews in Germany and Austria finally received full civil and legal rights. Challenging most scholarship to date, which either has refused to read "the Jew" in this text at all, or has steadfastly not read "the Jew" in this text in its complexity, I have argued that the play's programmatically conflicting representations of Jews has theoretical significance. In this text the Jews threaten to transgress all borders and ordering structures: this is precisely why they cannot be delimited, or represented, unambiguously. Like Arnim, Droste, and Stifter, Grillparzer constructs "the Jew" rhetorically and discursively as a shifty, shifting, morally ambivalent signifier. Strikingly, he does so in a drama that takes as its starting point an apparently Enlightened monarch who bucks popular opinion and welcomes Jews into his realm. Yet there is no sense in which the tensions inherent in the text can be interpreted as Enlightenment criticism in the spirit of Lessing. Grillparzer characterizes Alfonso's philo-Semitism as a misguided infatuation that will devastate: the play ends with the murder of the Jew and the downfall of the Christian state. Forebodingly, Grillparzer writes his contribution to the debate about the "Jewish Question" in the genre of the "historical tragedy." There will not be a happy end to this story.

The Word Unheard

"The Jew" is not, and cannot be, just another "other" in German discourse: the very fact of the Holocaust makes "the Jew" a privileged signifier, and lends urgency to the study of the genealogy of anti-Semitism in German letters. This is not to argue that all German literature is anti-Semitic, or that the Holocaust is preprogrammed in the eighteenth- and nineteenth-century literature under consideration here. I do not believe this to be the case, and I have not been making this argument in the preceding chapters. To read *The Word Unheard* as "just another book on anti-Semitism," as a book about "proving" that German authors and German literature are anti-Semitic, as a book that traces—or should trace—literary constructions of the *Blut und Boden* ideology that led to the Third Reich, is to miss the point entirely. This is a book about recognizing a different type of anti-Semitism, one that hides in plain view and silently informs key canonical texts of the German literary tradition. Precisely because this is canonical literature, the readings developed throughout this book will bother many people, and *should* bother many people. The preceding chapters reevaluate cherished classics in fundamentally new ways, and expose systematic blind spots in our understanding of literary anti-Semitism and its reception history. In so doing, *The Word Unheard* demonstrates how subtle forms of anti-Semitism become part of a cultural legacy.

Having the courage to confront prejudices in our thought patterns and in our reading practices lies at the core of Lessing's critical enterprise. We began this study with an analysis of an essential tension in Lessing's pro-Jewish Enlightenment writings, which programmatically turn back on themselves in a self-reflexive gesture, thereby emphasizing the importance of constantly questioning how texts construct meaning, of constantly questioning what we know and how we know it. If we read honestly and circumspectly, we must acknowledge the anti-Jewish moments in Lessing's own writing, the problematic elements that tinge the discursive construction of "the Jew" in his texts. From Lessing we traced the development of an increasingly sophisticated and nuanced theory of literary anti-Semitism. We briefly recall the contours of this trajectory: Schiller's trenchant critique of the origins of, and historical justification for, anti-Semitism in his rewriting of the Exodus account; Arnim's semiotic construction of "Jewishness" as a necessary and noxious sign against which German national identity forms by exclusion; Droste-Hülshoff's theorization of the power of language to create and transmit prejudice, and her concomitant identification of a hidden Jewishness in German society, an anti-Semitism of the blood; Stifter's hermeneutic theory of "the Jew" that naturalizes anti-Semitism as a physical and metaphysical phenomenon; and Grillparzer's dramatic staging of the cataclysmic dangers of philo-Semitism. Each of the texts analyzed presents a self-reflexive discourse on the structure and function of anti-Semitism in literature. Each grounds this theory in language, in the written word. Yet the language of anti-Semitism in these texts has remained unheard, unread.

The rhetoric of anti-Semitism resonates subliminally in this great literature, and this is why it is so important to recognize its presence. It is very easy to acknowledge obvious, virulent expressions of anti-Semitism, and to distance oneself from overt prejudice. It is much harder to confront subconscious biases that are transmitted canonically and perpetuated unquestioningly. This book has proposed a new approach to latent literary anti-Semitism by being attentive to words that are there, words that convey meaning. To gain a deeper understanding of the genealogy of anti-Semitism, these texts must be read in their complexity.

Introduction

1. For other studies of Jews in German literature in the time period under consideration see, for example, Ritchie Robertson's magisterial *The 'Jewish Question' in German Literature, 1749–1939* (Oxford and London: Oxford University Press, 1999), which concentrates on the years 1880–1939, and does not offer sustained textual analysis. Jeffrey Librett's *The Rhetoric of Cultural Dialogue* (Stanford, Calif.: Stanford University Press, 2000) provides an in-depth interpretation of the structure of German-Jewish dialogue in the era of emancipation; it does not focus on the rhetoric of anti-Semitism per se, and does not consider latent anti-Semitism in literature. Jonathan M. Hess's *Germans, Jews and the Claims of Modernity* (New Haven and London: Yale University Press, 2002) presents a groundbreaking analysis of the inception of the Jewish emancipation debate in Germany from a sociohistorical perspective, but offers relatively little discussion of literature. Gunnar Och's *Imago Judaica* (Würzburg: Königshausen & Neumann, 1995) provides thoughtful analyses of Jews in German literature from 1750 to 1812, but does not consider latent anti-Semitism. Irving Massey's *Philo-Semitism in Nineteenth-Century German Literature* (Tübingen: Niemeyer, 2000) and Alfred Low's *Jews in the Eyes of Germans from the Enlightenment to Imperial Germany* (Philadelphia: Institute for the Study of Human Issues, 1979) are both well-intentioned studies that fail to offer comprehensive analyses of the literary texts under discussion.

2. For an in-depth analysis of the rhetorical strategies that inform the discursive construction of the Jew in the tales of the Brothers Grimm and Clemens Brentano, see my "The Fairy Tale Jew," *Neue Lektüren/New Readings*, ed. Norbert Eke and Gerhard Knapp. *Amsterdamer Beiträge zur neueren Germanistik*, vol. 67 (Amsterdam and New York: Rodopi: 2009), 31–42.

3. For a theoretical discussion of textual latency grounded in Heideggerian philosophy, see Hans Ulrich Gumbrecht, "How (If at All) Can We Encounter What Remains Latent in Texts?" *Partial Answers: Journal of Literature and the History of Ideas* 7, no. 1 (2009): 87–96. Gumbrecht defines "latent" as "whatever we believe is in a text without being unproblematically graspable" (87). Gumbrecht proposes an approach to latency that abandons close textual analysis and "strenuous hermeneutic efforts," arguing that we may best encounter latency by "taking a passive stance and an attitude of composure (*Gelassenheit*)" (96).

4. The poem, presumably written by Klee, is itself dynamically beautiful, composed of mellifluous language and abstract images that are strikingly poignant and singularly difficult to understand and to translate: "Einst dem Grau der Nacht enttaucht / Dann schwer und teurer / und stark vom Feur / Abends

voll von Gott und gebeugt / Nun ätherlings vom Blau umschauert, / entschwebt über Firnen / zu klugen Gestirnen" ("Once emerged from the gray of night / Then grave [serious, heavy] and dearer / and strong from fire / Evenings full of God and bowed / Now ethereally showered all around by blue, / hovering away over snow-covered peaks / to wise stars [to knowing constellations]"). For a discussion of the painting, and Klee's self-understanding as a poet, see K. Porter Aichele, *Paul Klee, Poet/Painter* (Rochester, N.Y.: Camden House, 2006), 45–48. Aichele provides an alternate translation to the poem (45).

5. Mark H. Gelber, "What Is Literary Antisemitism?" *Jewish Social Studies* 47, no. 1 (1985): 1.

6. Ibid., 16. Emphasis in the original.

7. Helmut Walser Smith has used the metaphor of the "vanishing point" from painting to elegantly demonstrate how very different pictures of history emerge by shifting perspective: "In painting, a vanishing point focuses the viewer's attention and determines the relative size of detail throughout the canvas. By analogy, the vanishing point in history determines the central focus of a disciplinary community, establishing central questions and deciding the scope of what counts. It does this not only for events chronologically close to the vanishing point, but also for those at considerable distance. In this sense, vanishing points pattern the writing of history, whether or not we wish them to." Helmut Walser Smith, *The Continuities of German History: Nation, Religion, and Race Across the Long Nineteenth Century* (Cambridge, U.K., and New York: Cambridge University Press, 2008), 6.

8. *The New Shorter Oxford English Dictionary*, vol. 1, ed. Lesley Brown (Oxford: Oxford University Press, 1973, 1993), 88.

9. This in itself is not a new argument: as Jonathan Hess has shown in his incisive analysis of late eighteenth-century German political, philosophical, and religious discourse, "distinctly modern forms of anti-Semitism emerged not as a reaction to the Enlightenment, but as an integral component of it" (*Germans, Jews and the Claims of Modernity*, 208). See also Smith, *The Continuities of German History*.

10. Reinhard Rürup and Thomas Nipperdey, "Antisemitismus—Entstehung, Funktion und Geschichte eines Begriffs," in Reinhard Rürup, *Emanzipation und Antisemitismus. Studien zur "Judenfrage" der bürgerlichen Gesellschaft* (Göttingen: Vandenhoeck & Ruprecht, 1975), 112–13.

11. See, for example, Shmuel Almog, "What's in a Hyphen?" *SICSA Report: Newsletter of the Vidal Sassoon International Center for the Study of Antisemitism* 2 (Summer 1989): 1–2; and Richard S. Levy, "Forget Webster," *German Studies Review* 29, no. 1 (2006): 145–46. Levy argues that because the word "Semitism" was used pejoratively in the nineteenth century, *semitism* and *antisemitism* were essentially synonyms. Other scholars have opted to use terms like "allosemitism" or "semitism" to capture this ambivalence and avoid prejudicial vocabulary. See Bryan Cheyette, *Constructions of "The Jew" in English Literature and Society* (Cambridge, U.K.: Cambridge University Press, 1993), 8–9.

12. The term in fact predates Marr. Rürup and Nipperdey, "Antisemitismus," 95.

13. The following discussion is based on Reinhard Rürup, "The Tortuous and Thorny Path to Legal Equality. 'Jew Laws' and Emancipatory Legislation in Germany from the Late Eighteenth Century," *Leo Baeck Institute Yearbook* 31 (1986): 3–33.

14. See Jacob Katz, *From Prejudice to Destruction: Anti-Semitism 1700–1933* (Cambridge, Mass., and London: Harvard University Press, 1980), 223–29.

Chapter One

1. In 1753, in the wake of edicts of emancipation in Holland and England, a pamphlet published anonymously in Berlin, *Letter from a Jew to a Philosopher, Together with the Response* (*Schreiben eines Juden an einen Philosophen nebst der Antwort*), called for the complete equality of the Jews in Germany. The text very likely was authored by Aaron Salomon Gumpertz, possibly with Lessing's encouragement; Lessing may well have been directly involved in its publication. Lessing reviewed the piece very shortly after it appeared in the *Berliner privilegirte Zeitung*, the leading newspaper in Berlin. See Gad Freudenthal, "Aaron Salomon Gumpertz, Gotthold Ephraim Lessing, and the First Call for an Improvement of the Civil Rights of Jews in Germany," *Association of Jewish Studies Review* 29, no. 2 (2005): 299–353.

2. For readings of *Nathan the Wise* against *The Merchant of Venice* see Gunnar Och, *Imago judaica. Juden und Judentum im Spiegel der deutschen Literatur 1750–1812* (Würzburg: Königshausen & Neumann, 1995), 159–62; and Klaus Berghahn, *Grenzen der Toleranz: Juden und Christen im Zeitalter der Aufklärung* (Cologne, Weimar, Vienna: Böhlau, 2000), 102–26.

3. Barbara Fischer and Thomas C. Fox, "Lessing's Life and Work," in *A Companion to the Works of Gotthold Ephraim Lessing*, ed. Barbara Fischer and Thomas C. Fox (Rochester, N.Y.: Camden House, 2005), 33. Writing in 1940, Elisabeth Frenzel explained why a production of *Nathan* was simply not possible now: the play was "understood and exploited as philo-Semitic." Quoted in Berghahn, *Grenzen der Toleranz*, 126. As Berghahn notes, Frenzel's scholarship, with its pronounced anti-Semitism, is a prime example of Nazi *Germanistik*. This is the same Elisabeth Frenzel who coauthored one of the standard reference works used in *Germanistik* up through the present, *Daten deutscher Dichtung*. See Herbert A. Frenzel and Elisabeth Frenzel, *Daten deutscher Dichtung. Chronologischer Abriß der deutschen Literaturgeschichte*, 2 vols., 22nd ed. (Munich: Deutscher Taschenbuch Verlag, 1985).

4. Some scholars have questioned whether "tolerance" should be the organizing principle of a study of "Lessing and the Jews" or German-Jewish interactions in the eighteenth century, arguing that this approach in effect misreads Lessing and does not account for the agency of Jews in the emancipation process. I use the term here precisely because of the strong reception of Lessing as a symbol of tolerance. The focus of my own analysis is not on tolerance per se, but on the discursive construction of the figure of the Jew in Lessing's texts. See Jonathan M. Hess, *Germans, Jews and the Claims of Modernity*, 9–10 and 212 n. 20; and Willi Goetschel, "Lessing and the Jews," in *A Companion to*

the *Works of Gotthold Ephraim Lessing,* ed. Barbara Fischer and Thomas C. Fox (Rochester, N.Y.: Camden House, 2005), 200–201. For fine studies that take "tolerance" as their organizing principle, see Peter R. Erspamer, *The Elusiveness of Tolerance: The "Jewish Question" from Lessing to the Napoleonic Wars* (Chapel Hill and London: University of North Carolina Press, 1997), and Berghahn, *Grenzen der Toleranz.*

5. See Friedrich Schlegel, "Vom Wesen der Kritik" (1804): "Alles was Lessing getan, gebildet, versucht und gewollt hat, läßt sich am füglichsten unter den Begriff der Kritik zusammenfassen" ("Everything that Lessing did, formed, tried, and wanted is most appropriately summarized by the concept of criticism"). *Kritische Friedrich Schlegel Ausgabe,* vol. 3, *Charakteristiken und Kritiken II,* ed. Hans Eichner (Munich, Paderborn, Vienna: Schöningh, 1975), 51.

6. Lessing famously makes this argument about truth in *Eine Duplik* (*A Rejoinder*), arguing that it is not truth, which every person possesses, or presumes to possess, but the sincere effort expended to get behind truth that determines a person's worth: "Nicht die Wahrheit, in deren Besitz irgendein Mensch ist, oder zu sein vermeinet, sondern die aufrichtige Mühe, die er angewandt hat, hinter die Wahrheit zu kommen, macht den Wert des Menschen." Throughout this chapter all Lessing citations will reference *Gotthold Ephraim Lessing. Werke und Briefe in zwölf Bänden,* ed. Wilfried Barner (Frankfurt am Main: Deutscher Klassiker Verlag, 1985–2001). Here, vol. 8, 61. The translations are my own.

7. The first half of the essay was written in 1776 and published in 1777; Nisbett suggests that Lessing may have written the second half in 1776 as well. The complete text was published for the first time in 1780, anonymously. Lessing's contemporaries and friends, Elise Reimarus, Moses Mendelssohn, Johann Gottfried Herder, and Friedrich Jacobi, had no doubt that Lessing was the author. Hugh Barr Nisbett, *Lessing. Eine Biographie,* tr. Karl S. Guthke (Munich: Beck, 2008), 746–47.

8. My assertion that Lessing writes from a Protestant theological perspective should of course be qualified by the fact that he very clearly is critical of Protestantism and promotes the development of a new religion of reason in this essay and elsewhere in his oeuvre. That Lessing considers this new religion of reason to be fundamentally Christian is suggested by the framework of his argument, by his rhetoric calling for "a new eternal gospel" ("das neue ewige Evangelium" [§86: 96]), and by an earlier fragmentary essay entitled *The Christendom of Reason* (*Das Christentum der Vernnunft,* 1754). Lessing eschewed the label "theologian," arguing that he could not commit to one dogma: "I am a lover of theology," Lessing famously stated, "not a theologian." *Lessing. Werke,* vol. 9, 57. Parenthetical references are to *Die Erziehung des Menschengeschlechts,* in *Lessing. Werke,* vol. 10, 75–99. I have included the paragraph number, followed by the page number. The translations are my own.

9. For good discussions of the theological context of the essay, see Nisbett, *Lessing,* 745–63; and Arno Schilson, "Lessing and Theology," in *A Companion*

to the Works of Gotthold Ephraim Lessing, ed. Barbara Fischer and Thomas C. Fox (Rochester, N.Y.: Camden House, 2005), 157–83.

10. The most famous of these inconsistencies is the contradiction between §4 and §77.

11. Lessing is not particularly original in advancing this model linking the history of religion to the history of human development. See also Nisbett, *Lessing,* 748.

12. Nisbett points out that Lessing's interest in the transmigration of souls was not especially unusual or eccentric in the last few decades of the eighteenth century. Ibid., 757–58.

13. Nisbett also notes the text's self-reflexivity here. Ibid., 752–53.

14. In an excellent and informative discussion, Willi Goetschel analyzes Lessing's interest in Jews not simply as "a token of good will," but as playing a "crucial role in his critical rethinking of both the claims of Christianity and the groundwork of modern national identity." Goetschel reads Lessing as exposing a mechanism of prejudice independent of its object (i.e., the Jews), and argues that any analysis of the representation of the Jewish characters in Lessing must remain circular, since the Jewish characters "all point back to their origin as Christian constructions." Goetschel, "Lessing and the Jews," 186, 203. In his analysis of the early Lessing, Barner likewise suggests that Lessing's main motivation in depicting Jews is not primarily philo-Semitic, but a critique of the contemporary Christian majority, and that the Jews are representative of discriminated minorities in general. Wilfried Barner, "Vorurteil, Emperie, Rettung. Der junge Lessing und die Juden," in *Juden und Judentum in der Literatur,* ed. Herbert A. Strauss and Christhard Hoffmann (Munich: Deutscher Taschenbuch Verlag, 1985), 64, 68.

15. Lessing presents a very different argument about the validity of Judaism as a contemporary religion in *Nathan the Wise* (1779), which was written after *The Education of the Human Race. The Education of the Human Race* was published in its entirety in 1780, after *Nathan* appeared.

16. The pertinent excerpt of Mendelssohn's critique, which appeared in *Jerusalem,* is reprinted in *Lessing. Werke,* vol. 10, 835–36.

17. The pertinent excerpt from the Preface to the published edition of *The Jews* is reprinted in *Lessing. Werke,* vol. 1, 1152.

18. Before the play was published, Lessing's friend Naumann reported that Lessing was working on a text called *The Jew (Der Jude).* It is unclear whether Lessing changed the title of the play to *The Jews (Die Juden),* or whether Naumann erred in his report. *Lessing. Werke,* vol. 1, 1152.

19. Och, *Imago judaica,* 73–74.

20. A copy of the decree is reproduced in Henry Wasserman, "Prussia," in *Encylopedia Judaica,* vol. 13 (New York: Macmillan, 1978), 1291.

21. Goetschel offers a differing interpretation of the significance of the beard decree to Lessing's comedy, arguing that Lessing's play demonstrates the "absurdity" of this law and illustrates that this legislation undermines Frederick's aspirations to be an enlightened ruler. Goetschel, "Lessing and the Jews," 190. Horowitz notes that German Jews "had generally been more

loyal to their beards than others in Western Europe." Elliott Horowitz, "The Early Eighteenth Century Confronts the Beard: Kabbalah and Jewish Self-Fashioning," *Jewish History* 8, no. 1–2 (1994): 109.

22. Parenthetical references are to *Die Juden*, in *Lessing. Werke*, vol. 1, 447–88. I have included scene number, followed by page number. The translations are my own.

23. In scene 16 the traveler—whose Jewish identity is as yet undisclosed to the other characters—returns to the physiognomy argument. Holding a "Jew beard" disguise to his chin, he asks whether he now looks like a Jew.

24. Most scholars read the text from the perspective of its characters and argue that the traveler's Jewish identity is not revealed until the end of the play. See, for example, Karl S. Guthke, "Lessing und das Judentum. Rezeption. Dramatik und Kritik. Krypto-Spinozismus," in *Judentum im Zeitalter der Aufklärung, Wolfenbütteler Studien zur Aufklärung*, vol. 4, ed. Günter Schulz (Wolfenbüttel: Jacobi, 1977), 244; Wilfried Barner, "Lessings *Die Juden* im Zusammenhang seines Frühwerks," in *Humanität und Dialog. Lessing und Mendelssohn in neuer Sicht*, ed. Ehrhard Bahr, Edward P. Harris, and Lawrence G. Lyon (Detroit: Wayne State University Press, 1982), 199; Och, *Imago judaica*, 79; Berghahn, *Grenzen der Toleranz*, 71; Goetschel, "Lessing and the Jews," 190; and Nisbett, *Lessing*, 98.

25. Lessing's response is included in *Lessing. Werke*, vol. 1, 489–97.

26. This argument is indebted in part to an analysis David Wellbery sketched out in a graduate seminar on Lessing at Stanford University on April 11, 1989.

27. The scene opens with the following exchange: "Der Reisende: 'Daß man Euch doch allezeit eine Stunde suchen muß, wenn man Euch haben will.' / Christoph: 'Sie scherzen, mein Herr. Nicht wahr, ich kann nicht mehr, als an einem Ort zugleich sein? Ist es also meine Schuld, daß Sie sich nicht an diesen Ort begeben? Gewiß Sie finden mich allezeit da, wo ich bin' " ("The Traveler: 'I always have to look for you for an hour when I want you.' / Christoph: 'Surely you're joking, sir. Isn't it true that I can't be in more than one place at the same time? Is it my fault that you're not here? You'll certainly always find me where I am' " (4: 455).

28. *Alfanz*, "der aus der Fremde gekommene Schalk, Betrüger." Gerhard Wahrig, *Deutsches Wörterbuch* (Munich: Bertelsman, 1991), 316.

29. The 1754 version of the text does not contain this line; Lessing added it in the revised version of 1767 (second edition 1770). *Lessing. Werke*, vol. 1, 1151, 1163.

30. Robertson suggests "on a skeptical reading" that Christoph has "unwittingly blurted out the truth: Jews can be admitted to the society of Enlightenment if they are not Jews, that is, if they have no distinctively Jewish features." Robertson, *The 'Jewish Question,'* 36.

31. *The Oxford Dictionary of the Jewish Religion*, ed. R. J. Zwi Werblowsky and Geoffrey Wigoder. New York and London: Oxford University Press, 1997. http://www.cirp.org/library/cultural/JewishEnc (accessed July 9, 2007).

32. Parenthetical references are to *Nathan der Weise,* in *Lessing. Werke,* vol. 9, 483–627. I have included act, scene, and page number. The translations are my own.

33. Other scholars have offered differing interpretations of the fact that Nathan is left out of the natural family constructed at the end of the play. To cite a few recent examples, Robertson argues that Nathan must earn his membership in a community of which the others are already members by merit of blood (Robertson, *The 'Jewish Question,'* 45). Berghahn sees this as a "mistake" that draws attention to the dialectic of Enlightenment (Berghahn, *Grenzen der Toleranz,* 123). Garloff suggests that Nathan be viewed not as an outsider here, but as part of a longer historical chain established in the text. Katja Garloff, "Sublimation and Its Discontents: Christian-Jewish Love in Lessing's *Nathan der Weise,*" *Lessing Yearbook/Jahrbuch* 36 (2004/2005): 63. Nisbett argues that Nathan is left out because Judiasm, unlike Christianity and Islam, constitutes not just a religious community, but also an ethnic one (Nisbett, *Lessing,* 805).

34. For a good discussion of the Lavatar affair see Hess, *Germans, Jews and the Claims of Modernity,* 97–105.

35. Atkins is one notable exception, arguing that Nathan tells the parable as an evasive answer to Saladin's question. Stuart Atkins, "The Parable of the Rings in Lessing's *Nathan,*" *Germanic Review* 26, no. 4 (1951): 262. Robertson likewise maintains that Nathan "sidesteps" Saladin's question by telling the tale (Robertson, *The 'Jewish Question,'* 42). Leventhal reads the parable itself as "in part a rhetorical device, a diversionary tactic" which functions to direct "the focus away from the question of the one 'true' belief or religion" and to redirect "focus toward the question of the basis for any belief whatsoever." Robert S. Leventhal, "The Parable as Performance: Interpretation, Cultural Transmission and Political Strategy in Lessing's *Nathan der Weise,*" in *The German Quarterly* 61, no. 4 (1988): 507–8. It is worth emphasizing that Nathan himself does not identify the story as a parable, but as a "Märchen," a "fairy tale," or a "Geschichtchen," a "little story" or "little history." This is significant, in that the genre designation to a large extent determines how the text itself should (and will) be read. For a recent interpretation of the ring tale that does analyze the text as a "Märchen," within the context of the theory of experiments in the eighteenth century, see Christine Weder, "Ein manipulierter Versuch: Das Märchen vom Experiment in Lessings *Nathan* und die naturwissenschaftliche Methodenlehre der 'durch Fleiß hervorgebrachten Erfahrung,'" *Deutsche Vierteljahrsschrift für Literaturwissenschaft und Geistesgeschichte* 82 (2008): 237–61.

36. Nathan draws a distinction here between "uralte Münze" and "neue Münze," intimating that coins from time immemorial may still have truth value, while modern coins do not. This distinction arguably is important from a religious point of view as well: the tale he is about to tell positions Judaism as the "uralte" religion, and then calls into question the significance of this originary status.

Chapter Two

1. Friedrich Schiller, *Die Sendung Moses*, in *Friedrich Schiller Werke und Briefe in zwölf Bänden, Band 6: Historische Schriften und Erzählungen I*, ed. Otto Dann (Frankfurt am Main: Deutscher Klassiker Verlag, 2000), 468. All parenthetical references to Schiller's essay are to this edition; the translations are my own. For an English version of the essay see *The Mission of Moses*, trans. George Gregory, in *Friedrich Schiller: Poet of Freedom*, vol. 2 (Washington, D.C.: Schiller Institute, 1988), 307–29.

2. Schiller's argument about the importance of Judaism to the Enlightenment is indebted to Herder. See Otto Dann, "Stellenkommentar" to *Die Sendung Moses* [n. 1], 872.

3. See, for example: Benno von Wiese, *Friedrich Schiller* (Stuttgart: Metzler, 1959, 1963), 348–49; Lesley Sharpe, *Schiller and the Historical Character: Presentation and Interpretation in the Historiographical Works and in the Historical Dramas* (New York: Oxford University Press, 1982); Karl-Heinz Hahn, "Schiller als Historiker," in *Aufklärung und Geschichte. Studien zur deutschen Geschichtswissenschaft im 18. Jahrhundert*, ed. Hans Erich Bödeker, Georg G. Iggers, Jonathan B. Knudsen, and Peter H. Reill (Göttingen: Vandenhoeck & Ruprecht, 1986), 388–415; Jürgen Eder, "Schiller als Historiker," in *Schiller-Handbuch*, ed. Helmut Koopmann (Kroner: Stuttgart, 1998) 653–98; and Otto Dann, "Schiller the Historian," in *A Companion to the Works of Friedrich Schiller*, ed. Steven D. Martinson (Rochester, N.Y.: Camden House, 2005), 67–86.

4. Jan Assmann, *Moses the Egyptian: The Memory of Egypt in Western Monotheism* (London and Cambridge, Mass.: Harvard University Press, 1977); Jan Assmann, "Vorwort" and "Nachwort" to Carl Leonhard Reinhold, *Die Hebräischen Mysterien, oder die älteste religiöse Freymaurerey*, ed. Jan Assmann (Neckargemünd: Mnemosyne, 2001), 5–10, 157–99; Wolf-Daniel Hartwich, *Die Sendung Moses: Von der Aufklärung bis Thomas Mann* (Munich: Fink, 1997); Yvonne Wübben, "Moses als Staatsgründer. Schiller und Reinhold über die Arkanpolitik der Spätaufklärung," *Aufklärung: Interdisziplinäres Jahrbuch zur Erforschung des 18. Jahrhunderts und seiner Wirkungsgeschichte* 15 (2003): 125–58; Klaus Weimar, "Der Effekt Geschichte," in *Schiller als Historiker*, ed. Otto Dann, Norbert Oellers, and Ernst Osterkamp (Stuttgart and Weimar: Metzler, 1995), 191–204; Regine Otto, "Schiller und Herder als Geschichtsschreiber. Annäherungen und Differenzen," in *Schiller als Historiker*, 293–307.

5. Alexander Mathäs, "Faith and Reason: Schiller's 'Die Sendung Moses,'" *The German Quarterly* 81, no. 3 (2008): 283–301.

6. Otto Dann, "Stellenkommentar" to *Die Sendung Moses* [n. 1], 871. Regine Otto notes that Schiller rarely mentioned his Jena lectures (Otto, "Schiller und Herder als Geschichtsschreiber," 306).

7. As Liliane Weissberg points out, Freud frequently quotes or alludes to Schiller without identifying him by name, making him one of Freud's most-cited authors. Liliane Weissberg, "Freuds Schiller," in *Friedrich Schiller und der Weg in die Moderne*, ed. Walter Hinderer (Würzburg: Königshausen &

Neumann, 2006), 422. For a brief discussion of Freud's reception of Schiller's essay see Lewis W. Brandt, "Freud and Schiller," *Psychoanalysis and the Psychoanalytic Review* 46, no. 4 (1959): 97–101. For an elegant analysis of Freud's treatment of Moses see Yosef Hayim Yerushalmi, *Freud's Moses: Judaism Terminable and Interminable* (New Haven and London: Yale University Press, 1991).

8. For example, Benno von Wiese, who calls Schiller a "victim" of Enlightenment prejudice, a fact that "requires no mention": "Daß Schiller mit all diesen Konstruktionen, was die historischen Tatsachen betrifft, ein Opfer der Vorurteile der Aufklärung geworden ist, bedarf keiner Erwähnung" (von Wiese, *Friedrich Schiller,* 349). Wolf-Daniel Hartwich comments in passing that "neither Reinhold nor Schiller were philosemites" (Hartwich, *Die Sendung Moses,* 33). Klaus Berghahn, who reads Schiller's essay as pro-Jewish, concedes that in Schiller's praise of the Hebrews, mental reservations "shimmer through" that point to the "limits of Enlightenment": "Bei aller Verehrung der Hebräer schimmern auch bei Schiller noch mentale Vorbehalte durch, die auf die Grenzen der Aufklärung verweisen." Klaus L. Berghahn, *Grenzen der Toleranz. Juden und Christen im Zeitalter der Aufklärung* (Cologne, Weimar, Vienna: Böhlau, 2000), 66. In comparison, Ritchie Robertson directly addresses the essay's anti-Semitism. Robertson, *The 'Jewish Question,'* 24–25.

9. Goethe, too, will later use the Exodus story as a vehicle for his contribution to the debate about the "Jewish Question." See Karin Schutjer, "German Epic/Jewish Epic: Goethe's Exodus Narrative in *Hermann und Dorothea* and 'Israel in der Wüste,'" *The German Quarterly* 80, no. 2 (2007): 165–84.

10. Ludwig Geiger, "Schiller und die Juden," in Geiger, *Die deutsche Literatur und die Juden* (Berlin: Reimer, 1910), 125–60; Alfred D. Low, *Jews in the Eyes of Germans: From the Enlightenment to Imperial Germany* (Philadelphia: Institute for the Study of Human Issues, 1979), 87–92; Berghahn, *Grenzen der Toleranz,* 65–68. Norbert Oellers offers a more qualified assessment, asserting that Schiller was not an opponent of Judaism, but was far from a "friend of Judaism." Norbert Oellers, "Goethe und Schiller in ihrem Verhältnis zum Judentume," in *Conditio Judaica. Judentum, Antisemitismus und deutschsprachige Literatur vom 18. Jahrhundert bis zum 1. Weltkrieg,* Part I, ed. Hans Otto Horch and Horst Denkler (Tübingen: Niemeyer, 1988), 121.

11. See Geiger, "Schiller und die Juden"; Low, *Jews in the Eyes of Germans;* Noellers, "Goethe und Schiller"; and Berghahn, *Grenzen der Toleranz.* Schiller's fragmentary novel *Der Geisterseher* (*The Ghost-Seer,* first published serially in 1787–1789) arguably also invokes the myth of the Wandering Jew in the figure of the Armenian.

12. See also Robertson, *The 'Jewish Question,'* 27–28. Robertson also astutely argues that "Through Spiegelberg, the frustrated young Schiller also projects his own ambitions, thus simultaneously expressing, disavowing, and caricaturing them" (28).

13. Philipp F. Veit, "The Strange Case of Moritz Spiegelberg," *Germanic Review* 44 (1969): 171–85; for a German version of this article see Veit,

"Moritz Spiegelberg: Eine Charakterstudie zu Schillers *Räubern,*" *Jahrbuch der deutschen Schillergesellschaft* 17 (1973): 273–90. Gunnar Och questions Spiegelberg's Jewishness. Gunnar Och, *Imago judaica. Juden und Judentum im Spiegel der deutschen Literatur 1750–1812* (Würzburg: Königshausen & Neumann, 1995), 214–19.

14. Friedrich Schiller, *Die Räuber,* in *Friedrich Schiller Werke und Briefe in zwölf Bänden, Band 2: Dramen I,* ed. Gerhard Kluge (Frankfurt am Main: Deutscher Klassiker Verlag, 2000). The translations are my own.

15. For a nuanced discussion of circumcision and castration in anti-Semitic discourse see James Shapiro, *Shakespeare and the Jews* (New York: Columbia University Press, 1996), 113–30.

16. Sander L. Gilman, *The Jew's Body* (New York and London: Routledge, 1991), 99–100, 171–74. Grimm's Dictionary identifies a "Lappland nose" as thick and pressed flat, and cites Schiller's text as an example. *Deutsches Wörterbuch von Jacob Grimm und Wilhelm Grimm,* vol. 6 (Leipzig: Hirzel, 1885), 201.

17. The following discussion of Schiller reception among German Jews is based on Andreas B. Kilcher, "Ha-Gila: Hebräische und jiddishe Schiller-Übersetzungen im 19. Jahrhundert," *Monatshefte* 100, no. 1 (2008): 67–87.

18. Ibid., 83–84.

19. See also Manfred Misch, "Schiller und die Religion," in *Schiller heute,* ed. Hans-Jörg Knobloch and Helmut Koopmann (Tübingen: Stauffenberg, 1996), 33–35; and Norbert Oellers, Schiller und die Religion," in *Friedrich Schiller und der Weg in die Moderne,* ed. Walter Hinderer (Würzburg: Königshausen & Neumann, 2006), 176.

20. Friedrich Schiller, *Was heisst und zu welchem Ende studiert man Universalgeschichte?,* in *Friedrich Schiller Werke und Briefe in zwölf Bänden, Band 6: Historische Schriften und Erzählungen I,* ed. Otto Dann (Frankfurt am Main: Deutscher Klassiker Verlag, 2000), 411–31. All parenthetical references to the essay are to this edition; the translations are my own. For a good discussion of the origins of Schiller's notion of universal history see Hahn, "Schiller als Historiker." Schiller's inaugural lecture was a major event in Jena: several hundred students attended. Enthusiasm for the lectures dropped off as the series proceeded. Schiller was not known for his exciting lecture style, although his Swabian dialect apparently endeared him to some students.

21. Friedrich Schiller, *On the Aesthetic Education of Man in a Series of Letters (English and German Facing),* ed. and trans. Elizabeth M. Wilkinson and L. A. Willoughby (Oxford and New York: Oxford University Press, 1967). See especially Letter 6 and Letter 9.

22. The following discussion of the provenance of Schiller's essay is based on Jan Assmann's "Vorwort" and "Nachwort" to Carl Leonhard Reinhold, *Die Hebräischen Mysterien,* and Jan Assmann, *Moses the Egyptian,* 122–39.

23. The first two lectures were published in a Freemason journal; the complete text then was published in book form. For a brief discussion of the differences between these editions see Wübben, "Moses als Staatsgründer," 136–38.

24. Assmann, "Nachwort," 160.

25. Friedrich Schiller, *Etwas über die erste Menschengesellschaft nach dem Leitfaden der Mosaische Urkunde,* in *Friedrich Schiller Werke und Briefe in zwölf Bänden, Band 6: Historische Schriften und Erzählungen I,* ed. Otto Dann (Frankfurt am Main: Deutscher Klassiker Verlag, 2000), 432.

26. "Ich muß die Leser dieses Aufsatzes auf eine Schrift von ähnlichem Inhalt: *Über die ältesten hebräischen Mysterien von Br. Decius:* verweisen, welche einen berühmten und verdienstvollen Schriftsteller zum Verfasser hat, und woraus ich verschiedene der hier zum Grund gelegten Ideen und Daten genommen habe" (474). Schiller inaccurately cites the title of Reinhold's text, which was published as *Die Hebräischen Mysterien, oder die älteste religiöse Freymaurerey.* Hartwich (*Die Sendung Moses*) and Wübben ("Moses als Staatsgründer") both suggest that it may have been politically prudent to remain anonymous at the time: Freemasons were considered politically subversive, and were implicated in plotting the French Revolution.

27. For a thoughtful discussion and a comparison of Schiller's and Reinhold's texts see Hartwich, *Die Sendung Moses,* 21–49.

28. Assmann comments that Schiller "not only used, but paraphrased—one could almost say plagiarized" Reinhold's book. Assmann, *Moses,* 117.

29. In a letter to Körner dated June 11, 1789, Schiller complains he is spending astonishing amounts of time and energy on the lectures. *Friedrich Schiller Werke und Briefe in zwölf Bänden, Band 11, Briefe I, 1772–1795,* ed. Georg Kurscheidt (Frankfurt am Main: Deutscher Klassiker Verlag, 2000), 846.

30. Hartwich, *Die Sendung Moses,* 30.

31. Assmann, *Moses,* 126; see also Assmann, "Nachwort," 184. Wübben ("Moses als Staatsgründer") and Mathäs ("Faith and Reason") correctly take issue with Assmann's and Hartwich's analyses of Schiller's essay as largely replicating Reinhold's work, but do not consider in enough detail the implications of the fact that Schiller *does* lift large portions of his argument from Reinhold. Wübben analyzes Reinhold's and Schiller's works in the larger context of the late Enlightenment discussion of arcane practices.

32. Reinhold, *Die Hebräischen Mysterien,* 13–14.

33. Weimar, "Der Effekt Geschichte," 192. Weimar argues that Schiller thereby effects a critique of all revelation. Given Schiller's indirectness in his delineation of the relationship between Judaism, Christianity, and Islam, which I will discuss below, I see little textual evidence to support Weimar's assertion, and read the critique as pertaining to the specifically Mosaic context that Schiller identifies in the essay.

34. Assmann, *Moses,* 96.

35. This was a common argument in Enlightenment thought. See Assmann, *Moses,* 91–143, and Hartwich, *Die Sendung Moses,* 21–29, for brief discussions of Judaism and Moses in Enlightenment discourse.

36. Similarly, throughout the essay Schiller refers to "the Hebrews" ("die Ebräer") rather than "the Jews" ("die Juden"), thereby drawing a clear linguistic demarcation between "the Hebrews" of old and the Jews of today. Schiller does use the terms "Jewish state" (451) and "nation of the Jews" (455). Reinhold freely uses the term "Jews" ("Juden") throughout his study.

37. Reinhold questions how truth became "der gemeinste Besitz des dümmsten und bösartigen Pöbels [. . .], der uns aus der ältern und neueren Geschichte bekannt ist." Reinhold, *Die Hebräischen Mysterien*, 34.

38. See also ibid., 86.

39. With the metaphor of the "shattered vessel" Schiller alludes to Jeremiah 48, where the Lord shatters Moab like an undesirable vessel as punishment for its arrogance and degeneracy. Hartwich comments that Schiller's use of metaphors of water transport to describe the historical role of Judaism is linked to the fact that the water transportation system constituted the economic basis on which Egyptian civilization was founded, and was also part of Moses' education: "Schiller beschreibt die historische Rolle des Judentums in der Metaphorik der Wasserleitungskunst, mit der die Ägypter die ökonomischen Grundlagen ihrer Hochkulter schufen und die auch zum Bildungsplan Moses gehörte." Hartwich, *Die Sendung Moses*, 29.

40. See also Weimar, "Der Effekt Geschichte," 193. Reinhold, *Die Hebräischen Mysterien*, 27.

41. Dann notes that Schiller likely took the figures of two million Jews and six hundred thousand battle-ready men from Voltaire, but that his source for the four hundred years is not clear (Dann, "Stellenkommentar," 872–73). The biblical account begins with a listing of the names of the sons of Israel who came to Egypt, seventy in number. The population then expanded, fulfilling the Abrahamic covenant: "But the sons of Israel were fruitful and increased greatly, and multiplied, and became exceedingly mighty, so that the land was filled with them" (Exodus 1:7).

42. See Jacob Katz, "A State Within a State, the History of an anti-Semitic Slogan," in Katz, *Emancipation and Assimilation: Studies in Modern Jewish History* (Farnborough: Gregg, 1972), 47–76. Katz notes that the phrase was initially not applied to the Jews.

43. Schiller follows the biblical account here. "Now a new king arose over Egypt, who did not know Joseph. And he said to his people, 'Behold, the people of the sons of Israel are more and mightier than we. Come, let us deal wisely with them, lest they multiply and in the event of war, they also join themselves to those who hate us, and fight against us, and depart from the land.' So they appointed taskmasters over them to afflict them with hard labor" (Exodus 1:8–11).

44. "Diese barbarische Behandlung hinderte aber nicht, daß sie sich nicht immer stärker ausbreiteten" (453).

45. For an account of how leprosy came to be associated with the Jews, see Assmann, *Moses*, 42–44.

46. "Wie allgemein dieses Übel gewesen, erhellt schon aus der Menge der Vorkehrungen, die der Gesetzgeber dagegen gemacht hat; und das einstimmige Zeugnis der Profanskribenten, des Egyptiers Manetho, des Diodor von Sicilien, des Tacitus, des Lysimachus, Strabo und vieler andern, welche von der Jüdischen Nation fast gar nichts, als diese Volkskrankheit des Aussatzes kennen, beweist, wie allgemein und wie tief der Eindruck davon bei den Egyptern gewesen sei" (454).

47. "Das tausendjährige Familienübel, / Die aus dem Nylthal mitgeshleppte Plage, der altegyptisch ungesunde Glauben." Heinrich Heine, "Das neue Israelitische Hospital zu Hamburg," in *Heinrich Heine Historisch-Kritische Gesamtausgabe der Werke* (Düsseldorfer Ausgabe), ed. Manfred Windfuhr, vol. 2, *Neue Gedichte*, ed. Elisabeth Benton (Hamburg: Hoffman and Campe, 1983), 117. The translation is my own.

48. "Gegen Menschen, die der Zorn der Götter auf eine so schreckliche Art ausgezeichnet, hielt man sich alles für erlaubt, und man trug kein Bedenken, ihnen die heiligsten Menschenrechte zu entziehen" (454).

49. "Auf diesem Wege freilich mußte die egyptische Regierung doch zuletzt ihren Zweck durchsetzen, und wenn kein Retter sich ins Mittel schlug, die Nation der Juden in wenigen Generationen gänzlich vertilgt haben" (455).

50. Low, *Jews in the Eyes of Germans*, 87–92, here p. 89.

51. See also n. 37.

52. The verb for "murder" has a separate root in Hebrew (*resh-tsade-het*), as does the verb for "kill" (*he-resh-gimel*). I am grateful to Gary Rendsburg for help with the Hebrew citation.

53. The *Geist-Geiz* distinction illustrates *in nuce* the New Testament opposition between spirit and letter, *Geist und Buchstabe*.

54. "Der wahre Gott bekümmert sich um die Hebräer ja nicht mehr als um irgend ein andres Volk.—Der wahre Gott konnte nicht für sie kämpfen, ihnen zu Gefallen die Gesetze der Natur nicht umstürzen" (468).

55. "Freilich konnte er [Moses] seinen Hebräern mit dieser neuen Religion nicht auch zugleich den Verstand mitgeben, sie zu fassen, und darin hatten die Eyptischen Epopten einen großen Vorzug vor ihnen voraus. Die Epopten erkannten die Wahrheit durch ihre Vernunft; die Hebräer konnten höchstens nur blind daran glauben" (474).

Chapter Three

1. "Antisemitism was not merely a singular aspect of a worldview typical of a certain cultural camp in Germany; rather, it was an unequivocal indicator of that culture. By the late nineteenth century, it had a unique role in demarcating the borderline between the two major positions in the German public sphere, one that it had never had before." Shulamit Volkov, *Germans, Jews, and Antisemites: Trials in Emancipation* (Cambridge, U.K., and New York: Cambridge University Press, 2006), 115. Volkov argues that anti-Semitism becomes the hallmark of the right, opposed to the "camp of emancipation," which supported "democracy, parliamentarism, and an array of economic and cultural goods associated with modernization" (115). See also Birgit Erdle, who draws the same connection between Arnim and Volkov. Erdle, "'Über die Kennzeichen des Judenthums': Die Rhetorik der Unterscheidung in einem phantasmatischen Text von Achim von Arnim, *German Life and Letters* 49, no. 2 (1996): 157.

2. Cited in Amos Elon, *The Pity of It All: A Portrait of the German-Jewish Epoch 1743–1933* (New York: Picador, 2002), 98.

3. For an informative discussion of Grattenauer see Hess, *Germans, Jews and the Claims of Modernity*, 173–74. While Elon argues that Grattenauer

may have been the first to introduce the concept of "race" into the discourse of anti-Semitism (Elon, *The Pity of It All*, 97–98), Hess demonstrates that the notion of "race" already was evident in the Jewish emancipation debate at the end of the eighteenth century, before the publication of Grattenauer's pamphlet.

4. Elon, *The Pity of It All*, 98.

5. For nuanced discussions of Arnim's ambivalent attitudes toward Jews and the "Jewish Question" see Heinz Härtl, "Romantischer Antisemitismus: Arnim und die 'Tischgesellschaft,'" *Weimarer Beiträge* 33, no. 7 (1987): 1159–73; Ritchie Robertson, "Antisemitismus und Ambivalenz: Zu Achim von Arnims Erzählung 'Die Majoratsherren,'" in *Romantische Identitätskonstruktionen: Nation, Geschichte, und (Auto-)Biographie,* ed. Sheila Dickson and Walter Pape (Tübingen: Niemeyer, 2003), 51–63; and Katja Garloff, "Figures of Love in Romantic Antisemitism: Achim von Arnim," *The German Quarterly* 80, no. 4 (2007): 427–48.

6. Arnim, "Vorschlag zu einer deutschen Tischgesellschaft," in Ludwig Achim von Arnim, *Werke und Briefwechsel, Historisch-Kritische Ausgabe,* vol. 11, *Texte der deutschen Tischgesellschaft,* ed. Stefan Nienhaus (Tübingen: Niemeyer, 2008), 4–5. The translations are my own. Hereafter references to this edition will be cited as *KA*.

7. In his 1815 speech to the Table Society Arnim reports that he had tried to open up membership to converted Jews at the first meeting, but was voted down (*KA* 206). This may well be the case, and many scholars cite this passage as evidence of Arnim's ambivalent anti-Semitism, but it is significant that the initial proposal for the Table Society, penned by Arnim, limits membership to those "born into the Christian religion" (*KA* 4–5); in other words, Arnim himself excluded converted Jews from the Table Society in his initial proposal. Nienhaus notes that when Fichte became speaker of the Table Society in 1811, he tried to distance the Table Society from this anti-Semitic agenda (*KA* 265). Arnim's 1815 speech underscores precisely how central the anti-Jewish agenda was to the Society in its inception.

8. For a discussion of Prussian and German nationalism in the Table Society see Nienhaus, *KA* 259–62. Garloff ("Figures of Love," 429–30) emphasizes the tension between Prussian patriotism and German nationalism in the Table Society.

9. Most extant documents written by its members refer to the club simply as the German Table Society.

10. Arnim himself regarded the Table Society as the heir of the salon culture (*KA* 252).

11. See also Klaus Berghahn, *Die Grenzen der Toleranz. Juden und Christen im Zeitalter der Aufklärung* (Cologne, Weimar, Vienna: Böhlau, 2000), 285.

12. Notably, some leading figures of Berlin's intelligentsia, including Wilhelm von Humboldt, distanced themselves from the Table Society because of its anti-Jewish stance.

13. Jürgen Knaack has rectified the common misconception that the Table Society was a socially conservative, backward-looking, aristocratic men's club.

While Knaack corrects the record on the constitutional intentions and social structure of the Table Society, he does not address its anti-Semitism. Jürgen Knaack, *Achim von Arnim—Nicht nur Poet* (Darmstadt: Thesen Verlag, 1976). For an in-depth discussion of the history of the Table Society see Stefan Nienhaus, *Geschichte der deutschen Tischgesellschaft* (Tübingen: Niemeyer, 2003). A concise summary of Nienhaus's study appears in the critical edition of Arnim's "Table Society Writings," edited by Nienhaus. See especially *KA* 246–68. Nienhaus (*Geschichte*, 7) notes that the Table Society met until at least 1834.

14. *KA* 205, 207.

15. *KA* 246.

16. *KA* 154.

17. *KA* 151.

18. The speech is reproduced in the critical edition of Arnim's Table Society writings. Clemens Brentano, "Der Philister vor, in und nach der Geschichte," *KA* 38–90. Brentano's enormously popular speech was published and circulated in Berlin soon after it was presented.

19. See also Oesterle, who astutely argues that "Philistine" and "Jew" constitute a "unity in their opposition" in Brentano's speech. Günter Oesterle, "Juden, Philister und romantische Intellektuelle. Überlegungen zum Antisemitismus in der Romantik," *Athenäum: Jahrbuch für Romantik* 2 (1992): 58.

20. The precise date of the speech is uncertain. It was presented sometime between March 13 and June 1811 (*KA* 362).

21. *KA* 153. The reference to dueling alludes to the Itzig affair. Arnim had had a famous run-in with Moritz Itzig. Arnim showed up at a party given by Sara Levy, uninvited and inappropriately attired, and behaved poorly, mocking the guests. Levy's nephew, Moritz Itzig, wrote Arnim a letter demanding an apology, and Arnim sent him a derisive response. Itzig then challenged Arnim to a duel. Arnim declined, on the grounds that he was not obligated to accept the Jew's challenge. Itzig then attacked Arnim in a public bathhouse. The case ended up in court, with Arnim looking rather foolish. For a discussion of the Itzig affair see Deborah Hertz, *How Jews Became Germans: The History of Conversion and Assimilation in Berlin* (New Haven and London: Yale University Press, 2007), 82–87.

22. Heinz Härtl, "Romanischer Antisemitismus," labels the speech the "worst anti-Semitic text of German Romanticism" (1162) because of its joking, lighthearted tone and because it was presumably received in the same vein.

23. See also Hartwich, who argues that the speech is simply an assemblage of established anti-Semitic slurs, with no particular rhetorical structure or argumentative value. Wolf-Daniel Hartwich, *Romantischer Antisemitismus: Von Klopstock bis Richard Wagner* (Göttingen: Vandenhoeck & Ruprecht, 2005), 155.

24. See also Oesterle, who argues that language becomes deed: "die Sprache wird Tat," "Juden, Philister und romantische Intellektuelle," 63. Gisela Henckmann argues that the fact that Arnim chose not to publish the speech is evidence

that it should not be taken seriously. Gisela Henckmann, "Das Problem des 'Antismitismus' bei Achim von Arnim," *Aurora* 46 (1986): 62. Henckmann has been rightly criticized in the scholarship for her efforts to defend Arnim against charges of anti-Semitism; at the same time, she raises a serious question, echoed by other scholars in various forms, with regard to Arnim's decision not to publish the speech. This may have been a form of self-censorship under the French occupation, and Arnim, who did moderate his tone on the "Jewish Question" in later years, may have subsequently decided to distance himself from the speech. Published or not, the speech was part of the public record at the time, and Arnim obviously took its composition very seriously: four lengthy variants to the speech exist. The variants are reprinted in *KA* 129–47.

25. This is the case even for analyses of Arnim's anti-Semitism. Erdle's cogent essay "'Über die Kennzeichen des Judenthums'" is a significant exception.

26. The text of *Ueber die Kennzeichen des Judenthums* appears in *KA* 107–28. Parenthetical page references refer to this edition. The translations are my own. Erdle also comments on the dramatic aspect of the text, calling it a "revue." Ibid., 147.

27. Erdle interprets this "blackness" or "darkness" in conjunction with the text's semantic register of "hiding," arguing that the metaphor points to one of the essay's central themes, the indistinguishability of Christian and Jew (ibid., 149). I propose a different reading: "black" is an anti-Semitic stereotype in eighteenth- and nineteenth-century German discourse, and Arnim explicitly invokes this stereotype later in the essay (113).

28. The very same mechanisms Arnim ascribes to the Jews sneaking into Christian society arguably characterize the rhetorical techniques he himself uses to define the Jews: *Verstellung* (literally: dis-placement that is also a *mis*-placement) and *Wechselverhältnisse* (relations of exchange). Using *Verstellung*, Arnim displaces "the Jew" onto "the Caraiban" and "the cannibal" and then constructs an equivalence of exchange among these signifiers by citing a putative genealogy that establishes the Caraibans and cannibals as descendants of the Jews.

29. The German verb I have translated as "cackling" is *auerte*, a neologism. Nienhaus notes that in Western Yiddish the word for "to pray" is "oren," and he surmises that Arnim intentionally perverts the Yiddish to be derogatory (*KA* 366).

30. Garloff offers a differing interpretation of the fact that Arnim on the one hand tries to construct a scientific test for Jewishness grounded in the Jew's body, and on the other formulates a projection theory of anti-Semitism, arguing that Arnim's essay repeatedly admits its own impossibility ("Figures of Love," 430–33). I agree with this astute observation, but maintain that the tension in Arnim's essay is resolved on the rhetorical level of the text.

31. Erdle argues that Arnim attempts to produce an ethnic and national German homogeneity here ("'Über die Kennzeichen des Judenthums,'" 151).

32. As an example of apophasis in recent American politics during the Clinton-Bush presidential campaign, consider the statement made about Bill Clinton by Mary Matalin, the Bush campaign's political director: "The larger

issue is that Clinton is evasive and slick. We have never said to the press that he is a philandering, pot-smoking, draft-dodger. There's nothing nefarious or subliminal going on." (Quoted in *The Guardian*, 1992). http: grammar.about .com/od/ab/apophasis.htm (accessed September 1, 2009).

33. *KA* 381; Helmut Walser Smith, *The Continuities of German History: Nation, Religion, and Race across the Long Nineteenth Century*, 75 and 81.

34. See Jacob Katz, *Jews and Freemasons in Europe, 1723–1939*, tr. Leonard Oschry (Cambridge, Mass.: Harvard University Press, 1970).

35. See also Dorothea E. von Mücke, *The Seduction of the Occult and the Rise of the Fantastic Tale* (Stanford, Calif.: Stanford University Press, 2003), 212–18. Von Mücke offers an insightful analysis of "the uses of blood" in *Isabella of Egypt* and emphasizes the anti-Semitic dimension of the novella, concentrating on "blood," i.e., racial anti-Semitism. I suggest a broader reading of Arnim's conception of anti-Semitism here.

36. For an incisive reading of the frame narrative, *The Reconcilation at the Summer Resort* (*Die Versöhnung in der Sommerfrische*) see Garloff, "Figures of Love."

37. "Zueignung an meine Freunde Jakob Grimm und Wilhelm Grimm," *Die Novellensammlung von 1812*, in Achim von Arnim, *Werke in sechs Bänden*, vol. 3, *Sämtliche Erzählungen 1802–1817*, ed. Renate Moering (Frankfurt am Main: Deutscher Klassiker Verlag, 1990). Subsequent references to *Isabella of Egypt* will be to this edition; the novella appears on pp. 622–744. The translations are my own. The critical Arnim edition of *Isabella* has not yet been published. For discussions of Arnim's historical and legendary sources see Peter Horst Neumann, "Legende, Sage und Geschichte in Achim von Arnims 'Isabella von Ägypten,'" *Jahrbuch der deutschen Schillergesellschaft* 12 (1968): 296–314; and Ernst Schürer, "Quellen und Fluss der Geschichte: Zur Interpretation von Arnims *Isabella von Ägypten*," in *Lebendige Form, Festschrift für Heinrich E. K. Henel*, ed. Jeffrey L. Sammons and Ernst Schürer (Munich: Fink, 1970), 189–210.

38. Cited in Azade Seyhan, *Representation and Its Discontents: The Critical Legacy of German Romanticism* (Berkeley and Los Angeles: University of California Press, 1992), 127.

39. Seyhan argues that in the narrative "the line between the real and the imaginary, the historical and the fictional, and the discursive and the occult is canceled and everything is subsumed by poetic representation." Her analysis focuses on the text's doubling strategies, but does not take "the Jewish" to be a fundamental structuring principle of the narrative (ibid., 127).

40. Saul notes that a Prussian edict of 1724 mandated that Gypsies and robbers caught stealing be hanged without question. Nicholas Saul, *Gypsies and Orientalism in German Literature and Anthropology of the Long Nineteenth Century* (London: Legenda, 2007), 4.

41. The "French" provenance of these Gypsies arguably marks them doubly as Jews, since, as indicated in the discussion of the origins of the Table Society above, hostility toward the French during the Napoleonic era was displaced onto the Jews.

42. Heinrich Moritz Gottlieb Grellmann, *Die Zigeuner. Ein historischer Versuch über die Lebensart und Verfassung, Sitten und Schiksale dieses Volks in Europa, nebst ihrem Ursprung* (Dessau und Leipzig, 1783). Cited in Arnim, *Werke in sechs Bänden,* vol. 3, 1254. In drawing this connection between Gypsies, Jews, and Egyptians, Arnim arguably also invokes the ancient tradition that casts Jews as leprous Egyptians, banished from their country. Robertson, *The 'Jewish Question,'* 23.

43. Arnim uses the word "Zigeuner" ("Gypsies"), precisely to invoke stereotypical associations. For this reason the accurate translation is "Gypsies" rather than "Roma." Arnim likely was familiar with Johann Jacob Schudt's anti-Semitic treatise *Jüdische Merkwürdigkeiten* (1714), which poses the question whether the Gypsies are descended from the Jews. A number of critics have commented on the connection between Gypsies and Jews in the narrative in terms of similarity and opposition, but do not analyze the rhetorical implications of this connection to the same extent that I do. At the same time, some of these scholars provide excellent discussions of the status of Gypsies in nineteenth-century discourse. See especially Neumann, "Legende, Sage und Geschichte"; Claudia Breger, *Ortlosigkeit des Fremden. 'Zigeunerinnen' und 'Zigeuner' in der deutschsprachigen Literatur um 1800* (Cologne, Weimar, Vienna: Böhlau Verlag, 1998), 265–301; and Saul, *Gypsies and Orientalism,* 30–32. For an excellent reading of *Isabella of Egypt* that situates the novella within the context of contemporaneous debates about the connection between Gypsies and Jews, see Cathy Gelbin, *The Golem Returns: From German Romantic Literature to Global Jewish Culture, 1808–2008* (Ann Arbor: University of Michigan Press, 2011), 29–34.

44. "Die Zigeuner waren damals in der Verfolgung, welche die vertriebenen Juden ihnen zuzogen, die sich für Zigeuner abgaben, um geduldet zu werden, schon sündlich verwildert; oft hatte Herzog Michael darüber geklagt und alle seine Klugheit angewendet, sie aus dieser Zerstreuung nach ihrem Vaterland zurückzuführen" (624).

45. As numerous scholars have noted, Isabella, and not her son, leads the Gypsies back to Egypt. It is worth pointing out that Isabella, herself the product of a mixed marriage—her mother was Belgian (628) and her father a Gypsy—needs Charles's Christian "seed" to become the leader of her people, and to become the "pure" symbol of innocence and leadership at the end of the narrative.

46. See n. 21.

47. "In der Mitte des Zimmers hing eine wunderliche gedrehte Messingskrone, sie hatte sonst die aufgehobene jüdische Synagoge zu Gent beleuchtet, jetzt steckte ein gewundenes buntes Wachslicht zu Ehren der Mutter Gottes darauf" (661–62).

48. The Gypsies become equated with Abyssinians at the end of the text (740), thereby underscoring the amorphous nature of the signifiers "Gypsy" and "Jew" in this text.

49. See also Hartwich, who argues that when Arnim draws a narrative connection between the mandrake root man and Germany's current problems, he

is not citing a Jewish stereotype, but a general mythical symbol. Hartwich bolsters this assertion by noting that Charles V was financed by Fugger money, and not by Jewish lenders (*Romantischer Antisemitismus,* 187). Hartwich does not recognize the extensive anti-Semitic semantic register that runs throughout the text, and the argument about Charles V's finances does not take into account Arnim's programmatic distortion of historical facts.

50. Arnim argues elsewhere too that it is impossible for Jews to truly convert to Christianity. In his "student play" *Halle and Jerusalem* (1811) Arnim converts Ahasverus to Christianity, but the Wandering Jew still bears "powerful traces" of his Jewishness, as he himself notes at the Church of the Holy Sepulchure. Ludwig Achim von Arnim, *Halle und Jerusalem,* in *Dramen von Clemens Brentano und Ludwig Achim von Arnim,* ed. Paul Kluckhohn (Reclam: Leipzig, 1938), 259. In *The Reconcilation at the Summer Resort,* the frame narrative Arnim drafted to introduce the novella collection of 1812, the Enlightened Jew Rabuni gives voice to an anti-assimilationist political agenda clearly designed as a refutation of Dohm's *On the Civic Betterment of the Jews.* Even when given a fair chance, Rabuni argues, Jews are unable to become effective or trustworthy citizens, and he indicates that he is unable to become truly Christian. Arnim of course intensifies his anti-assimilationist critique by having a Jew voice these words. *Die Versöhnung in der Sommerfrische,* in Arnim, *Werke in sechs Bänden,* vol. 3, 554–61.

51. Friedrichsmeyer also comments on the sham nature of Isabella's innocence in her excellent reading of the novella, and hence argues that "despite its idealization of Isabella, this novella should in no way be construed as intimating that von Arnim is dreaming of a woman to lead the German-speaking peoples to their destiny as a nation-state." Sara Friedrichsmeyer, "Romantic Nationalism: Achim von Arnim's Gypsy Princess Isabella," in *Gender and Germanness: Cultural Productions of Nation,* ed. Patricia Herminghouse and Magda Mueller (Providence and Oxford: Berhgahn, 1997), 60. See also von Mücke, who offers a differing interpretation: stressing the importance of the Astraea legend to the narrative, von Mücke argues for a gendered reading in which Arnim does privilege the feminine as a ground for a future unified Germany (*The Seduction of the Occult,* 199–212). Von Mücke's cogent analysis does not take into account the fact that the text programmatically undermines Isabella's innocence, and hence its own truth value, yet she rightly emphasizes the importance of Isabella as a political symbol of the future.

52. Neumann, "Legende, Sage und Geschichte," 310–11.

Chapter Four

The title of this chapter, "Reading Blood," is a paraphrase of a line from *Die Judenbuche,* in *Annette von Droste-Hülshoff Historisch-Kritische Ausgabe,* 13 vols., ed. Walter Huge (Tübingen: Niemeyer, 1978–1988), vol. 5.1, 3. Hereafter cited as *HKA.*

1. The theme of hidden Jews in literature is, of course, not new, and we have explored this motif extensively in previous chapters. For a study of the "camouflaged Jew" in relation to Jewish emancipation and assimilation see

Charlene A. Lea, *Emancipation, Assimilation and Stereotype: The Image of the Jew in German and Austrian Drama (1800–1850)* (Bonn: Bouvier, 1978). In her reading of Balzac's "Sarrasine," Esther Rashkin uses her psychoanalytic theory of the phantom to trace hidden Jewish identity by reconstructing discursive elements of Balzac's text and situating her analysis within the historical context of Jewish emancipation and assimilation in nineteenth-century France. Rashkin proposes a paradigm for interpreting other literary texts, stating that a major result of her reading of "Sarrasine" is "to suggest how psychoanalysis can participate in the exploration and exposure, within certain literary works, of heretofore unseen narratives of religious identity and prejudice." Esther Rashkin, "Tracing Phantoms: Religious Secrets and the (Un)veiling of Jewish Identity in Balzac's 'Sarrasine,' " *Religion and the Arts* 1, no. 4 (1997): 41. Additional exposition of her methodology can be found in Rashkin, "The Occulted Jew: Symbolism and Anti-Semitism in Villiers de l'Isle-Adam's *Axël,*" *Nineteenth-Century French Studies* 26 (1998): 398–416. Conversations with Rashkin about her reading of "Sarrasine" and Karoline Krauss's reading of *The Jews' Beech Tree* contributed to my interest in anti-Semitism in Droste-Hülshoff's novella. See Karoline Krauss, "Das offene Geheimnis in Annette von Droste-Hülshoff's *Die Judenbuche,*" *Zeitschrift für deutsche Philologie* 114 (1995): 542–59.

2. The literature on *Die Judenbuche* is vast, and the following references are not comprehensive. For analyses concerned with genre see Benno von Wiese, "Annette von Droste-Hülshoff: Die Judenbuche," in *Die deutsche Novelle von Goethe bis Kafka. Interpretationen,* vol. 1 (Düsseldorf: Bagel, 1956), 154–75; Karl Philipp Moritz, *Droste-Hülshoff. Die Judenbuche: Sittengemälde und Kriminalnovelle* (Paderborn, Munich, Vienna, and Zürich: Schöningh, 1980); Walter Huge, " 'Die Judenbuche' als Kriminalgeschichte: Das Problem von Erkenntnis und Urteil im Kriminalschema," *Zeitschrift für Deutsche Philologie Sonderheft* 99 (1980): 49–70; and Helmut Koopmann, "Die Wirklichkeit des Bösen in der 'Judenbuche' der Droste: Zu einer moralischen Erzählung des 19. Jahrhunderts," *Zeitschrift für Deutsche Philologie Sonderheft* 99 (1980): 71–85. For discussions of the text's sociohistorical background and genealogy see Alan P. Cottrell, "The Significance of the Name 'Johannes' in *Die Judenbuche,*" *Seminar* 6 (1970): 207–15; Janet K. King, "Conscience and Conviction in 'Die Judenbuche,' " *Monatshefte* 64 (1972): 349–55; Betty Nance Weber, "Droste's *Judenbuche:* Westphalia in International Context," *Germanic Review* 50 (1975): 203–12; Gerard Oppermann, "Die Narbe des Friedrich Mergel: Zur Aufklärung eines literarischen Motivs in Annette von Droste-Hülshoffs *Die Judenbuche,*" *Deutsche Vierteljahrsschrift für Literaturwissenschaft und Geistesgechichte* 13 (1976): 449–64; Larry D. Wells, "Annette von Droste-Hülshoff's Johannes Niemand: Much Ado About Nobody," *Germanic Review* 52 (1977): 109–21; Bernd Kortländer, "Wahrheit und Wahrscheinlichkeit: Zu einer Schreibstrategie in der *Judenbuche* der Droste," *Zeitschrift für Deutsche Philologie Sonderheft* 99 (1980): 86–99; Michael Werner, "Dichtung oder Wahrheit?: Empirie und Fiktion in A. von Haxthausens *Geschichte eines Algierer-Sklaven,* der Hauptquelle zur

Judenbuche der Droste," *Zeitschrift für Deutsche Philologie Sonderheft* 99 (1980): 21–31; Winfried Woesler, "Die Literarisierung eines Kriminalfalles," *Zeitschrift für Deutsche Philologie Sonderheft* 99 (1980): 5–21; and Horst-Dieter Krus, *Mordsache Soistmann Berend. Zum historischen Hintergrund der Novelle "Die Judenbuche" von Annette von Droste-Hülshoff* (Münster: Aschendorff, 1990). For attempts to resolve the text's ambiguities see Wells, "Annette von Droste-Hülshoff's Johannes Niemand"; Raleigh Whitinger, "From Confusion to Clarity: Further Reflections on the Revelatory Function of Narrative Technique and Symbolism in Annette von Droste-Hülshoff's *Die Judenbuche," Deutsche Vierteljahrsschrift für Literaturwissenschaft und Geistesgeschichte* 54 (1980): 259–83; Benno von Wiese, "Porträt eines Mörders: Zur *Judenbuche* der Annette von Droste-Hülshoff," *Zeitschrift für Deutsche Philologie Sonderheft* 99 (1980): 32–48; Doris Brett, "Friedrich, the Beech, and Margreth in Droste-Hülshoff's 'Judenbuche,'" *Journal of English and Germanic Philology* (1985): 157–65; Wolfgang Wittkowski, "Das Rätsel der 'Judenbuche' und seine Lösung: Religiöse Geheimsignale in Zeitangaben der Literatur um 1840," *Sprachkunst. Beiträge zur Literaturwissenschaft* 16 (1985): 175–92; and Wolfgang Wittkowski, "*Die Judenbuche: Das Ärgernis des Rätsels und der Auflösung," Droste-Jahrbuch* 1 (1986/87): 107–28. For interpretations focusing on indeterminacy see Heinrich Henel, "Annette von Droste-Hülshoff: Erzählstil und Wirklichkeit," in *Festschrift für Bernhard Blume: Aufsätze zur deutschen und europäischen Literatur,* ed. Egon Schwarz, Hunter G. Hannum, and Edgar Lohner (Göttingen: Vandenhoeck & Ruprecht, 1967), 146–72; Heinz Rölleke, "Erzähltes Mysterium: Studie zur 'Judenbuche' der Annette von Droste-Hülshoff," *Deutsche Vierteljahrsschrift für Literaturwissenschaft und Geistesgeschichte* 42 (1968): 399–426; N.P. Belchamber, "A Case of Identity: A New Look at *Die Judenbuche* by Annette von Droste-Hülshoff," *Modern Languages: Journal of the Modern Language Association* 55 (1974): 80–82; Jane K. Brown, "The Real Mystery in Droste-Hülshoff's 'Die Judenbuche,'" *Modern Language Review* 73 (1978): 835–46; and Inge Diersen, "'. . . ein arm verkümmert Sein': Annette von Droste-Hülshoffs 'Die Judenbuche,'" *Zeitschrift für Germanistik* 3 (1983): 299–313.

    3. Brown asserts the Jews are not part of the text's mystery; the novella's title has misled us (Brown, "The Real Mystery," 835). Lietina-Ray proposes prejudice is the main theme of the novella, without taking the text's treatment of Jews into consideration (Maruta Lietina-Ray, "Das Recht der öffentlichen Meinung: Über das Vorurteil in der *Judenbuche," Zeitschrift für Deutsche Philologie Sonderheft* 99 [1980]: 99–109). Franzos argues the novella is a masterpiece in every respect, even in its depiction of the Jews, and that hatred of Jews is a secondary theme of the novella (Karl Emil Franzos, "Eine Novelle und ihre Quellen," *Allgemeine Zeitung des Judentums* 61, no. 51–53 [1897]: 609, 634). Wells identifies the text as a "tale of anti-Semitism," but does not pursue the topic further (Wells, "Annette von Droste-Hülshoff's Johannes Niemand," 488). Low maintains Droste "asks for forbearance toward the people's fateful hostility toward the Jews" (Alfred D. Low, *Jews in the Eyes of Germans from the Enlightenment to Imperial Germany* [Philadelphia: Institute for the Study

of Human Issues, 1979], 208). A number of scholars suggest Droste tries to counter the anti-Semitism rampant in her society. See Wittkowski ("Das Rätsel," 188); Raymond Immerwahr, "'Die Judenbuche' als Gewebe von Begegnungen mit dem Fremden," in *Begegnung mit dem 'Fremden': Grenzen, Traditionen, Vergleiche. Akten des VIII. Internationalen Germanisten-Kongresses Tokyo 1990*, ed. Eijiro Iwaski, vol 11: 144–45); and Clemens Heselhaus, "Die Golem-Gespenster der Droste-Hülshoff," *Droste-Jahrbuch* 1 (1986/87): 131–32. Palmieri concludes Droste herself was not anti-Semitic, but the *Judenbuche* exhibits an anti-Semitic thought-structure. (Aldo Palmieri, "Die Judenbuche—eine antisemitische Novelle?" in *Gegenbilder und Vorurteil: Aspekte des Judentums im Werk deutschsprachiger Schriftstellerinnen*, ed. Renate Heuer and Ralph-Rainer Wuthenow, 9–39 [Frankfurt am Main and New York: Campus, 1995], 137). Chase offers a discussion of a number of stereotypes associated with Jews in the narrative, yet maintains that Droste opposes segregation and Jewish non-citizenship (Jefferson S. Chase, "Part of the Story: The Significance of the Jews in Annette von Droste-Hülshoff's *Die Judenbuche*," *Deutsche Vierteljahrsschrift für Literaturwissneschaft und Geistesgeschichte* 71 [1997]: 127–45).

4. Karin Doerr, "The Specter of Anti-Semitism in and Around Annette von Droste-Hülshoff's *Judenbuche*," *German Studies Review* 17 (1994): 447–71. I am indebted to Doerr's analysis for much of the background information that follows. Chase's thoughtful article ("Part of the Story,"), which appeared after this essay was completed, covers much of the same ground as Doerr's. Two additional articles that offer significant new interpretations of the novella's anti-Semitism appeared after my analysis was first published in 1998. See William Collins Donahue, "'Ist er kein Jude, so verdiente er einer zu sein': Droste-Hülshoff's *Die Judenbuche* and Religious Anti-Semitism," *The German Quarterly* 72, no. 1 (1999): 44–73; and Richard T. Gray, "Red Herrings and Blue Smocks: Ecological Destruction, Commercialism, and Anti-Semitism in Annette von Droste-Hülshoff's *Die Judenbuche*," *German Studies Review* 26, no. 3 (2003): 515–42.

5. Sander L. Gilman, *Difference and Pathology: Stereotypes of Sexuality, Race, and Madness* (Ithaca and London: Cornell University Press, 1985), 27.

6. Huge (*HKA* 5.2: 213) and Moritz (*Droste-Hülshoff,* 89) argue that Goethe's definition ("eine sich ereignete unerhörte Begebenheit" ["an unheard-of event that really occurred"]) is not applicable to *Die Judenbuche.*

7. Quoted in *Erläuterungen und Dokumente: Annette von Droste-Hülshoff, Die Judenbuche*, ed. Walter Huge (Stuttgart: Reclam, 1979), 63–64.

8. In one of the standard reference works on *Die Judenbuche* Moritz argues against contextualizing the storyline historically, claiming such an approach would be useless and misleading since these historical developments are not reflected in the novella and Droste did not intend to present a picture of contemporary society (Moritz, *Droste-Hülshoff,* 17–18).

9. Reinhard Rürup, "The Tortuous and Thorny Path to Legal Equality. 'Jew Laws' and Emancipatory Legislation in Germany from the Late Eighteenth Century," *Leo Baeck Institute Year Book* 31 (1986): 9.

10. Ibid., 15n. 24. For a brief discussion of the history of Jews in Westphalia see Röthert, who quotes a leading government official, Vincke, making an anti-Semitic statement that the Jews have seized control of the Paderborn economy (Hermann Röthert, *Westfälische Geschichte* [Gütersloh: Bertelsmann, 1962], 161).

11. Rürup, "The Tortuous and Thorny Path," 21.

12. Ibid., 6–7.

13. Lewis W. Tusken, *Annette von Droste-Hülshoff's 'Die Judenbuche': A Study of Its Background* (Boulder: University of Colorado Press, 1968), 37–38.

14. For a discussion of the role of Jewish artists in Germany beginning in the 1830s see Jacob Katz, *From Prejudice to Destruction: Anti-Semitism, 1700–1933* (Cambridge, Mass., and London: Harvard University Press, 1980), 175–94.

15. "[I]st der Laube nicht ein Jude? Er hat wenigstens Alles was die Schriftsteller dieses Volkes bezeichnet, – Geist, Witz, Grimm gegen alle bestehende Formen, sonderlich die christlichen und bürgerlichen, – Haschen nach Effect, – Aufgeblasenheit und eine Stentorische Manier das Wort in der litterarischen Welt an sich zu reißen, – Einseitigkeit, die aber nicht aus dem Verstande, sondern aus reinem Dünkel hervorgeht, – kurz – ist er kein Jude, so verdiente er Einer zu seyn [. . .]" (*HKA* 9.1: 28).

16. Katz, *From Prejudice to Destruction*, 183.

17. *HKA* 5.2: 199–214.

18. Haxthausen's *Geschichte eines Algierer-Sklaven* is reprinted in *HKA* 5.2: 214–25. For analyses of Haxthausen's account see Werner ("Dichtung oder Wahrheit?"), Woesler ("Die Literarisierung eines Kriminalfalles"), and Krus (*Mordsache Soistmann Berend*).

19. *HKA* 5.2: 200.

20. In partial opposition to Woesler ("Die Literarisierung eines Kriminal-falles"), who surmises this religious dimension reflects Droste's unconscious recognition of the endangered position of the Catholic nobility in her sociohistorical context (16), I suggest Droste consciously recognizes this danger, and that the relevant sociohistorical context is the debate centered around the "Jewish Question."

21. In the first edition of the novella the year was printed as 1788; because of time references cited in the narrative most editors assume this to be an error, and have corrected the year to 1789. The editors of *HKA* retain the original year (*HKA* 5.2: 246–48); I have chosen to cite the date as 1789. Droste's choice of year is clearly significant: in an earlier draft of the manuscript the narrative action ends in 1795 (*HKA* 5.2: 433).

22. *HKA* 9.1: 293.

23. For a discussion of the legend and the popular pilgrimage to Maria Buchen see Wolfgang Brückner, ed., *Maria Buchen. Eine fränkishe Wallfahrt* (Würzburg: Echter Verlag, 1979). Doerr ("The Specter of Anti-Semitism," 458) correctly criticizes Wittkowski's assertion ("Das Rätsel," 188) that Droste attempted to counter this anti-Semitic legend with her novella.

24. The article, "Die Judenstadt in Prag," written by F. G. Kohl, was published in six installments in the *Morgenblatt für gebildete Leser* in May 1842. The essay begins with a general discussion of the number of Jews living in Prague and other European cities. The next two installments describe the Jews' city in Prague by focusing on their cemetery. After remarking the graveyard would be the perfect backdrop for painting a picture of "the resurrection of the dead," "die Auferstehung der Todten" (467), Kohl tours the spooky graveyard and points out headstones of outstanding members of the Jewish community, commenting that Jewish children are playing among the maggots in the cemetery and wondering what kind of effect this will have on them as adults. The fourth installment discusses a young boy Lebel, who was found "verwildert," "wild," and taken in by the community, where he slowly is becoming civilized. The author, puzzled how this could be possible, remarks that he does not dare to ascribe the boy's condition to the community's moral depravation: "Alles der Unordnung in der Gemeinde Schuld zu geben und den Lebel als eine Blüthe der moralischen Versumpfung in jenem Judenviertel zu betrachten, wage ich nicht" (475). Kohl then compares the dusty, dirty, dark synagogue to a catacomb, adding that the old rabbi who prays there moves around in a manner that would be inappropriate in Protestant churches, speaking in a loud voice without "Geist" (476). The fifth installment addresses the Reform movement in the Prague Jewish community, which the author hopes will lead to improvements in their schools and hospitals. After this grand tour of the "Judenstadt" Kohl concludes the Jews always have been oppressed, and hopes perhaps that his century can reverse this oppression (483). The same ambivalent attitude toward Jews is reflected in the newspaper's mastheads, which frequently include quotes about Jews that seem to promote their emancipation, yet often are anti-Semitic. F. G. Kohl, "Die Judenstadt in Prag," *Morgenblatt für gebildete Leser* (Stuttgart and Tübingen) May 16–21, 1842: 461–83.

25. *HKA* 5.2: 209.

26. *HKA* 5.1: 1.

27. *HKA* 5.2: 200.

28. Quoted in Wittkowski ("Das Rätsel," 176). Droste actually made this statement with reference to her poetic production. See Moritz (*Droste-Hülshoff*) and Wittkowski for discussions of "Verrätselung" in Droste's oeuvre.

29. Page references are to *HKA* 5.1. The translations are my own, though I consulted Annette von Droste-Hülshoff, *The Jews' Beech Tree*, tr. Michael Bullock, in *Three Eerie Tales from 19th Century Germany* (New York: Ungar, 1975), 101–51.

30. The verse instantiates its own lexical challenge to read semantic registers in the series of "measure" words that runs throughout the poem: *wagen, messen, wägen, Wagschal'*.

31. Three times the text steadfastly refuses to "prove" facts critical to the narrative. The first instance, which I discuss in detail below, occurs when Margreth tries to disprove the similarity between Johannes and Friedrich: "Aehnlichkeiten wollen nichts beweisen" (15). The other instances occur in

conjunction with the death of the Jew Aaron: the second serves to identify Mergel as the probable murderer ("die Anzeigen gegen ihn zwar gravirend, doch ohne persönliches Geständniß nicht beweisend" [33]), while the third draws this conclusion into doubt by suggesting Lumpenmoises may have been the perpetrator ("Leider fehlen die Beweise, aber die Wahrscheinlichkeit ist groß" [34]).

32. The original Boileau quote reads: "Jamais au Spectateur n'offrez rien d'incroyable. Le Vrai peut quelquefois n'estre pas vraisemblable" (*HKA* 5.2: 243). Droste modifies the quote such that it resonates with Kleist's famous "Kant crisis" statement: "Wir können nicht entscheiden, ob das, was wir Wahrheit nennen, wahrhaft Wahrheit ist, oder ob es uns nur so scheint." Heinrich von Kleist, *Sämtliche Werke und Briefe in Vier Bänden,* ed. Helmut Sembdner (Munich and Vienna: Hanser, 1982), 634.

33. For an analysis that summarily dismisses the present interpretation see Norbert Mecklenburg, *Der Fall 'Judenbuche': Revision eines Fehlurteils* (Bielefeld: Aisthesis Verlag, 2008), 112. Focusing on the novella's thematization of ethics, Mecklenburg attacks all other critics for incorrectly reading the novella and advances an unoriginal thesis that exonerates Friedrich of the Jew Aaron's murder.

34. See Moritz, *Droste-Hülshoff,* 21–29.

35. See Immerwahr ("'Die Judenbuche' als Gewebe") for a discussion of "Fremdheit" as a leitmotif in the novella. Freund also comments on the theme of foreignness, arguing the problem of social integration is one of the novella's main themes. Winfried Freund, "Der Außenseiter 'Friedrich Mergel': Eine sozialpsychologische Studie zur *Judenbuche* der Annette von Droste-Hülshoff," *Zeitschrift für Deutsche Philologie Sonderheft* 99 (1980): 110–18.

36. For a differing interpretation defending Margreth's character see Gertrud Bauer Pickar, "The Battering and Meta-Battering of Droste's Margreth: Covert Misogyny in *Die Judenbuche*'s Critical Reception," *Women in German Yearbook* 9 (1993): 71–90.

37. *HKA* 5.2: 265.

38. See also Rölleke, "Erzähltes Mysterium," 421.

39. Jacob Grimm and Wilhelm Grimm, *Deutsches Wörterbuch,* vol. 8 (Leipzig: Hirzel, 1936), 2506–10.

40. In light of subsequent narrative details that suggest his real parentage, it may not be too far-fetched to read Friedrich's stabbing gesture as a gloss on the Maria Buchen legend, in which Jews are identified as such when they unwittingly stab Christian images.

41. This "not at home-ness" resonates subliminally with the text's first description of the Jews as not "angessesen," not resident.

42. "Händel suchend" can, of course, also mean "quarrel-seeking," but following the prologue's call to read the roots of words, I have chosen to translate the phrase as "deal-seeking." I believe it fortuitous that Simon shares the last name of the Protestant theologian Johann Salomo Semler (1725–1791): although the area around Paderborn is a Catholic enclave in a predominantly Protestant region, there is no evidence in the text to suggest a thematic tension

between Protestants and Catholics, while the polarization of Christian and Jew is overt.

43. Joshua Trachtenberg, *The Devil and the Jews: The Medieval Conception of the Jew and Its Relation to Modern Anti-Semitism*, 2nd ed. (Philadelphia and Jerusalem: The Jewish Publication Society, 1983), 11–54.

44. Rölleke, "Erzähltes Mysterium," 405.

45. Trachtenberg, *The Devil and the Jews*, 57–155 and 231n. 19.

46. "Die Juden zaubern" (*HKA* 5.2: 257).

47. *The Anchor Bible Dictionary*, ed. David Noel Freedman, vol. 6 (New York, London, Toronto: Doubleday, 1992), 27–31.

48. Trachtenberg, *The Devil and the Jews*, 32–43.

49. Rölleke, "Erzähltes Mysterium," 404.

50. I thank Michaela Welk for this observation.

51. One might argue Margreth rejects Simon's comparison by proudly contrasting his "red brush" to her son's "blond locks," yet her actions surrounding this exchange suggests this is not the case. Having just remarked that Friedrich "hat viel von dir, Simon, viel" ("has a lot of you Simon, a lot") she warns Friedrich to behave well for his uncle, indicating she is eager to promote their bonding.

52. In a convincing analysis not well received in the critical literature McGlatherty has explored this incest theme, citing much of the textual evidence I introduce here, and suggested Friedrich and Johannes may be brothers or half brothers. James M. McGlathery, "Fear of Perdition in Droste-Hülshoff's *Judenbuche*," in *Lebendige Form: Interpretationen zur deutschen Literatur. Festschrift für E. K. Henel*, ed. Jeffrey L. Sammons and Ernst Schürer (Munich: Fink, 1970), 229–44.

53. My thanks to Eva Bates, Ann-Marie Paul, and Christina Schreiber for drawing my attention to this detail of the narrative.

54. The extant prepublication drafts of the manuscript indicate this sentence was added late in the text's genealogy, suggesting it introduces a significant detail into the narrative (*HKA* 5.2: 403).

55. Moritz, *Droste-Hülshoff*, 39. Certainly Westphalia is known for its linen industry, yet it is significant that these textile signifiers are repeatedly linked to both the "Hechelkrämer" and the Mergel family throughout the text, and not to the general population.

56. Frank Felsenstein, *Anti-Semitic Stereotypes: A Paradigm of Otherness in English Popular Culture, 1660–1830* (Baltimore and London: Johns Hopkins University Press, 1995), 75.

57. This association is also underscored on the phonological level: <u>Hecht</u>, <u>Hech</u>elkrämer.

58. Strictly speaking this definition may not be fully valid, since no textual evidence indicates Margreth and Simon's mother was Jewish, and it is also unclear whether Margreth herself is Jewish.

59. These plot developments are obliquely anticipated in the conclusion of the scene. As the two unchristian travelers walk through the dark forest, the weak moon gives the objects it illuminates a "fremdartiges Ansehen" ("foreign

appearance" [12]), an attribute later transferred to Johannes appearing as Friedrich, described as having a "widriges Ansehen" ("unpleasant appearance" [13]). Friedrich trips over "Baumwurzeln" ("tree roots") as he proceeds down the slippery path, suggesting in light of the prologue's challenge to consider the roots of words that we read the roots of these trees. The two come to a clearing where "die Axt unbarmherzig gewüthet hatte" ("the axe had raged unmercifully" [12]), a graphic foreshadowing of the axe murder of Brandis that will take place in the woods. Simon stops to look at a fallen beech tree with quaking leaves that lies across their path, while an old oak remains standing in the middle of the clearing: "Simon blieb einen Augenblick stehen und betrachtete den gefällten Stamm mit Aufmerksamkeit. In der Mitte der Lichtung stand eine alte Eiche mehr breit als hoch" (12). In light of the ensuing narrative the arboreal metaphorics are clear: the fallen Jewish stem struck down in its prime is juxtaposed to the old Germanic oak, which, hollow as it may be, is still standing.

60. Rölleke unknowingly comes close to the conclusion that Friedrich is a Jew when he argues that Mergel is stuck in pre-Christian and unchristian realms and that the prepublication drafts of the manuscript show a systematic elimination of all of Mergel's connections to the Christian realm ("Erzähltes Mysterium," 422 and 420–421n. 66).

61. Doerr ("The Specter of Anti-Semitism," 454–55) and Palmieri ("Die Judenbuche," 37) both note this association. To be sure, members of the corrupt Christian society occasionally engage in "Jewish" behavior as well (e.g., the marriage of the old man and the young girl is described as a "Geschäft" [29] and the villagers join forces to protect the murderer of Brandis the forester), yet only Friedrich is condemned for his actions.

62. The lexeme also occurs in the scene where Margreth, stung by Brandis's accusations of her poverty, defensively calls him a "Lump" (22), thereby projecting her own impoverished status onto the forester.

63. Doerr, "The Specter of Anti-Semitism," 451. For an extensive discussion of the stereotypical association of Jews with pigs see Felsenstein, *Anti-Semitic Stereotypes,* 126–37.

64. The narrative sequence immediately following this scene corroborates this reading. The squire, who has witnessed the confrontation between Aaron and Friedrich, is on his way home when he notices two figures running in front of his wagon. The squire identifies the two as "Auch ein paar selige Schweine aus unserm eigenen Stall!" ("A couple of holy pigs from our own barn!" [29]). The phrase "selige Schweine," "holy pigs," stands in implicit opposition to the presumably unholy Jew maligned as a pig in the previous scene. The men, unwitting witnesses to Aaron's death, claim they were spooked by the ghost of Hermann Mergel (obliquely established as a "Schelm" in the text), and ruin a fountain searching for a horse's skull said to ward off evil spirits. The squire, surveying the damaged fountain, remarks, "was die Schelme nicht stehlen, das verderben die Narren" ("what *Schelme* don't steal, fools ruin" [30]), thereby setting up an opposition between Christian fools and thieving "Schelme," a signifier previously identified as "Jewish" in the text.

65. To be sure, the Mergel household is not a particularly "light" space, but it is a Christian one, even though the hand that raises Friedrich (i.e., Margreth) is pious only on the surface. The narrative pits this empty Christian piety against the threatening alterity of Judaism, which is indirectly described as "sehr dunkel," "düster," and "ganz finster" ("very dark," "gloomy," and "completely black") in the text (11–12). The final lines of the verse might equally apply to the judgmental Christian reader.

66. Doerr, "The Specter of Anti-Semitism," 452–53.

67. See also ibid.

68. The signifier also occurs in Kapp's remark that his servant knew about Mergel's escape following Aaron's death an hour before he did: "allerdings hatte meine Anne Marie den Handel um eine Stunde früher erfahren als ich" (32).

69. Doerr, "The Specter of Anti-Semitism," 456.

70. Droste's source material, Haxthausen's *Geschichte eines Algierer-Sklaven*, also glosses the returning man as a Christ figure: he is confronted by a female Wandering Jew who demands he wear a heavy wreath of thorns and prods him when he stands still, and then disappears into the night (*HKA* 5.2: 223).

71. Sander Gilman, "The Jewish Foot: A Foot-Note to the Jewish Body," in Gilman, *The Jew's Body* (New York and London: Routledge, 1991), 38–59.

72. According to Haxthausen's account Hermann Winkelhannes witnessed the "Revolution gegen die Juden," a pogrom in 1805 in which hundreds of Jews were killed, and was then freed several months later after Jérôme Bonaparte forced the Dei Mustapha to release his Christian slaves (*HKA: 5.2: 221–22*). Werner has concluded this account is not accurate: Haxthausen's chronology of events leading from the pogrom to the freeing of the slaves does not match the historical record, and extant historical documents do not list Winkelhannes among the 231 Christian slaves who were freed ("Dichtung oder Wahrheit?" 23–26). Krus (*Mordsache Soistmann Berend*) takes issue with Werner's analysis, arguing for the historical validity of Haxthausen's account.

73. The narrative leaves one member of the Friedrich/Johannes duo roaming in the world unaccounted for, a cipher, perhaps, of the Wandering Jew.

74. Trachtenberg, *The Devil and the Jews*, 47–50. Certainly a two-week-old corpse would stink, but the term "schändlich" ("shameful, morally reprehensible") suggests much more is at stake here than merely organic decomposition.

75. Moritz, *Droste-Hülshoff*, 49.

76. "Nicht von derselben Familie, unedel geboren, also übel von Charackter und Sitte" (Grimm and Grimm 11.3: 846–49). Krauss ("Das offene Geheimnis") points to this etymology as evidence that the psychopathological behavior Friedrich exhibits in carving the wood results from the open secret that Johannes is a bastard.

77. Doerr, "The Specter of Anti-Semitism," 457.

78. Wells ("Johannes Niemand") reads the scar as a reference to Friedrich as the Ulysses figure mentioned at the beginning of the narrative, since Ulysses was identified by his scar when he returned from his adventures. *HKA*

5.2: 246 notes that in the Gospel of St. John the doubting disciple Thomas recognizes the resurrected Christ by his scars.

79. *HKA* 5.2: 214 and 224.

80. *HKA* 5.2: 216.

81. The two other possible reasons for Mergel's unceremonious interment lack explanatory force. If Mergel committed suicide or was a murderer, he may well have been denied a Catholic burial, but it is doubtful his corpse would have been interred in the knacker's yard (see also *Erläuterungen*, 20): in such cases the remains usually were buried in unconsecrated ground next to the Catholic graveyard. Moreover, in the case of suicide canon law allows for burial in hallowed ground when the suicide can be attributed to derangement, as is the case with Mergel (*HKA* 5.2: 39–40). For manifest sins like murder the deceased may be granted Catholic burial if he or she has shown any remorse, as is arguably the case with Mergel, who explicitly returns home seeking reentry into Christian society (*HKA* 5.2: 39). *New Catholic Encyclopedia*, vol. 2 (New York: McGraw-Hill, 1967), 896–97.

82. "Lauge zum Entfernen natürlicher Verunreinigungen aus Textilien." Gerhard Wahrig, *Deutsches Wörterbuch* (Munich: Bertelsman, 1991), 780–81 and 667.

83. See Nancy A. Lauckner, "The Surrogate Jew in the Postwar German Novel," *Monatshefte* 66 (1974): 133–44.

84. For a discussion of the text's reception see *Erläuterungen*, 55–68. Katz identifies 1879 as the year that marks the beginning of modern anti-Semitism (*From Prejudice to Destruction*, 245).

Chapter Five

1. The volume, *Österreichischer Novellenalmanach für 1843*, edited by Andreas Schumacher, actually was published in 1842.

2. The cited reviews are reprinted in Moriz Enzinger, *Adalbert Stifter im Urteil seiner Zeit* (Vienna: Bühlau, Kommissionsverlag der Österreichischen Akademie der Wissenschaften in Wien, 1968): the quote from the *Allgemeine Zeitung*, pp. 36–37; from the *Sonntagsblätter*, p. 34.

3. Citations are from the reviews reprinted in Enzinger, *Adalbert Stifter*, 33–37: "unstreitig der bedeutendste und beste Beitrag der ganzen Sammlung; eine recht eigentlich geistreiche, durch und durch gediegene Arbeit"; written "mit seltener Originalität"; "[eine] seltene Eigentümlichkeit"; "durchaus eigentümlich"; "eine finstere Originalität"; "kühn und originell"; "prägnant"; "glänzend"; "entzück[end]"; "frisch[] und kräftig[]"; "vorzüglich[]"; Stifter is "ein Sohn der Zeit."

4. Enzinger, *Adalbert Stifter*, 13–15.

5. For a recent analysis that takes issue with the present interpretation, denies the centrality of anti-Semitism to the text, and argues that Stifter counteracts the mythical construct of the Wandering Jew in *Abdias*, see Sylvain Guarda, "Stifters *Abdias*: Kindheit in ästhetischer Spiegelung," *German Life and Letters* 61, no. 3 (2008): 297–310.

6. The cited reviews are reprinted in Enzinger, *Adalbert Stifter,* 33–34, 102–3, and 117. For a more recent (though not current) overview of secondary literature on *Abdias* see H. R. Klienberger, "Stifter's *Abdias* and Its Interpreters," *Forum for Modern Language Studies* 14 (1978): 332–48.

7. Margarete Susman, "Nachwort," in *Abdias: Erzählung von Adalbert Stifter* (Berlin: Schocken, 1935), 108–13.

8. Urban Roedl, "Stifter und die Juden," *Jüdische Revue* 3, no. 3 (1938): 182.

9. Wolfgang Heybey, "Adalbert Stifters 'Abdias' und 'Das Heidedorf': Ein Beitrag zum Welt- und Menschbild des Dichters aus rassischer Grundlage," *Zeitschrift für Deutschkunde* 56, no. 6 (1942): 195.

10. John Urzidil, "Adalbert Stifter and Judaism," *The Menorah Journal* 36, no. 4 (1948): 329.

11. Kurt Gerhard Fischer, "Der jüdische Mensch in Stifters Dichtungs-Denken," *Vierteljahrsschrift des Adalbert-Stifter-Instituts des Landes Oberösterreich* 14 (1965): 109–18.

12. Ruth K. Angress, "Wunsch- und Angstbilder: Jüdische Gestalten aus der deutschen Literatur des neunzehnten Jahrhunderts," in *Kontroversen, alte und neue. Akten des VII. Internationalen Germanisten-Kongresses,* vol. 1, ed. Albrecht Schöne (Tübingen: Niemeyer, 1985), 85–96.

13. Joseph Metz, "The Jew as Sign in Stifter's *Abdias,*" *Germanic Review* 77, no. 3 (2002): 220–21. I am grateful to Joseph Metz for our invigorating discussion of *Abdias.*

14. Martin Swales and Erica Swales, *Adalbert Stifter: A Critical Study* (Cambridge, U.K., and New York: Cambridge University Press, 1984), 36.

15. Eva Geulen, *Worthörig wider Willen: Darstellungsproblematik und Sprachreflexion in der Prosa Adalbert Stifters* (Munich: Iudicum, 1992), 68.

16. Cornelia Blasberg, *Erschriebene Tradition: Adalbert Stifter oder das Erzählen im Zeichen verlorener Geschichten* (Freiburg im Breisgau: Rombach, 1998), 232.

17. Metz, "The Jew as Sign," 230.

18. Ibid., 220.

19. Walter Benjamin, "Karl Kraus," in *Gesammelte Schriften,* ed. Rolf Tiedemann and Hermann Schweppenhäuser, vol. II,1 (Frankfurt am Main: Suhrkamp, 1972), 339–41.

20. Eric Downing, *Double Exposures: Repetition and Realism in Nineteenth-Century German Fiction* (Stanford, Calif.: Stanford University Press, 2000), 25.

21. Ibid. Like Benjamin, Downing presents a reading of the *Vorrede* to *Bunte Steine* to develop this theory, arguing that this tendency is also present in Stifter's pre-1848 writings.

22. Some two thousand five hundred books, pamphlets, and essays devoted to the "Jewish Question" were published between 1815 and 1850. Rürup, "The Tortuous and Thorny Path to Legal Equality: 'Jew Laws' and Emancipatory Legislation in Germany from the Late Eighteenth Century," in *Leo Baeck Institute Yearbook* 31 (1986): 21.

23. The following discussion is drawn from Jacob Katz, *From Prejudice to Destruction: Anti-Semitism, 1700–1933* (Cambridge, Mass., and London: Harvard University Press, 1980), 223–29.

24. Ibid., 224.

25. Ibid., 226.

26. Quoted ibid., 226.

27. Paul Lawrence Rose, *German Question/Jewish Question: Revolutionary Antisemitism from Kant to Wagner* (Princeton, N.J.: Princeton University Press, 1990), 62–69.

28. See also Metz, "The Jew as Sign," 231 n. 2. Metz bases these observations on Sander L. Gilman, *Freud, Race, Gender* (Princeton, N.J.: Princeton University Press, 1993), 18–20, and Sander L. Gilman, *The Jew's Body* (New York and London: Routledge, 1991), 99–100 and 171–74.

29. Adalbert Stifter, *Abdias*, in *Adalbert Stifter Werke und Briefe: Historisch-Kritische Gesamtausgabe*, 38 vols., ed. Alfred Doppler and Wolfgang Frühwald (Stuttgart: Kohlhammer, 1978f.), vol. I,5: 334. All parenthetical references to Stifter's writings in this essay refer to this edition, hereafter cited as *HKG*. The translations are my own, though I consulted Adalbert Stifter, *Brigitta; with Abdias; Limestone; and The Forest Path*, trans. Helen Watanabe-O'Kelly (London: Angel Books, 1990).

30. I make this argument against Benno von Wiese, "Adalbert Stifter: *Abdias*," in von Wiese, *Die deutsche Novelle*, vol. 2 (Düsseldorf: August Bagel, 1962), 130, and Swales and Swales, *Adalbert Stifter*, 61, who maintain that the narrator remains strictly objective.

31. See Geulen, *Worthörig wider Willen*, 57–81, for a discussion of "hiding" in *Abdias*.

32. The phrase resonates strongly with the narrator's description of "düstre Juden" (240) living in holes in the ground, unearthing money from earth and stones. See my discussion of the text's discursive construction of "Jewishness" below.

33. See also Swales and Swales, *Adalbert Stifter*; Blasberg, *Erschriebene Tradition*; Geulen, *Worthörig wider Willen*; and Metz, "The Jew as Sign."

34. See also Swales and Swales, *Adalbert Stifter*, 59–67, who argue that the text both invites and withholds judgment and interpretation.

35. The narrator likewise uses water metaphors to describe Abdias's entry into Austrian culture. On arriving in Austria, the Jews are "*ver*schlungen," "flung," again in a perverse natural act, as the prefix *ver* indicates, by a stream of people and carried off on a wave: "Einen Augenblick staunten die vielen, die da standen und zuschauten, die Fremdlinge an—im nächsten waren dieselben von dem Strom des menschenwimmelnden Welttheiles verschlungen und in seinen Wogen fortgeführt. Das Bild zeigte wieder sonst nichts, als was es den ganzen Tag zeigt [. . .]" (300). This scene also rewrites the narrative's opening description of nature glossing over the drowning boy with a silver mirror (237).

36. When Abdias returns home after his fifteen-year absence, he carries carrion with him to keep the jackals from his own body, indicating that the jackals

regard the Jews as prey: "[er] trug Stücke eines Pferdeaases in der Hand, um davon den Schakalen zuzuwerfen, daß er sie von seinem Leibe hielte" (245).

37. His father planned to bring the boy to a doctor to be educated, as were the prophets and leaders of his race, but nothing became of this because he forgot about it: "[E]r dachte, er wolle den Knaben [. . .] zu einem Arzte bringen, daß er weise würde, wie es die alten Propheten und Führer seines Geschlechtes gewesen. Aber auch aus dem ist wieder nichts geworden, weil es in Vergessenheit gerathen war."

38. See, for example, Enzinger, *Adalbert Stifter,* 103; and von Wiese, "Adalbert Stifter," 133.

39. See Sander L. Gilman, *Jewish Self-Hatred: Anti-Semitism and the Hidden Language of the Jews* (Baltimore and London: Johns Hopkins University Press, 1986), for a discussion of the structure of self-hatred.

40. The Jew's comment about hoping to become richer than ever appears in oblique form in the revised *Studienfassung:* "wenn er der Mann sei, der sie ins Verderben gebracht, so könne er ihnen auch wieder empor helfen, er muß ersetzen, sie wollen ihn sparen und in der Zukunft zwingen" (257).

41. For a discussion of the affinities between the mark of Cain and the Wandering Jew marked by the sign of the cross see Frank Felsenstein, *Anti-Semitic Stereotypes: A Paradigm of Otherness in English Popular Culture, 1660–1830* (Baltimore and London: Johns Hopkins University Press, 1995), 85.

42. Gilman, *Freud, Race, and Gender,* 33.

43. Two of the three of these details—the description of Deborah dressing Abdias as a girl and the names of the section headings—were added to the later *Studienfassung,* indicating the importance of this feminizing gesture to Abdias's characterization.

44. In the *Journalfassung* the accusation does not receive the same structural emphasis.

45. This second accusation was added to the *Studienfassung.*

46. As I will discuss in the next chapter, the discursive construction of the Jew in Grillparzer's *Die Jüdin von Toledo* relies on similar rhetorical strategies.

47. "Der Iltis ist Seelen- und Totentier." Gerhard Wahrig, *Deutsches Wörterbuch* (Munich: Bertelsman, 1991), 1922.

48. See also Metz, "The Jew as Sign," 220.

49. Ibid., 228.

50. "Judith gilt als die Repräsentantin des wahren Gottesvolkes, und ist als solche eine Vorläuferin Mariens, deren Farbe [blau] und Blume [die Lilie] auch hier Ditha zugeordnet werden" (*HKG* 1,9: 292).

51. The Judith story was dramatized by Hebbel in an eponymous play dating from 1839 to 1840, shortly before *Abdias* was written.

52. Gilman, *Jewish Self-Hatred,* 30–31.

53. See also Metz, "The Jew as Sign," 220.

54. See Downing for a discussion of Stifter's paradoxical recourse to God in his realist aesthetic program (*Double Exposures,* 24–40). Metz proposes a differing interpretation, suggesting that the narrative presents the possibility that God in fact is not operating "behind the scenes," as it were ("The

Jew as Sign," 222–24). In contrast, Fenves argues that Stifter's narratives all pose the same question concerning the consequences of removing the theological framework entirely: "Was geschieht, wo die theologische Fragestellung sich entzieht?" Peter Fenves, "Die Scham der Schönheit: Einige Bemerkungen zu Stifter," in *"Geteilte Aufmerksamkeit": Zur Frage des Lesens,* ed. Thomas Schestag (Frankfurt am Main: Peter Lang, 1997), 94.

55. The description of the second rainbow in the *Journalfassung* mirrors the description of the first, underscoring the significance of the revision in the later *Studienfassung:* "Das Gewitter, welches dem Kinde mit einer weichen Flamme das Leben von dem Haupte geküßt hatte, schüttete dann noch auf alle Wesen reichlichen Segen herab, und hatte, wie jenes, das ihr das Augenlicht gebracht, mit einem schönen Sonnenuntergang im Westen und einem Regenbogen im Osten geschlossen" (J156–57).

56. Ditha is struck down in a flax field in the midst of her discussion of flax and how linen houses the human body in life and in death (339–40).

57. In the *Journalfassung* the narrator states that Abdias "in part" sows the seeds of his own fate ("was zum Theile er selber, zum Theile der Lauf der Dinge gesäet hatte" [J114]). The quote also resonates with the narrator's comment in the opening paragraphs of the novella that Abdias has reaped both "Fluch" and "Segen" in the course of his life: "er hat beides in seinem Leben reichlich geerndet" (239).

58. That Stifter added this word to the revised *Studienfassung* underscores its semantic significance. In the *Journalfassung* the verb is "hervorsproßen" ("sprouted forth"): "da er sieben und neunzig Jahre alt geworden, schien die Sonne eines Tages auf den leeren Platz und auf seinen Grabeshügel, aus dem eben das erste Gras hervorsproßte" (J157–58).

59. Karl Marx, "Zur Judenfrage," in *Karl Marx, Friedrich Engels, Werke,* 42 vols. (Berlin: Institut für Marxismus-Leninismus beim ZK der SED, 1961), vol. 1, 347–77. Also: Karl Marx, "On the Jewish Question," in Karl Marx, *Selected Writings,* ed. David McLellan (Oxford, London, and New York: Oxford University Press, 1977), 39–62.

Chapter Six

1. A number of critics have noted the title figure functions as a scapegoat, but have not attributed her sacrificial murder to the fact she is a Jew. The one scholar who offers an extensive discussion of the Jew as scapegoat is Dagmar C. G. Lorenz, "'Schafe im Wolfpelz' oder die Bösewichte, die keine waren: Die Juden in Grillparzers *Die Jüdin von Toledo," Jahrbuch der Grillparzer-Gesellschaft,* 3. Folge, 15 (1983): 79–87. For analyses that focus on the political and sexual matter informing the text without addressing the significance of the "Jewish Question" to these themes see Heinz Politzer, "Das Spiel vom Fall: *Die Jüdin von Toledo,"* in Politzer, *Franz Grillparzer oder das abgründige Biedermeier* (Vienna, Munich, Zurich: Fritz Molden, 1972), 328–50; B. Thompson, "An Ironic Tragedy: An Examination of Grillparzer's *Die Jüdin von Toledo," German Life and Letters* 25 (1971–1972): 210–19; Heinz Lippuner, "Grillparzers 'Jüdin von Toledo'. Untersuchung eines Paradigmas," *Orbis Litterarum* 27

(1972): 202–23; Joachim Müller, "Die Staatsthematik in Grillparzers Drama *Die Jüdin von Toledo*," in *Die andere Welt. Aspekte der österreichischen Literatur des 19. und 20. Jahrhunderts*, ed. Kurt Barsch, Dietmar Goltschnigg, Gerhard Melzer, and Wolfgang Heinz Schober (Bern and Munich: Hanser, 1979), 71–96; Dieter Borchmeyer, "Franz Grillparzer: Die Jüdin von Toledo," in *Deutsche Dramen. Interpretationen zu Werken von der Aufklärung bis zur Gegenwart*, vol. 1, ed. Harro Müller-Michaels (Königstein: Athenäum, 1981), 200–38; and Dieter Kafitz, "Die subversive Kraft der Sinnlichkeit in Franz Grillparzers 'Die Jüdin von Toledo,'" *Zeitschrift für deutsche Philologie* 112 (1993): 188–214. For an incisive analysis that confronts the play's anti-Semitism and intreprets the text's programmatic emphasis on hybridity and mixture, see Eva Geulen, "Das Geheimnis der Mischung: Grillparzers *Jüdin von Toledo*," in *Die deutsche Tragödie. Neue Lektüren einer Gattung im europäischen Kontext*, ed. Volker C. Dörr and Helmut J. Schneider (Bielefeld: Aisthesis, 2006), 157–73. Geulen's essay was published after the present analysis first appeared in 2002.

2. "[D]as Weib als solches, nichts, als ihr Geschlecht." Parenthetical references to the play (act, line, and page number) are to Franz Grillparzer, *Sämtliche Werke*, ed. Peter Frank and Karl Pörnbacher, 4 vols. (Munich: Hanser, 1960), here volume 2. The translations are my own. Konstanze Lauterbach's 2007 production at the Staatstheater Wiesbaden focused on the erotic dimension of the play, and apparently deleted most of the dialogue concerned with the "Jewish Question." Eva-Marie Magel, "Da beißt der König in den Kronleuchter," FAZ.net 19. November 2007, http://www.faz.net/s/RubFBF9 3A39DCA8403FB78B7625AD0646C5/Doc~EA10D51CB9E0A46FB9EB584 638FFF183B~ATpl~Ecommon~Scontent.html (accessed July 28, 2010).

3. "Trauerspiel. Die Geschichte Alonso des Guten von Kastilien und jener Rahel, *die ihn nicht ohne Verdacht der Zauberei* [b: 3 unterstr.], so lange umstrickt, und die zuletzt von den Großen des Reichs im Einverständniße mit der Königin, ermordet wurde." Parenthetical references to the "Apparat zur Jüdin von Toledo" from the Grillparzer critical edition (vol. 21, part 1) are cited as *HKA*. The translations are my own. See also Grillparzer's diary entry for a sketch of the play dating from 1827: "Rahels Verhältniß zum König gewißermaßen Bezauberung" (*HKA* 369). Franz Grillparzer, *Sämtliche Werke. Historisch-kritische Gesamtausgabe*, ed. August Sauer and Reinhold Backmann, vol. 21, part 1 (Vienna: Anton Schroll, 1940).

4. Dorothy Lasker-Schlitt, *Grillparzer's Attitude Toward the Jews* (Diss., New York University, 1936), 119, 121, 88. For a recent analysis that interprets the play within the context of Roman Catholic attitudes toward the Jews, see Eda Sagarra, "Grillparzer, the Catholics, and the Jews: A Reading of *Die Jüdin von Toledo (1851)*," *Leo Baeck Institute Yearbook* 46 (2001): 67–79.

5. Sigurd Paul Scheichl, "Franz Grillparzer zwischen Judenfeindschaft und Josephinismus," in *Conditio Judaica. Judentum, Antisemitismus und deutschsprachige Literatur vom 18. Jahrhundert bis zum Ersten Weltkrieg*, part 1, ed. Hans Otto Horch and Horst Denkler (Tübingen: Niemeyer, 1988), 135, 145.

6. For analyses that downplay the significance of the characters' religion see Lasker-Schlitt, *Grillparzer's Attitude Toward the Jews;* Harold F. Lenz, *Grillparzer's Political Ideas and "Die Jüdin von Toledo"* (Diss., New York University, published privately, 1938); Eric A. Blackall, "Grillparzer: *Die Jüdin von Toledo,*" in *Deutsche Dramen von Gryphius bis Brecht: Interpretation,* vol. 2, ed. Jost Schillemeit (Frankfurt am Main and Hamburg: Fischer, 1965), 240–52; Charlene A. Lea, *Emancipation, Assimilation and Stereotype: The Image of the Jew in German and Austrian Drama 1800–1850* (Bonn: Bouvier, 1978); and Scheichl, "Franz Grillparzer." To varying degrees these analyses also subscribe to the second strand of criticism that situates the text as wavering between a Josephinist tolerance of Jews and an ingrained anti-Semitism. Recently Florian Krobb has argued that the text's self-contradictory statements are a reflection of its protracted genesis, and that it would be incorrect to try to resolve these inconsistencies. Florian Krobb, "'Bleib zurück, geh nicht in' Garten!': Grillparzers *Jüdin von Toledo* als Traktat über die 'Judenfrage,'" in *Judenrollen: Darstellungsformen im europäischen Theater von der Restauration bis zur Zwischenkriegszeit,* ed. Hans-Peter Bayerdörfer and Jens Malte Fischer (Tübingen: Niemeyer, 2008), 125.

7. Angress cites the play's most pro-Jewish passage—the eloquent speech in which the king defends the Jews—and then remarks: "Doch werden damit die stereotyp-schlechten Eigenschaften der Juden, die Gefahr, die von ihnen ausgehen soll, ja nicht abgestritten, sondern im Gegenteil durch eine josefinisch-aufgeklärt Geisteshaltung bestätigt. 'Die Jüdin von Toledo' ist das merkwürdigste Gemisch solcher Bestätigungen und beschwichtigender Rücknahmen." Ruth K. Angress, "Wunsch- und Angstbilder: Jüdische Gestalten aus der deutschen Literatur des neunzehnten Jahrhunderts," in *Kontroversen, alte und neue. Akten des VII. Internationalen Germanisten-Kongresses,* vol. 1, ed. Albrecht Schöne (Tübingen: Niemeyer, 1985), 94.

8. The text's stereotypical characterizations of the Jews was noted in a review of the play's Prague premiere in 1872, which characterizes Rahel as a devilish siren whose "orientalische Üppigkeit" ("Oriental voluptuousness") is opposed to northern "Tugend" ("virtue"); Isaak as a Shylock figure; and Esther as a "weiblicher Nathan" (a "female Nathan" [*HKA* 330–31]).

9. "[D]ie Bösewichte, die keine waren." Lorenz, "'Schafe im Wolfpelz,'" 79.

10. That Grillparzer had begun to work on sketches of the play as early as 1809 or 1813, that he was heavily influenced by Lope de Vega's drama, and that the title figure was modeled after one of Grillparzer's non-Jewish mistresses in no way invalidates the significance of the "Jewish Question" to the text; to reason so strikes me as illogical, given the centrality of the emancipation debate to the politics and discourse of the era. Oddly, the three critics who contextualize Grillparzer's works with reference to his attitudes toward Jews, Jewish emancipation, and politics (Lasker-Schlitt, Lenz, and Lea) cite these reasons as grounds for dismissing the "Jewish Question" in interpreting the text.

11. *The New Shorter Oxford English Dictionary,* ed. Lesley Brown, 2 vols. (Oxford University Press, 1993), 1019.

12. The following historical overview is drawn from Wolfgang von Wurzbach, "Die 'Jüdin von Toledo' in Geschichte und Dichtung," *Jahrbuch der Grillparzer-Gesellschaft* 9 (1899): 86–89.

13. Jean de Mariana, *Histoire Generale D'Espagne*, trans. P. Joseph-Nicolas Charenton (Paris: 1725), 5 vols, here vol. 2: 632–33.

14. Scheichl proposes a differing interpretation, arguing that we may surmise that Grillparzer thought historically enough that he did not use the term "free of prejudice" ironically, that in seventeenth-century Spain the only way to depict a Jew positively was by converting him or her to Christianity : "Man kann davon ausgehn, daß Grillparzer historisch genug dachte, um 'Vorurteilsfreiheit' hier nicht ironisch zu meinen: im Spanien des 17. Jahrhunderts gab es eben keine andere Möglichkeit als ein solches Taufbegehren, um eine jüdische Figur positiv zu zeichnen" (Scheichl, "Franz Grillparzer," 141).

15. The designation is not Grillparzer's own, but was probably added by Josef Weilen. In the critical edition Backmann postulates that Grillparzer never would have called his play a "historical" tragedy: "Gr. würde sein Stück nie als 'historisches' Trauerspiel überschrieben haben" (*HKA* 372–73). This assertion may well be true, but the fact remains that Grillparzer did choose historical subject matter for his play.

16. Backmann states it is unclear Grillparzer was aware of the parallels between the Danish and Spanish stories, but was aware of the parallels with the Dutch account (*HKA* 319, 321). See also Wurzbach, "Die 'Jüdin von Toledo,'" 99.

17. The following discussion draws heavily from Jacob Katz, *From Prejudice to Destruction: Anti-Semitism, 1700–1933* (Cambridge, Mass., and London: Harvard University Press, 1980), 223–29.

18. Acccording to Pauley, Jews played a more prominent role in every stage of the 1848 revolution in Austria than in any other European country. As a result of the events of 1848 Jews in both Austria and Germany were termed "revolutionaries." Bruce F. Pauley, *From Prejudice to Persecution: A History of Austrian Anti-Semitism* (Chapel Hill and London: University of North Carolina Press, 1992), 20. See also James F. Harris, *The People Speak! Anti-Semitism and Emancipation in Nineteenth-Century Bavaria* (Ann Arbor: University of Michigan Press, 1994), 74–75, 130–31.

19. Katz, *From Prejudice to Destruction*, 229.

20. Grillparzer, perhaps reacting to negative criticism he had received for some of his work, chose not to publish three major manuscripts, among them *The Jewess of Toledo*.

21. Katz, *From Prejudice to Destruction*, 210–11.

22. See Lasker-Schlitt, *Grillparzer's Attitude Toward the Jews*, for a summary of these statements.

23. Irving Massey, *Philo-Semitism in Nineteenth-Century German Literature* (Tübingen: Niemeyer, 2000), 114–16. Massey notes that Grillparzer identifies the main theme of *Esther* as "die Ideen von Staatsreligion und Duldung" ("the ideas of a state religion and toleration"); the historical impetus for this examination of religious toleration was not the "Jewish Question" per se, but

the marriage of the Grand Duke Karl to Henriette, who was Protestant (115). Grillparzer's plans for the continuation of *Esther* are reprinted in Karl Pörnbacher, ed., *Dichter über ihre Dichtungen: Franz Grillparzer* (Munich: Heimeran, 1970), 239–52. The word "Kanaille" is derived from the Latin *canis*, "dog." Gerhard Wahrig, *Deutsches Wörterbuch* (Munich: Bertelsman, 1991), 2032.

24. Grillparzer, *Sämtliche Werke*, ed. Frank and Pörnbacher, vol. 1, 577. Grillparzer wrote the quatrain in 1865, when the Jews in the Habsburg empire had been granted legal rights. In his study of the 1848 revolutions in Bavaria, Harris analyzes the rhetoric of emancipation legislation and remarks: "One could support emancipation in 1849–50 and still be anti-Judaic and perhaps even anti-Semitic" (*The People Speak!* 65). This comment might also apply to Grillparzer's quatrain.

25. Scheichl makes this assertion, noting the epigram was written some ten years after Grillparzer finished the manuscript of the play ("Franz Grillparzer," 144).

26. In her 2007 production of the play at the Hans Otto Theater in Potsdam, Jacqueline Kornmüller emphasized the play's conflation of Jew and Muslim by having Rahel and Esther make their first appearance clad in burka-like robes. Rahel then drops her robe and remains naked for the remainder of the play. Wolfgang Behrens, "Hüllenlos in einem Meer vom Schaum," nachtkritik.de, http://www.nachtkritik.de/index.php?option=com_content&view=article&id =451:die-juedin-von-toledo—jacqueline-kornmueller-grillparzt-zu -saisonbeginn&catid=3 (accessed July 28, 2010).

27. I make this argument in partial opposition to Lorenz, who regards Rahel's capriciousness, rather than her Jewishness, as the threat to the Christian state, to the structure of Spain's first family, and thus to the Christian family system and to the society's general repression: "Ihre Freizügigkeit macht sie zur Feindin des Staates. Sie gefährdet die Ordnung der ersten Familie Spaniens und damit das christliche Familiensystem und die allgemeine Repression." Dagmar C. G. Lorenz, *Grillparzer: Dichter des sozialen Konflikts* (Vienna: Böhlau, 1986), 99.

28. "Gr. hat das Stück "Die Jüdin von Toledo" genannt. Nicht ohne bestimmte Absicht. [. . .] Daß Gr. das moderne, ihn umgebende Judenthum mit im Auge gehabt, diese poetische Perfidie kann man nicht von der Hand weisen. Bestimmte ihn doch wohl dazu die Bedeutung des Judenthums in dem modernen Leben, die heutige Macht der Nation, die basaltartig, vulkanisch, die Völkerlagerung Europa's durchbrach." Review by "D.R." in the *Wiener Abendpost* (Beilage der *Wiener Zeitung*) of January 23, 1873 (*HKA* 346).

29. "Hinter Rahels Sippe lauert ein ganzes Volk auf den Einbruch in den Staatskörper." Quoted in Scheichl, "Franz Grillparzer," 132.

30. The poem appears in Grillparzer, *Sämtliche Werke*, ed. Frank and Pörnbacher, vol. 1, 310–11. Lorenz interprets the poem in relation to the play in terms of its celebration of the liberalization of sexual mores. I concur, but note the poem was written in 1847, before the full extent of the affair was apparent. I suggest Grillparzer's assessment of Montez would have changed after Ludwig I was forced to abdicate in 1848.

31. The following summary is drawn from Jim Yardley, "Lola, Long Dead, Is Still Getting Attention," *New York Times* (April 26, 1998): 31; and Bruce Seymour, *Lola Montez: A Life* (New Haven and London: Yale University Press, 1996).

32. For discussions of Montez as a sorceress and a spy see Ishbell Ross, *The Uncrowned Queen: The Life of Lola Montez* (New York: Harper & Row, 1972), 86–122. Vogt's pamphlet, published in Munich in 1848, contains descriptions of Montez being led by a demon into Bavaria and threatening the purity of the Bavarian people, "eine unvermischte deutsche Nation" ("an unmixed German nation"). Karl Wilhelm Vogt, *Lola Montez mit ihrem Anhange und Münchens Bürger und Studenten: Ein dunkler Fleck und ein Glanzpunkt in Baierns Geschichte* (Munich, 1848), 14, 7.

33. At the time, Bavaria was a Catholic state, and citizenship was limited to Catholics. Accordingly, in the debate over Montez's citizenship, the question was raised whether she was indeed Catholic.

34. This semantic network is introduced in the king's first appearance in act 1: in the space of thirty lines (I, 157–86: 455–56) the words *Fehl, Fehler,* and *fleckenlos* are repeated seven times to describe Alfonso as a man without flaws and faults, a characterization that will be called into question on the semiotic level through the repetition and transformation of these descriptors throughout the text.

35. The king originally had intended to house the Jews only until night fell and they could be escorted safely back to their own home in the Judenstraße under the cover of darkness, but between acts 2 and 3 moves Rahel to the Lustschloß Retiro, site of his ancestor Don Sancho's renowned affair with a Mooress. From this remote venue—marked by its name as a place removed from the court—the Jews threaten the Christian state.

36. "Die Lanze paßte gut für meinen Zweck" (III, 1002: 486). The phallic symbolism of the king's weapons is suggested throughout this scene and elsewhere in the text (I, 178: 456).

37. See also Manrike's justification for killing Rahel, that her death is divinely ordained because she has committed a transgression against the divine order: "Gott geizt mit seiner Menschen Leben nicht, / Und soll man ängstlich sein, da wo sein Wort, / Die heil'ge Ordnung die er selbst gesetzt / Den Tod des Einen fordert, der gefrevelt" (IV, 1236–39: 494). The king also is criticized for going against the natural order in constructing the "Lustgarten" that will lead to his downfall.

38. See Politzer, "Das Spiel vom Fall" for an extensive discussion of the play's framed structure and its treatment of the Fall motif.

39. To be sure, this schema is relativized in the larger historical context: the Battle of Alarcos marked a setback for the Christian state, but the Moors ultimately were driven from Spain.

40. Alfonso unwittingly anticipates Rahel's demonic transformation at the start of the play when he remarks: "Doch soll den Tag man nicht vor den Abend loben / Und malen nicht den Teufel an die Wand" ("But one should not praise the day before evening / And not paint the Devil on the wall" [I,

188–89: 456]), a seemingly innocuous homily that takes on significance in light of the *Bildertausch* in which Rahel replaces the king's framed portrait with her own, in some sense becoming a painted Devil.

41. Grillparzer adopts the *Bild* motif from Cazotte, who uses the Jewess's picture as a talisman, a clear sign of the Jews' necromancy. Jacques Cazotte, *Rahel ou la belle juive. Oeuvres badines et morales,* vol. 7 (London: 1798), 141–232.

42. At the beginning of the play Esther states that she and her family are not spies for the Moors, and the king readily accepts this assertion. Indeed, the text never suggests the Jews in this play are spies, but it does repeatedly link the Jews and the Moors to the point where the two religious groups are virtually interchangeable as "Andersgläubige"("those of other faiths"). In act 1 the Moors mass at the borders of the realm, and the Jews in the kingdom are roughed up as a result. The king objects strenuously to their mistreatment, claiming he will protect all subjects in his realm, regardless of their beliefs, and he attacks Garceran for calling Rahel "eine schöne Heidin" ("a beautiful heathen" [I, 371: 463]). But the queen, referring to Rahel, asserts that "Der Mauren Volk und all was ihnen ähnlich" ("The Moorish people and all like them" [IV, 1424: 499]) practice black magic, a claim that is lent a certain amount of credence by the fact that when Esther utters her curse at the close of the play, the Moors defeat Alfonso.

43. Massey characterizes Esther's change of heart here as "an unintelligible, almost ridiculous, volte-face" (*Philo-Semitism,* 114).

44. The groundwork for this transformation is laid at the beginning of the text. Alfonso sets himself up as a signifier in his very first speech of the play: "Laßt näher nur das Volk! Es stört mich nicht. / Denn wer mich einen König nennt, bezeichnet / Als höchsten unter Vielen mich, und Menschen / Sind so ein Teil von meinen eigen selbst" ("Let the people nearer! It doesn't bother me. / Since whoever calls me a king signifies / Me as the highest among many, and people / Are thus a part of my own self" [I, 94–97: 454]).

45. Wurzbach notes there were also rumors the boy was poisoned by his older sister ("Die 'Jüdin von Toledo,' " 92–93).

46. The characterization of Rahel as a Christ figure is historically accurate in that Jesus was a Jew, but serves to emphasize the challenge the Jews pose to the Christians from a historical theological perspective: as Alfonso remarks in his impassioned defense of the Jews, the Jews, as the guarantors of a divine, prelapsarian truth, are closer to God on a chronological scale than are the Christians. This is why Rahel's transformation into a Christ figure represents a challenge to the Christian state: Alfonso, as God's earthly representative, should be the Christ figure, but he is supplanted by a Jew, thereby suggesting the Jews are closer to God than the Christians not only on a chronological scale, but also on an absolute scale.

47. For a discussion of the figure of the "Schwelle" in the play see Wolfgang Wittkowski, "Motiv und Strukturprinzip der Schwelle in Grillparzers *Die Jüdin von Toledo," Modern Austrian Literature* 23, no. 3/4 (1995): 105–30.

48. Lorenz, *Grillparzer: Dichter des sozialen Konflikts,* 111.

BIBLIOGRAPHY

Aichele, Kathryn Porter. *Paul Klee, Poet/Painter.* Rochester, N.Y.: Camden House, 2006.

Almog, Shmuel. "What's in a Hyphen?" *SICSA Report: Newsletter of the Vidal Sassoon International Center for the Study of Antisemitism* 2 (Summer 1989): 1–2.

The Anchor Bible Dictionary. Edited by David Noel Freedman. New York, London, Toronto: Doubleday, 1992.

Angress, Ruth K. "Wunsch- und Angstbilder: Jüdische Gestalten aus der deutschen Literatur des neunzehnten Jahrhunderts." In *Kontroversen, alte und neue. Akten des VII. Internationalen Germanisten-Kongresses,* vol. 1, edited by Albrecht Schöne, 85–96. Tübingen: Niemeyer, 1985.

Arnim, Ludwig Achim von. *Halle und Jerusalem.* In *Dramen von Clemens Brentano und Ludwig Achim von Arnim,* edited by Paul Kluckhohn, 49–298. Reclam: Leipzig, 1938.

———. *Werke in sechs Bänden,* vol. 3, *Sämtliche Erzählungen 1802–1817,* edited by Renate Moering. Frankfurt am Main: Deutscher Klassiker Verlag, 1990.

———. *Werke und Briefwechsel, Historisch-Kritische Ausgabe,* vol. 11, *Texte der deutschen Tischgesellschaft,* edited by Stefan Nienhaus. Tübingen: Niemeyer, 2008.

Assmann, Jan. *Moses the Egyptian: The Memory of Egypt in Western Monotheism.* London and Cambridge, Mass.: Harvard University Press, 1977.

———. "Vorwort" and "Nachwort" to Carl Leonhard Reinhold, *Die Hebräischen Mysterien, oder die älteste religiöse Freymaurerey,* edited by Jan Assmann, 5–10, 157–99. Neckargemünd: Mnemosyne, 2001.

Atkins, Stuart. "The Parable of the Rings in Lessing's *Nathan.*" *Germanic Review* 26, no. 4 (1951): 259–67.

Barner, Wilfried. "Lessings *Die Juden* im Zusammenhang seines Frühwerks." In *Humanität und Dialog. Lessing und Mendelssohn in neuer Sicht,* edited by Ehrhard Bahr, Edward P. Harris, and Lawrence G. Lyon, 182–209. Detroit: Wayne State University Press, 1982.

———. "Vorurteil, Emperie, Rettung. Der junge Lessing und die Juden." In *Juden und Judentum in der Literatur,* edited by Herbert A. Strauss and Christhard Hoffmann, 52–77. Munich: Deutscher Taschenbuch Verlag, 1985.

Behrens, Wolfgang. "Hüllenlos in einem Meer vom Schaum," nachtkritik.de, http://www.nachtkritik.de/index.php?option=com_content&view=article &id=451:die-juedin-von-toledo—jacqueline-kornmueller-grillparzt -zu-saisonbeginn&catid=3 (accessed July 28, 2010).

Belchamber, N.P. "A Case of Identity: A New Look at *Die Judenbuche* by Annette von Droste-Hülshoff." *Modern Languages: Journal of the Modern Language Association* 55 (1974): 80–82.

Benjamin, Walter. "Karl Kraus." In *Gesammelte Schriften,* edited by Rolf Tiedemann and Hermann Schweppenhäuser, vol. II,1, 334–67. Frankfurt am Main: Suhrkamp, 1972.

Berghahn, Klaus. *Grenzen der Toleranz: Juden und Christen im Zeitalter der Aufklärung.* Cologne, Weimar, Vienna: Böhlau, 2000.

Blackall, Eric A. "Grillparzer: *Die Jüdin von Toledo.*" In *Deutsche Dramen von Gryphius bis Brecht: Interpretation,* vol. 2, edited by Jost Schillemeit, 240–52. Frankfurt am Main and Hamburg: Fischer, 1965.

Blasberg, Cornelia. *Erschriebene Tradition: Adalbert Stifter oder das Erzählen im Zeichen verlorener Geschichten.* Freiburg im Breisgau: Rombach, 1998.

Borchmeyer, Dieter. "Franz Grillparzer: Die Jüdin von Toledo." In *Deutsche Dramen. Interpretationen zu Werken von der Aufklärung bis zur Gegenwart,* vol. 1, edited by Harro Müller-Michaels, 200–38. Königstein: Athenäum, 1981.

Brandt, Lewis W. "Freud and Schiller." In *Psychoanalysis and the Psychoanalytic Review* 46, no. 4 (1959): 97–101.

Breger, Claudia. *Ortlosigkeit des Fremden. 'Zigeunerinnen' und 'Zigeuner' in der deutschsprachigen Literatur um 1800.* Cologne, Weimar, Vienna: Böhlau Verlag, 1998.

Brentano, Clemens. "Der Philister vor, in und nach der Geschichte." In *Ludwig Achim von Arnim. Werke und Briefwechsel, Historisch-Kritische Ausgabe,* vol. 11, *Texte der deutschen Tischgesellschaft,* edited by Stefan Nienhaus, 38–90. Tübingen: Niemeyer, 2008.

Brett, Doris. "Friedrich, the Beech, and Margreth in Droste-Hülshoff's 'Judenbuche.'" *Journal of English and Germanic Philology* (1985): 157–65.

Brown, Jane K. "The Real Mystery in Droste-Hülshoff's 'Die Judenbuche.'" *Modern Language Review* 73 (1978): 835–46.

Brückner, Wolfgang, ed. *Maria Buchen. Eine fränkishe Wallfahrt.* Würzburg: Echter Verlag, 1979.

Cazotte, Jacques. *Rahel ou la belle juive. Oeuvres badines et morales,* vol. 7, 141–232. London: 1798.

Chase, Jefferson S. "Part of the Story: The Significance of the Jews in Annette von Droste-Hülshoff's *Die Judenbuche.*" *Deutsche Vierteljahrsschrift für Literaturwissenschaft und Geistesgeschichte* 71 (1997): 127–45.

Cheyette, Bryan. *Constructions of 'The Jew' in English Literature and Society.* Cambridge, U.K.: Cambridge University Press, 1993.

Cottrell, Alan P. "The Significance of the Name 'Johannes' in *Die Judenbuche.*" *Seminar* 6 (1970): 207–15.

Dann, Otto. "Schiller the Historian." In *A Companion to the Works of Friedrich Schiller,* edited by Steven D. Martinson, 67–86. Rochester, N.Y.: Camden House, 2005.

———. "Stellenkommentar" to *Die Sendung Moses.* In *Friedrich Schiller Werke und Briefe in zwölf Bänden, Band 6: Historische Schriften und*

Erzählungen I, edited by Otto Dann. Frankfurt am Main: Deutscher Klassiker Verlag, 2000.

Diersen, Inge. "'. . . ein arm verkümmert Sein': Annette von Droste-Hülshoffs 'Die Judenbuche.'" *Zeitschrift für Germanistik* 3 (1983): 299–313.

Doerr, Karin. "The Specter of Anti-Semitism in and Around Annette von Droste-Hülshoff's *Judenbuche.*" *German Studies Review* 17 (1994): 447–71.

Donahue, William Collins. "'Ist er kein Jude, so verdiente er einer zu sein': Droste-Hülshoff's *Die Judenbuche* and Religious Anti-Semitism." *The German Quarterly* 72, no. 1 (1999): 44–73.

Downing, Eric. *Double Exposures: Repetition and Realism in Nineteenth-Century German Fiction.* Stanford, Calif.: Stanford University Press, 2000.

Droste-Hülshoff, Annette von. *Historisch-Kritische Ausgabe.* 13 vols., edited by Walter Huge. Tübingen: Niemeyer, 1978–1988.

———. *The Jews' Beech Tree.* Translated by Michael Bullock, in *Three Eerie Tales from 19th Century Germany,* 101–51. New York: Ungar, 1975.

Eder, Jürgen. "Schiller als Historiker." In *Schiller-Handbuch,* edited by Helmut Koopmann, 653–98. Kroner: Stuttgart, 1998.

Elon, Amos. *The Pity of It All: A Portrait of the German-Jewish Epoch 1743–1933.* New York: Picador, 2002.

Enzinger, Moriz. *Adalbert Stifter im Urteil seiner Zeit.* Vienna: Bühlau, Kommissionsverlag der Österreichischen Akademie der Wissenschaften in Wien, 1968.

Erdle, Birgit. "'Über die Kennzeichen des Judenthums': Die Rhetorik der Unterscheidung in einem phantasmatischen Text von Achim von Arnim." *German Life and Letters* 49, no. 2 (1996): 147–58.

Erspamer, Peter R. *The Elusiveness of Tolerance: The "Jewish Question" from Lessing to the Napoleonic Wars.* Chapel Hill and London: University of North Carolina Press, 1997.

Felsenstein, Frank. *Anti-Semitic Stereotypes: A Paradigm of Otherness in English Popular Culture, 1660–1830.* Baltimore and London: Johns Hopkins University Press, 1995.

Fenves, Peter. "Die Scham der Schönheit: Einige Bemerkungen zu Stifter." In *"Geteilte Aufmerksamkeit": Zur Frage des Lesens,* edited by Thomas Schestag, 91–111. Frankfurt am Main: Peter Lang, 1997.

Fischer, Barbara, and Thomas C. Fox. "Lessing's Life and Work." In *A Companion to the Works of Gotthold Ephraim Lessing,* edited by Barbara Fischer and Thomas C. Fox, 13–39. Rochester, N.Y.: Camden House, 2005.

Fischer, Kurt Gerhard. "Der jüdische Mensch in Stifters Dichtungs-Denken." *Vierteljahrsschrift des Adalbert-Stifter-Instituts des Landes Oberösterreich* 14 (1965): 109–18.

Franzos, Karl Emil. "Eine Novelle und ihre Quellen." *Allgemeine Zeitung des Judentums* 61, no. 51–53 (1897): 609 ff.

Frenzel, Herbert, and Elisabeth Frenzel. *Daten deutscher Dichtung. Chronologischer Abriß der deutschen Literaturgeschichte.* 2 vols. 22nd ed. Munich: Deutscher Taschenbuch Verlag, 1985.

Freudenthal, Gad. "Aaron Salomon Gumpertz, Gotthold Ephraim Lessing, and the First Call for an Improvement of the Civil Rights of Jews in Germany." *Association of Jewish Studies Review* 29, no. 2 (2005): 299–353.

Freund, Winfried. "Der Außenseiter 'Friedrich Mergel': Eine sozialpsychologische Studie zur *Judenbuche* der Annette von Droste-Hülshoff." *Zeitschrift für Deutsche Philologie Sonderheft* 99 (1980): 110–18.

Friedrichsmeyer, Sara. "Romantic Nationalism: Achim von Arnim's Gypsy Princess Isabella." In *Gender and Germanness: Cultural Productions of Nation*, edited by Patricia Herminghouse and Magda Mueller, 51–65. Providence and Oxford: Berhgahn, 1997.

Garloff, Katja. "Figures of Love in Romantic Antisemitism: Achim von Arnim." *The German Quarterly* 80, no. 4 (2007): 427–48.

———. "Sublimation and Its Discontents: Christian-Jewish Love in Lessing's *Nathan der Weise*." *Lessing Yearbook/ Jahrbuch* 36 (2004/2005): 51–68.

Geiger, Ludwig. "Schiller und die Juden." In Geiger, *Die deutsche Literatur und die Juden*, 125–60. Berlin: Reimer, 1910.

Gelber, Mark H. "What Is Literary Antisemitism?" *Jewish Social Studies* 47, no. 1 (1985): 1–20.

Gelbin, Cathy S. *The Golem Returns: From German Romantic Literature to Global Jewish Culture, 1808–2008*. Ann Arbor: University of Michigan Press, 2011.

Geulen, Eva. "Das Geheimnis der Mischung: Grillparzers *Jüdin von Toledo*." In *Die deutsche Tragödie. Neue Lektüren einer Gattung im europäischen Kontext*, edited by Volker C. Dörr and Helmut J. Schneider, 157–73. Bielefeld: Aisthesis, 2006.

———. *Worthörig wider Willen: Darstellungsproblematik und Sprachreflexion in der Prosa Adalbert Stifters*. Munich: Iudicum, 1992.

Gilman, Sander L. *Difference and Pathology: Stereotypes of Sexuality, Race, and Madness*. Ithaca and London: Cornell University Press, 1985.

———. *Freud, Race, Gender*. Princeton, N.J.: Princeton University Press, 1993.

———. *Jewish Self-Hatred: Anti-Semitism and the Hidden Language of the Jews*. Baltimore and London: Johns Hopkins University Press, 1986.

———. *The Jew's Body*. New York and London: Routledge, 1991.

Goetschel, Willi. "Lessing and the Jews." In *A Companion to the Works of Gotthold Ephraim Lessing*, edited by Barbara Fischer and Thomas C. Fox, 185–208. Rochester, N.Y.: Camden House, 2005.

Gray, Richard T. "Red Herrings and Blue Smocks: Ecological Destruction, Commercialism, and Anti-Semitism in Annette von Droste-Hülshoff's *Die Judenbuche*." *German Studies Review* 26, no. 3 (2003): 515–42.

Grillparzer, Franz. *Sämtliche Werke*, edited by Peter Frank and Karl Pörnbacher. 4 vols. Munich: Hanser, 1960.

———. *Sämtliche Werke. Historisch-kritische Gesamtausgabe*, edited by August Sauer and Reinhold Backmann, vol. 21, part 1. Vienna: Anton Schroll, 1940.

Grimm, Jacob, and Wilhelm Grimm. *Deutsches Wörterbuch*. Leipzig: Hirzel, 1936.

Guarda, Sylvain. "Stifters *Abdias*: Kindheit in ästhetischer Spiegelung." *German Life and Letters* 61, no. 3 (2008): 297–310.

Gumbrecht, Hans Ulrich. "How (If at All) Can We Encounter What Remains Latent in Texts?" *Partial Answers: Journal of Literature and the History of Ideas* 7, no. 1 (2009): 87–96.

Guthke, Karl S. "Lessing und das Judentum. Rezeption. Dramatik und Kritik. Krypto-Spinozismus." In *Judentum im Zeitalter der Aufklärung. Wolfenbütteler Studien zur Aufklärung,* vol. 4, edited by Günter Schulz, 229–71. Wolfenbüttel: Jacobi, 1977.

Hahn, Karl-Heinz. "Schiller als Historiker." In *Aufklärung und Geschichte. Studien zur deutschen Geschichtswissenschaft im 18. Jahrhundert,* edited by Hans Erich Bödeker, Georg G. Iggers, Jonathan B. Knudsen, and Peter H. Reill, 388–415. Göttingen: Vandenhoeck & Ruprecht, 1986.

Harris, James F. *The People Speak! Anti-Semitism and Emancipation in Nineteenth-Century Bavaria.* Ann Arbor: University of Michigan Press, 1994.

Härtl, Heinz. "Romantischer Antisemitismus: Arnim und die 'Tischgesellschaft.'" *Weimarer Beiträge* 33, no. 7 (1987): 1159–73.

Hartwich, Wolf-Daniel. *Romantischer Antisemitismus: Von Klopstock bis Richard Wagner.* Göttingen: Vandenhoeck & Ruprecht, 2005.

———. *Die Sendung Moses: Von der Aufklärung bis Thomas Mann.* Munich: Fink, 1997.

Heine, Heinrich. "Das neue Israelitische Hospital zu Hamburg." In *Heinrich Heine Historisch-Kritische Gesamtausgabe der Werke* (Düsseldorfer Ausgabe), vol. 2, *Neue Gedichte,* edited by Elisabeth Benton, 117–18. Hamburg: Hoffman and Campe, 1983.

Helfer, Martha B. "The Fairy Tale Jew." In *Neue Lektüren/New Readings,* edited by Norbert Eke and Gerhard Knapp, 31–42. Amsterdamer Beiträge zur neueren Germanistik, vol. 67. Amsterdam and New York: Rodopi: 2009.

———. "Framing the Jew: Grillparzer's *Die Jüdin von Toledo.*" *The German Quarterly* 75, no. 2 (2002): 160–80.

———. "Natural Anti-Semitism: Stifter's *Abdias.*" *Deutsche Vierteljahrsschrift für Literaturwissenschaft und Geistesgeschichte* 78, no. 2 (2004): 261–86.

———. *"Wer wagt es, eitlen Blutes Drang zu messen?:* Reading Blood in Annette von Droste-Hülshoff's *Die Judenbuche.*" *The German Quarterly* 71, no. 3 (1998): 228–53.

Henckmann, Gisela. "Das Problem des 'Antismitismus' bei Achim von Arnim." *Aurora* 46 (1986): 48–69.

Henel, Heinrich. "Annette von Droste-Hülshoff: Erzählstil und Wirklichkeit." In *Festschrift für Bernhard Blume: Aufsätze zur deutschen und europäischen Literatur,* edited by Egon Schwarz, Hunter G. Hannum, and Edgar Lohner, 146–72. Göttingen: Vandenhoeck & Ruprecht, 1967.

Hertz, Deborah. *How Jews Became Germans: The History of Conversion and Assimilation in Berlin.* New Haven and London: Yale University Press, 2007.

Heselhaus, Clemens. "Die Golem-Gespenster der Droste-Hülshoff." *Droste-Jahrbuch* 1 (1986/87): 129–56.

Hess, Jonathan M. *Germans, Jews and the Claims of Modernity.* New Haven and London: Yale University Press, 2002.

Heybey, Wolfgang. "Adalbert Stifters 'Abdias' und 'Das Heidedorf': Ein Beitrag zum Welt- und Menschbild des Dichters aus rassischer Grundlage." *Zeitschrift für Deutschkunde 56*, no. 6 (1942): 195–203.

Horowitz, Elliott. "The Early Eighteenth Century Confronts the Beard: Kabbalah and Jewish Self-Fashioning." *Jewish History* 8, no. 1–2 (1994): 96–115.

Huge, Walter, ed. *Erläuterungen und Dokumente: Annette von Droste-Hülshoff, Die Judenbuche.* Stuttgart: Reclam, 1979.

———. "'Die Judenbuche' als Kriminalgeschichte: Das Problem von Erkenntnis und Urteil im Kriminalschema." *Zeitschrift für Deutsche Philologie Sonderheft* 99 (1980): 49–70.

Immerwahr, Raymond. "'Die Judenbuche' als Gewebe von Begegnungen mit dem Fremden." In *Begegnung mit dem 'Fremden': Grenzen, Traditionen, Vergleiche. Akten des VIII. Internationalen Germanisten-Kongresses Tokyo 1990*, edited by Eijiro Iwaski, vol. 11, 137–46. Tokyo: 1990.

Kafitz, Dieter. "Die subversive Kraft der Sinnlichkeit in Franz Grillparzers 'Die Jüdin von Toledo.'" *Zeitschrift für deutsche Philologie* 112 (1993): 188–214.

Katz, Jacob. *From Prejudice to Destruction: Anti-Semitism 1700–1933.* Cambridge, Mass., and London: Harvard University Press, 1980.

———. *Jews and Freemasons in Europe, 1723–1939.* Translated by Leonard Oschry. Cambridge, Mass.: Harvard University Press, 1970.

———. "A State Within a State, the History of an Anti-Semitic Slogan." In Katz, *Emancipation and Assimilation: Studies in Modern Jewish History,* 47–76. Farnborough: Gregg, 1972.

Kilcher, Andreas B. "Ha-Gila: Hebräische und jiddische Schiller-Übersetzungen im 19. Jahrhundert." *Monatshefte* 100 (2008): 67–87.

King, Janet K. "Conscience and Conviction in 'Die Judenbuche.'" *Monatshefte* 64 (1972): 349–55.

Kleist, Heinrich von. *Sämtliche Werke und Briefe in Vier Bänden,* edited by Helmut Sembdner. Munich and Vienna: Hanser, 1982.

Klienberger, H. R. "Stifter's *Abdias* and Its Interpreters." *Forum for Modern Language Studies* 14 (1978): 332–48.

Knaack, Jürgen. *Achim von Arnim—Nicht nur Poet.* Darmstadt: Thesen Verlag, 1976.

Kohl, F. G. "Die Judenstadt in Prag." *Morgenblatt für gebildete Leser* (Stuttgart and Tübingen) May 16–21, 1842: 461–83.

Koopmann, Helmut. "Die Wirklichkeit des Bösen in der 'Judenbuche' der Droste: Zu einer moralischen Erzählung des 19. Jahrhunderts." *Zeitschrift für Deutsche Philologie Sonderheft* 99 (1980): 71–85.

Kortländer, Bernd. "Wahrheit und Wahrscheinlichkeit: Zu einer Schreibstrategie in der *Judenbuche* der Droste." *Zeitschrift für Deutsche Philologie Sonderheft* 99 (1980): 86–99.

Krauss, Karoline. "Das offene Geheimnis in Annette von Droste-Hülshoff's *Die Judenbuche*." *Zeitschrift für deutsche Philologie* 114 (1995): 542–59.

Krobb, Florian. "'Bleib zurück, geh nicht in' Garten!': Grillparzers *Jüdin von Toledo* als Traktat über die 'Judenfrage.'" In *Judenrollen: Darstellungsformen im europäischen Theater von der Restauration bis zur Zwischenkriegszeit,* edited by Hans-Peter Bayerdörfer and Jens Malte Fischer, 125–42. Tübingen: Niemeyer, 2008.

Krus, Horst-Dieter. *Mordsache Soistmann Berend. Zum historischen Hintergrund der Novelle "Die Judenbuche" von Annette von Droste-Hülshoff.* Münster: Aschendorff, 1990.

Lasker-Schlitt, Dorothy. *Grillparzer's Attitude Toward the Jews.* Diss. New York University, 1936.

Lauckner, Nancy A. "The Surrogate Jew in the Postwar German Novel." *Monatshefte* 66 (1974): 133–44.

Lea, Charlene A. *Emancipation, Assimilation and Stereotype: The Image of the Jew in German and Austrian Drama 1800–1850.* Bonn: Bouvier, 1978.

Lenz, Harold F. *Grillparzer's Political Ideas and "Die Jüdin von Toledo."* Diss. New York University, published privately, 1938.

Lessing, Gotthold Ephraim. *Werke und Briefe in zwölf Bänden,* edited by Wilfried Barner. Frankfurt am Main: Deutscher Klassiker Verlag, 1985–2001.

Leventhal, Robert S. "The Parable as Performance: Interpretation, Cultural Transmission and Political Strategy in Lessing's *Nathan der Weise*." *The German Quarterly* 61, no. 4 (1988): 502–27.

Levy, Richard S. "Forget Webster." *German Studies Review* 29, no. 1 (2006): 145–46.

Librett, Jeffrey. *The Rhetoric of Cultural Dialogue.* Stanford, Calif.: Stanford University Press, 2000.

Lietina-Ray, Maruta. "Das Recht der öffentlichen Meinung: Über das Vorurteil in der *Judenbuche*." *Zeitschrift für Deutsche Philologie Sonderheft* 99 (1980): 99–109.

Lippuner, Heinz. "Grillparzers 'Jüdin von Toledo'. Untersuchung eines Paradigmas." *Orbis Litterarum* 27 (1972): 202–23.

Lorenz, Dagmar C. G. *Grillparzer: Dichter des sozialen Konflikts.* Vienna: Böhlau, 1986.

———. "'Schafe im Wolfpelz' oder die Bösewichte, die keine waren: Die Juden in Grillparzers *Die Jüdin von Toledo*." *Jahrbuch der Grillparzer-Gesellschaft,* 3. Folge, 15 (1983): 79–87.

Low, Alfred D. *Jews in the Eyes of Germans from the Enlightenment to Imperial Germany.* Philadelphia: Institute for the Study of Human Issues, 1979.

Magel, Eva-Marie. "Da beißt der König in den Kronleuchter," FAZ.net 19. November 2007. http://www.faz.net/s/RubFBF93A39DCA8403FB78B76 25AD0646C5/Doc~EA10D51CB9E0A46FB9EB584638FFF183B~ATpl ~Ecommon~Scontent.html (accessed July 28, 2010).

Mariana, Jean de. *Histoire Generale D'Espagne.* Translated by P. Joseph-Nicolas Charenton. 5 vols. Paris: 1725.

Marx, Karl. "On the Jewish Question." In Karl Marx, *Selected Writings,* edited by David McLellan, 39–62. Oxford, London, and New York: Oxford University Press, 1977.

————. "Zur Judenfrage." In *Karl Marx, Friedrich Engels, Werke*, vol. 1, 347–77. Berlin: Institut für Marxismus-Leninismus beim ZK der SED, 1961.

Massey, Irving. *Philo-Semitism in Nineteenth-Century German Literature.* Tübingen: Niemeyer, 2000.

Mathäs, Alexander. "Faith and Reason: Schiller's 'Die Sendung Moses.'" *The German Quarterly* 81, no. 3 (2008): 283–301.

McGlathery, James M. "Fear of Perdition in Droste-Hülshoff's *Judenbuche.*" In *Lebendige Form: Interpretationen zur deutschen Literatur. Festschrift für E. K. Henel,* edited by Jeffrey L. Sammons and Ernst Schürer, 229–44. Munich: Fink, 1970.

Mecklenburg, Norbert. *Der Fall 'Judenbuche': Revision eines Fehlurteils.* Bielefeld: Aisthesis Verlag, 2008.

Metz, Joseph. "The Jew as Sign in Stifter's *Abdias.*" *Germanic Review* 77, no. 3 (2002): 219–32.

Misch, Manfred. "Schiller und die Religion." In *Schiller heute,* edited by Hans-Jörg Knobloch and Helmut Koopmann, 27–43. Tübingen: Stauffenberg, 1996.

Moritz, Karl Philipp. *Droste-Hülshoff. Die "Judenbuche": Sittengemälde und Kriminalnovelle.* Paderborn, Munich, Vienna, and Zürich: Schöningh, 1980.

Mücke, Dorothea E. von. *The Seduction of the Occult and the Rise of the Fantastic Tale.* Stanford, Calif.: Stanford University Press, 2003.

Müller, Joachim. "Die Staatsthematik in Grillparzers Drama *Die Jüdin von Toledo.*" In *Die andere Welt. Aspekte der österreichischen Literatur des 19. und 20. Jahrhunderts,* edited by Kurt Barsch, Dietmar Goltschnigg, Gerhard Melzer, and Wolfgang Heinz Schober, 71–96. Bern and Munich: Hanser, 1979.

Neumann, Peter Horst. "Legende, Sage und Geschichte in Achim von Arnims 'Isabella von Ägypten.'" *Jahrbuch der deutschen Schillergesellschaft* 12 (1968): 296–314.

New Catholic Encyclopedia. New York: McGraw-Hill, 1967.

The New Shorter Oxford English Dictionary, edited by Lesley Brown. Oxford: Oxford University Press, 1973, 1993.

Nienhaus, Stefan. *Geschichte der deutschen Tischgesellschaft.* Tübingen: Niemeyer, 2003.

Nisbett, Hugh Barr. *Lessing. Eine Biographie.* Translated by Karl S. Guthke. Munich: Beck, 2008.

Och, Gunnar. *Imago judaica. Juden und Judentum im Spiegel der deutschen Literatur 1750–1812.* Würzburg: Königshausen & Neumann, 1995.

Oellers, Norbert. "Goethe und Schiller in ihrem Verhältnis zum Judentume." In *Conditio Judaica. Judentum, Antisemitismus und deutschsprachige Literatur vom 18. Jahrhundert bis zum 1. Weltkrieg,* part 1, edited by Hans Otto Horch and Horst Denkler, 108–30. Tübingen: Niemeyer, 1988.

Oesterle, Günter. "Juden, Philister und romantische Intellektuelle. Überlegungen zum Antisemitismus in der Romantik." *Athenäum: Jahrbuch für Romantik* 2 (1992): 55–89.

Oppermann, Gerard. "Die Narbe des Friedrich Mergel: Zur Aufklärung eines literarischen Motivs in Annette von Droste-Hülshoffs *Die Judenbuche.*" *Deutsche Vierteljahrsschrift für Literaturwissenschaft und Geistesgechichte* 13 (1976): 449–64.

Otto, Regine. "Schiller und Herder als Geschichtsschreiber. Annäherungen und Differenzen." In *Schiller als Historiker,* edited by Otto Dann, Norbert Oellers, and Ernst Osterkamp, 293–307. Stuttgart and Weimar: Metzler, 1995.

The Oxford Dictionary of the Jewish Religion. Edited by R. J. Zwi Werblowsky and Geoffrey Wigoder. New York and London: Oxford University Press, 1997.

Palmieri, Aldo. "Die Judenbuche—eine antisemitische Novelle?" In *Gegenbilder und Vorurteil: Aspekte des Judentums im Werk deutschsprachiger Schriftstellerinnen,* edited by Renate Heuer and Ralph-Rainer Wuthenow, 9–39. Frankfurt am Main and New York: Campus, 1995.

Pauley, Bruce F. *From Prejudice to Persecution: A History of Austrian Anti-Semitism.* Chapel Hill and London: University of North Carolina Press, 1992.

Pickar, Gertrud Bauer. "The Battering and Meta-Battering of Droste's Margreth: Covert Misogyny in *Die Judenbuche*'s Critical Reception." *Women in German Yearbook* 9 (1993): 71–90.

Politzer, Heinz. "Das Spiel vom Fall: *Die Jüdin von Toledo.*" In Politzer, *Franz Grillparzer oder das abgründige Biedermeier,* 328–50. Vienna, Munich, Zurich: Fritz Molden, 1972.

Pörnbacher, Karl, ed. *Dichter über ihre Dichtungen: Franz Grillparzer.* Munich: Heimeran, 1970.

Rashkin, Esther. "The Occulted Jew: Symbolism and Anti-Semitism in Villiers de l'Isle-Adam's Axël." *Nineteenth-Century French Studies* 26 (1998): 398–416.

———. "Tracing Phantoms: Religious Secrets and the (Un)veiling of Jewish Identity in Balzac's 'Sarrasine.'" *Religion and the Arts* 1, no. 4 (1997): 40–61.

Reinhold, Carl Leonhard. *Die Hebräischen Mysterien, oder die älteste religiöse Freymaurerey,* edited by Jan Assmann. Neckargemünd: Mnemosyne, 2001.

Robertson, Ritchie. "Antisemitismus und Ambivalenz: Zu Achim von Arnims Erzählung 'Die Majoratsherren.'" In *Romantische Identitätskonstruktionen: Nation, Geschichte, und (Auto-)Biographie,* edited by Sheila Dickson and Walter Pape, 51–63. Tübingen: Niemeyer, 2003.

———. *The 'Jewish Question' in German Literature, 1749–1939.* Oxford and New York: Oxford University Press, 1999.

Roedl, Urban. "Stifter und die Juden." *Jüdische Revue* 3, no. 3 (1938): 182–84.

Rölleke, Heinz. "Erzähltes Mysterium: Studie zur 'Judenbuche' der Annette von Droste-Hülshoff." *Deutsche Vierteljahrsschrift für Literaturwissenschaft und Geistesgeschichte* 42 (1968): 399–426.

Rose, Paul Lawrence. *German Question/Jewish Question: Revolutionary Antisemitism from Kant to Wagner.* Princeton, N.J.: Princeton University Press, 1990.

Ross, Ishbell. *The Uncrowned Queen: The Life of Lola Montez.* New York: Harper & Row, 1972.

Röthert, Hermann. *Westfälische Geschichte.* Gütersloh: Bertelsmann, 1962.

Rürup, Reinhard. "The Tortuous and Thorny Path to Legal Equality: 'Jew Laws' and Emancipatory Legislation in Germany from the Late Eighteenth Century." *Leo Baeck Institute Yearbook* 31 (1986): 3–33.

Rürup, Reinhard, and Thomas Nipperdey. "Antisemitismus—Entstehung, Funktion und Geschichte eines Begriffs." In Reinhard Rürup, *Emanzipation und Antisemitismus. Studien zur "Judenfrage" der bürgerlichen Gesellschaft,* 95–114. Göttingen: Vandenhoeck & Ruprecht, 1975.

Sagarra, Eda. "Grillparzer, the Catholics, and the Jews: A Reading of *Die Jüdin von Toledo (1851).*" *Leo Baeck Institute Yearbook* 46 (2001): 67–79.

Saul, Nicholas. *Gypsies and Orientalism in German Literature and Anthropology of the Long Nineteenth Century.* London: Legenda, 2007.

Scheichl, Sigurd Paul. "Franz Grillparzer zwischen Judenfeindschaft und Josephinismus." In *Conditio Judaica. Judentum, Antisemitismus und deutschsprachige Literatur vom 18. Jahrhundert bis zum Ersten Weltkrieg,* part 1, edited by Hans Otto Horch and Horst Denkler, 131–49. Tübingen: Niemeyer, 1988.

Schiller, Friedrich. *The Mission of Moses.* Translated by George Gregory. In *Friedrich Schiller: Poet of Freedom,* vol. 2, 307–29. Washington, D.C.: Schiller Institute, 1988.

———. *On the Aesthetic Education of Man in a Series of Letters (English and German Facing).* Edited and translated by Elizabeth M. Wilkinson and L. A. Willoughby. Oxford and New York: Oxford University Press, 1967.

———. *Werke und Briefe in zwölf Bänden,* edited by Otto Dann, Heinz Gerd Ingenkamp, Rolf-Peter Janz, Gerhard Kluge, Herbert Kraft, Georg Kurscheidt, Matthias Luserke, Norbert Oellers, Mirjam Springer, and Frithjof Stock. Frankfurt am Main: Deutscher Klassiker Verlag, 1992–2004.

Schilson, Arno. "Lessing and Theology." In *A Companion to the Works of Gotthold Ephraim Lessing,* edited by Barbara Fischer and Thomas C. Fox, 157–83. Rochester, N.Y.: Camden House, 2005.

Schlegel, Friedrich. "Vom Wesen der Kritik." In *Kritische Friedrich Schlegel Ausgabe,* vol. 3, *Charakteristiken und Kritiken II,* edited by Hans Eichner, 51–60. Munich, Paderborn, Vienna: Schöningh, 1975.

Schürer, Ernst. "Quellen und Fluss der Geschichte: Zur Interpretation von Arnims *Isabella von Ägypten.*" In *Lebendige Form, Festschrift für Heinrich E. K. Henel,* edited by Jeffrey L. Sammons and Ernst Schürer, 189–210. Munich: Fink, 1970.

Schutjer, Karin. "German Epic/Jewish Epic: Goethe's Exodus Narrative in *Hermann und Dorothea* and 'Israel in der Wüste.'" *The German Quarterly* 80, no. 2 (2007): 165–84.

Seyhan, Azade. *Representation and Its Discontents: The Critical Legacy of German Romanticism.* Berkeley and Los Angeles: University of California Press, 1992.

Seymour, Bruce. *Lola Montez: A Life.* New Haven and London: Yale University Press, 1996.

Shapiro, James. *Shakespeare and the Jews.* New York: Columbia University Press, 1996.

Sharpe, Lesley. *Schiller and the Historical Character: Presentation and Interpretation in the Historiographical Works and in the Historical Dramas.* New York: Oxford University Press, 1982.

Smith, Helmut Walser. *The Continuities of German History: Nation, Religion, and Race Across the Long Nineteenth Century.* Cambridge, U.K., and New York: Cambridge University Press, 2008.

Stifter, Adalbert. *Brigitta; with Abdias; Limestone; and The Forest Path.* Translated by Helen Watanabe-O'Kelly. London: Angel Books, 1990.

———. *Werke und Briefe: Historisch-Kritische Gesamtausgabe,* 38 vols., edited by Alfred Doppler and Wolfgang Frühwald. Stuttgart: Kohlhammer, 1978f.

Susman, Margarete. "Nachwort." In *Abdias: Erzählung von Adalbert Stifter,* 108–13. Berlin: Schocken, 1935.

Swales, Martin, and Erica Swales. *Adalbert Stifter: A Critical Study.* Cambridge, U.K., and New York: Cambridge University Press, 1984.

Thompson, B. "An Ironic Tragedy. An Examination of Grillparzer's *Die Jüdin von Toledo.*" *German Life and Letters* 25 (1971–1972): 210–19.

Trachtenberg, Joshua. *The Devil and the Jews: The Medieval Conception of the Jew and Its Relation to Modern Anti-Semitism,* 2nd ed. Philadelphia and Jerusalem: The Jewish Publication Society, 1983.

Tusken, Lewis W. *Annette von Droste-Hülshoff's 'Die Judenbuche': A Study of Its Background.* Boulder: University of Colorado Press, 1968.

Urzidil, John. "Adalbert Stifter and Judaism." *The Menorah Journal* 36, no. 4 (1948): 327–38.

Veit, Philipp F. "Moritz Spiegelberg: Eine Charakterstudie zu Schillers *Räubern.*" *Jahrbuch der deutschen Schillergesellschaft* 17 (1973): 273–90.

———. "The Strange Case of Moritz Spiegelberg." *Germanic Review* 44 (1969): 171–85.

Vogt, Karl Wilhelm. *Lola Montez mit ihrem Anhange und Münchens Bürger und Studenten: Ein dunkler Fleck und ein Glanzpunkt in Baierns Geschichte.* Munich: 1848.

Volkov, Shulamit. *Germans, Jews, and Antisemites: Trials in Emancipation.* Cambridge, U.K., and New York: Cambridge University Press, 2006.

Wahrig, Gerhard. *Deutsches Wörterbuch.* Munich: Bertelsman, 1991.

Wasserman, Henry. "Prussia." In *Encylopedia Judaica,* vol. 13, 1287–93. New York: Macmillan, 1978.

Weber, Betty Nance. "Droste's *Judenbuche:* Westphalia in International Context." *Germanic Review* 50 (1975): 203–12.

Weder, Christine. "Ein manipulierter Versuch: Das Märchen vom Experiment in Lessings *Nathan* und die naturwissenschaftliche Methodenlehre der 'durch Fleiß hervorgebrachten Erfahrung.'" *Deutsche Vierteljahrsschrift für Literaturwissenschaft und Geistesgeschichte* 82 (2008): 237–61.

Weimar, Klaus. "Der Effekt Geschichte." In *Schiller als Historiker*, edited by Otto Dann, Norbert Oellers, and Ernst Osterkamp, 191–204. Stuttgart and Weimar: Metzler, 1995.

Weissberg, Liliane. "Freuds Schiller." In *Friedrich Schiller und der Weg in die Moderne*, edited by Walter Hinderer, 421–34. Würzburg: Königshausen & Neumann, 2006.

Wells, Larry D. "Annette von Droste-Hülshoff's Johannes Niemand: Much Ado About Nobody." *Germanic Review* 52 (1977): 109–21.

Werner, Michael. "Dichtung oder Wahrheit?: Empirie und Fiktion in A. von Haxthausens *Geschichte eines Algierer-Sklaven*, der Hauptquelle zur *Judenbuche* der Droste." *Zeitschrift für Deutsche Philologie Sonderheft* 99 (1980): 21–31.

Whitinger, Raleigh. "From Confusion to Clarity: Further Reflections on the Revelatory Function of Narrative Technique and Symbolism in Annette von Droste-Hülshoff's *Die Judenbuche*." *Deutsche Vierteljahrsschrift für Literaturwissenschaft und Geistesgeschichte* 54 (1980): 259–83.

Wiese, Benno von. "Adalbert Stifter: *Abdias*." In von Wiese, *Die deutsche Novelle von Goethe bis Kafka. Interpretationen*, vol. 2, 127–48. Düsseldorf: August Bagel, 1962.

———. "Annette von Droste-Hülshoff: Die Judenbuche." In von Wiese, *Die deutsche Novelle von Goethe bis Kafka. Interpretationen*, vol. 1, 154–75. Düsseldorf: Bagel, 1956.

———. *Friedrich Schiller*. Stuttgart: Metzler, 1959, 1963.

———. "Porträt eines Mörders: Zur *Judenbuche* der Annette von Droste-Hülshoff." *Zeitschrift für Deutsche Philologie Sonderheft* 99 (1980): 32–48.

Wittkowski, Wolfgang. "Das Rätsel der 'Judenbuche' und seine Lösung: Religiöse Geheimsignale in Zeitangaben der Literatur um 1840." *Sprachkunst. Beiträge zur Literaturwissenschaft* 16 (1985): 175–92.

———. "*Die Judenbuche*: Das Ärgernis des Rätsels und der Auflösung." *Droste-Jahrbuch* 1 (1986/87): 107–28.

———. "Motiv und Strukturprinzip der Schwelle in Grillparzers *Die Jüdin von Toledo*." *Modern Austrian Literature* 23, no. 3/4 (1995): 105–30.

Woesler, Winfried. "Die Literarisierung eines Kriminalfalles." *Zeitschrift für Deutsche Philologie Sonderheft* 99 (1980): 5–21.

Wübben, Yvonne. "Moses als Staatsgründer. Schiller und Reinhold über die Arkanpolitik der Spätaufklärung." *Aufklärung: Interdisziplinäres Jahrbuch zur Erforschung des 18. Jahrhunderts und seiner Wirkungsgeschichte* 15 (2003): 125–58.

Wurzbach, Wolfgang von. "Die 'Jüdin von Toledo' in Geschichte und Dichtung." *Jahrbuch der Grillparzer-Gesellschaft* 9 (1899): 86–127.

Yardley, Jim. "Lola, Long Dead, Is Still Getting Attention." *New York Times* (April 26, 1998): 31.

Yerushalmi, Yosef Hayim. *Freud's Moses: Judaism Terminable and Interminable*. New Haven and London: Yale University Press, 1991.

ABOUT THE AUTHOR

Martha B. Helfer is an associate professor of German and the chair of the Department of Germanic, Russian, and East European Languages and Literatures at Rutgers University.